The World of Mexican Migrants

Also by Judith Adler Hellman

Mexican Lives

Mexico in Crisis

Journeys Among Women: Feminism in Five Italian Cities

The World of Mexican Migrants

The Rock and the Hard Place

Judith Adler Hellman

THE NEW PRESS

NEW YORK
LONDON

Requests for permission to reproduce selections from this book should be mailed to:
Permissions Department, The New Press, 38 Greene Street, New York, NY 10013.

Published in the United States by The New Press, New York, 2007
Distributed by W. W. Norton & Company, Inc., New York

Library of Congress Cataloging-in-Publication Data

Hellman, Judith Adler.
The world of Mexican migrants : the rock and the hard place / Judith Adler Hellman.
p.   cm.
Includes bibliographical references.
ISBN 978-1-56584-838-2 (hc.)
1. Mexican Americans—Interviews. 2. Immigrants—United States—Interviews.
3. Mexicans—Interviews. 4. Mexican Americans—Social conditions—Anecdotes.
5. Immigrants—United States—Social conditions—Anecdotes. 6. Migrant labor—United States—
Anecdotes. 7. Migrant labor—Mexico—Anecdotes. 8. United States—Emigration and
immigration—Anecdotes. 9. Mexico—Emigration and immigration—Anecdotes. I. Title.
E184.M5H385 2008
305.868'72073—dc22
2007028947

The New Press was established in 1990 as a not-for-profit alternative to the large, commercial
publishing houses currently dominating the book publishing industry. The New Press operates in
the public interest rather than for private gain, and is committed to publishing, in innovative ways,
works of educational, cultural, and community value that are often deemed insufficiently profitable.

www.thenewpress.com

Composition by NK Graphics, a Black Dot Company
This book was set in Minion

Printed in the United States of America

2   4   6   8   10   9   7   5   3   1

For Steve

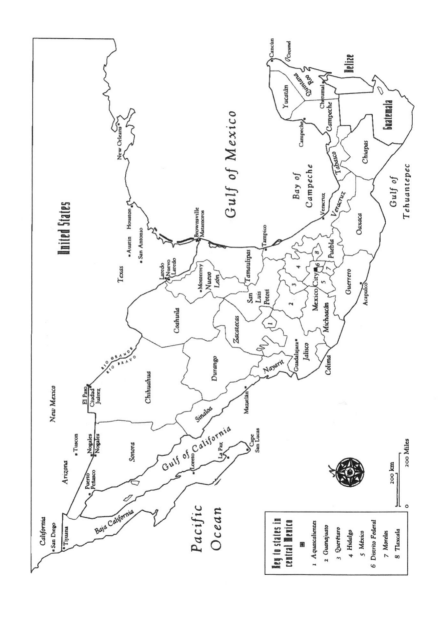

Contents

Acknowledgments

This book is constructed on a foundation of remarkable solidarity and kindness shown to me by friends in Mexico and the United States.

Leigh Binford, Nancy Churchill, Blanca Cordero Díaz, Sergio Cortés, María Eugenia d'Aubeterre Buznego, Delfina Martínez Alba, Alison Lee, Gonzalo Llamas Bernal, Sandra Verónica García Cabrera, Juan Ramón Ortiz, and Liliana Rivera packed me into their cars and spent whole days taking me around to meet returned migrants, prospective migrants, and migrant-sending families in Puebla, Morelos, Veracruz, Jalisco, and Zacatecas. They introduced me to people I could never have met, let alone interviewed, were it not that I was presented to them by friends who had worked long and hard to develop warm relations of confidence and trust in widely scattered villages and towns. Under the circumstances, the term "generous" is hardly adequate to describe those who took me to places I would never have known and shared with me their own contacts so that I could meet and interview the kinds of people whose experiences would illuminate this study.

With other colleagues and friends I had discussions that went on for hours and, in some cases, days, as they shared their knowledge and their writings and offered opinions on my preliminary impressions and tentative findings. Jerónimo Cabrera, Rocio Córdova, Wayne Cornelius, Alyshia Galvéz, Rodolfo García Zamora, Gustavo López Angel, Juanadelos Angeles Mejía Marenco, Cristina Núñez Madrazo, Frances Rothstein, David Skerrit, Ofelia Woo, and Patricia Zermuda all gave invaluable help of this kind. Kirsten Appendini, Adriana Alcántara, and Saul Macías shared preliminary research findings, which greatly enriched my own understanding of the data I was collecting. Carlos Garrido's vivid description of his own participant observation in a household of migrants in New York pointed me toward many questions I might otherwise never have thought to ask.

The scope of this project, which involved interviews in five locations in Mexico and another five in the United States, created for me a whole other category of people to whom the most heartfelt thanks are due. These are friends and relations who hosted me in their homes during periods of fieldwork and offered not only food and shelter but also indispensable encouragement through their willingness, indeed, sometimes eagerness, to hear and comment upon the stories that I was collecting. These wonderfully supportive people are Nancy Churchill and Leigh Binford, Ann Craig and Wayne Cornelius, Fran and Bob Rothstein, Kirsten and Mario Appendini, Janet and David Carruthers, Carole Bender, Silvia Gómez Tagle, Nora Hamilton, Alma Maldonado, Jennifer Parker and Jerry Litwak, Fred Rosen, and, as always, Cynthia Hewitt de Alcántara and Sergio Alcántara Ferrer.

Ira Baumel, Carole Bender, Eduardo Canel, Pablo Idahosa, Esther Jennis, John Lear, Grace Lewis, Jean Rapp, Dennis Rodgers, Ray Seidelman, Miriam Slipowitz, Emily Sugerman, Sid Tarrow, and Patrick Taylor all read chapters of the book and provided helpful feedback. My sister, Nancy Baumel, and my husband, Steve Hellman, both read the entire manuscript, offering invaluable comments. I am also indebted to Paula Hevia, Luz María Vázquez, Carlos Velásquez, and Leandro Vergara Camus for careful transcriptions of many hours of interview tapes, and to Liam Mitchell, Blake Robichaud, and Ellen Shub for monitoring the immigration debate online.

I am grateful for the help of Brother Joel Magallán, Esperanza Chacón, and the late Joe McNulty at Associación Tepeyac, and at Project Hospitality, for the kindness of Patrice Pica, Terry Troia, and especially, Gonzalo Mercado, who went to great lengths to connect me to the community of day workers. Hillary Greene and Brook Mead of the

Berkshire Immigrant Center offered valuable help. I owe thanks as well to the Mexican consuls general in New York, Salvador Beltrán del Rio and Javier Díaz, and the consul of Mexico in Tucson, Juan M. Calderón-Jaime, as well as their staff for the data they provided for this study.

I wish to acknowledge the support of the Social Science and Humanities Research Council of Canada, which, together with the Faculty of Arts of York University, provided the funding that made this research possible. I am also grateful to the Center for Latin American and Caribbean Studies at New York University, which hosted me as a Visiting Scholar during two periods of fieldwork in New York, and particularly to Maritza Colón, Patty Oscategui, and the director of CLACS, George Yudice, for making me feel so welcome in that center and for facilitating my work.

André Schiffrin is justly famous for conveying to authors both his enthusiasm and his belief in the importance of what they have to say, and I am very grateful for his unflagging commitment to this project. Joel Ariaratnam, at The New Press, brings an exuberance to his work as an editor that has made our collaboration as much fun as it has been productive, and his careful reading of the manuscript has been of the greatest help to me.

Of course, I also owe a debt of gratitude to a group of people I cannot mention by name. These are the scores of Mexicans who welcomed me into their lives, patiently answered my questions, and reinforced my belief that their experiences are important to share. The warmth and encouragement of the research subjects themselves was the element that made this project so gratifying for me.

This book is dedicated with love to my husband, Steve Hellman, whose love, support, and humor have *always* provided the underpinning for everything in life that ever seemed to me worth doing—most recently, the work on this project.

Prologue

Luis: Keeping Your Head Down

Luis figured out an escape plan the day that a fight broke out in the deli where he had worked his way up to grillman. Luis couldn't even tell me what the fight was about, but he remembers that Alex, a Dominican who was normally expansive and secure in his privileged role as the only person who could bridge the gap between the Greek owner and the Latinos in the kitchen, actually threw a punch at Rolando, a Salvadoran. There was a lot of shouting and none of the Mexicans said anything to Alex or Rolando or to each other, but Luis was deeply shaken.

Of course Luis had seen lots of fights in the *cantina* in his barrio in "Tenango"* in the Mixteca, the arid region of the states of Puebla Oaxaca, and Guerrero. He had seen punches thrown and a lot worse: men who fought with machetes and knives. He had seen neighbors who were *compadres*, and who played on the same soccer team, get drunk and draw knives and cut each other on the face! Luis had seen a

---

*All but two of the names of people in this book are invented, as are the names of small towns and villages in Mexico and the United States. The invented place names appear in quotation marks the first time they are used.

lot of foolish, drunken fistfights in his day and he, himself, had gotten into punch-ups as a teenager.

But this was different. This wasn't a cantina or a *pulqueria* where men throw back one *copa* after another of intoxicating *pulque* extracted from maguey plants. The deli was a workplace, a place to which Luis and the others had traveled three thousand miles to find jobs, a place for which he had paid a *coyote*, a smuggler, $1,500 and walked forty hours across the Arizona-Sonora desert to reach, and a place from which, in a flash, he could be expelled and lose everything. Luis knew that at any moment the doors to the kitchen could swing open and agents of the *migra* could walk in, seize him, take him off to a detention center in New Jersey, and send him back to Tenango.

This was not a place to throw a punch, Luis thought. This was a place to keep your head down and work hard and be inconspicuous and to move steadily up from delivering menus to dishwashing to salad prep to grillman and maybe, with enough English, to work at the deli counter or wait tables. This is a city, Luis says, where you can ride the number 7 subway line from Jackson Heights to midtown Manhattan, and you could meet all kinds of strange and sometimes crazy people who might shout at you, or might curse someone who wasn't visible to anyone else on the train, or who might grab you by the front of your sweatshirt, put his face one inch from yours, and insist that you accept Jesus Christ as your personal savior. Even worse, this is a city where you can meet someone who doesn't look at all crazy, but is very unhappy to share the subway car with a person he takes to be an undocumented migrant from Puebla.

Luis says, "Basically, this is why I just try to go along quietly and keep out of other people's faces."

> I have this friend, Humberto, who every time I see him, he's got a new job. First he's working in a dry cleaners pressing pants, and then he's delivering menus for a Thai restaurant, and then he's working as a stock boy in a supermarket. And I say to him: "Berto, why are you working a new job? What happened to the old one?" and he always says something like: "The manager was disrespectful to me" or "The boss ordered me to pick stuff up, but he didn't say 'Please.'"

"You know Humberto's not wrong to demand respect," Luis says. "Let's face it: whatever job he gets, it's going to be hard work and he's going to make between $300 and $350 a week. So he might as well work in a place where people are polite to him."

> But I have a different way of doing things. Whatever happens at work, or on the way to work, anywhere you go, you don't want to call attention to yourself. Even if someone insults you, you just make out like you don't understand that you've been insulted. It makes me laugh because I remember how, when I was a kid, the priest used to go on about how we should turn the other cheek, but we weren't into that at all. Sometimes you would pound the shit out of your closest friend for a disrespectful remark. But not here. Not given the sacrifices you make to get here and to stay here.

Luis knows about sacrifices. His own began at age 5 when his father left Tenango for Mexico City to work as a street vendor selling candied fruits and cigarettes—by the pack or by the single cigarette. Then his mother found work as a laundress and joined her husband in Nezahualcóyotl, which was, at that point, no more than a shantytown of almost 3 million residents that had sprung up on a dried lake bed just east of the international airport. At best, Luis would see them a few times a year at festivals for the village saint, at Christmas, and at Easter. For the rest, he lived with his grandparents and worked with his grandfather in his *milpa*, his cornfield. He was also in charge of herding the goats to their grazing patch at five in the morning, a job he had to complete before making his way to elementary school. In *primaria*, Luis managed to complete six years of studies before going to work full-time with his grandfather at odd construction jobs and growing watermelon, sesame, and peanuts for market.

> Because my parents were migrants to the city who worked to sustain their own parents and us kids back in the village, I guess I always imagined that when I grew to be a man, I would also migrate. What I couldn't have imagined was that

I wouldn't just go to the state capital, Puebla City, or to Mexico City, but all the way *al otro lado*, to the "other side."

However, Luis had no wish to emulate his parents in all respects. He was determined, among other things, that he would never leave his children behind.

As a kid I always had lots of friends, but I never had a steady girlfriend, a *novia*, in the village, because I didn't want to marry young, like my parents, and then have to leave my family behind when I left Tenango. This is because all of us understood, even as young men, that without land, we would need to get out and find some way to make a living someplace else. But I didn't want to live out my life separated from my wife and my kids.

And so, in 1994, at age twenty, Luis crossed the border near Eagle Pass, Texas. In this very first trip he walked only thirteen hours through the desert night with five neighbors from Tenango in a journey that he remembers as "easy."

In those days, all you had to do was to walk along the *linea*, the demarcation line between the two countries, and snip through a barbwire fence. That was it. Back then it was simple. We just walked north with the coyote until his partner, a Chicano, picked us up in his van. I admit I was frightened in that first crossing, but I had been in the army for three years so I knew how to march along whether I felt like it or not, and I had another big advantage, which was that I've always been a person who could go for three days without sleep.

When he arrived, Luis joined his two brothers, who shared a one-bedroom apartment in the Crown Heights neighborhood of Brooklyn with five other men from Tenango, one of whom brought Luis along to his workplace, thus securing for him the classic entry-level position for a new Mexican migrant to New York: washing pots and pans.

Basically, all the kitchen jobs in those days paid the same $5.15 an hour, right up to subchef. It's just that some were more disgusting or tough than others, like scrubbing the grease that had been cooked onto the pans.

But if you kept your eyes and ears open you could learn things that would get you a better job, even in the same place. I came with no English, but within a couple of days, I had studied the order slips and figured out all the codes: "SC" for scrambled eggs, "OV" for over easy, "S-up" for sunny-side up, "HF" for home fries. Then I just kept my eye on the grillman as he worked, and when he went back to Mexico I convinced the boss to give me his job.

In those first months, there were a lot of things that Luis needed to learn beyond how to read the order for scrambled eggs and how to cook them properly. He had to figure out how to get around on the subway, how to shop for food, and how to wash clothing at a laundromat.

Well, for sure there was no one like my *abuelita* in Crown Heights who was going to prepare my tortillas or wash my clothes! In fact, in my first year in New York, I really got fat from eating too many Big Macs and pizza slices and stuff like ravioli straight from a can. You know, in Mexico my family only ate meat if there was a fiesta. But the foods we did eat all the time in Tenango—the tortillas and beans and vegetables—are a lot better for you than the junk that the other guys and I prepared for ourselves in that kitchen in Brooklyn—a kitchen, by the way, that was also the bedroom of two of the guys.

We used to eat a lot of ham and pork and white bread and "Spanish rice" out of a can. And even though half the guys in that apartment were working in restaurants, we couldn't figure out how to cook rice for ourselves! Can you imagine? There were guys like Gustavo who did salad prep all day in a deli—just standing at a counter all day cutting up vegetables for six different kinds of salad. But none of the guys—and especially *not* Gustavo—seemed to think that we might prepare vegetables for ourselves. Actually, Gustavo was big on bringing in Chinese food. He used to say, "God put Chinese people on earth so that Mexicans wouldn't starve to death."

The three big things, however, that Luis says he learned in that first year were how to stay out of trouble, how to hold onto his job, and how his earnings would really mount up if he could just manage to do the first two things.

When my brothers went back to Tenango, I started living with twelve guys in a house in Jackson Heights, and that worked out very well. In that kind of situation you really need to be respectful in your behavior because that's a lot of people in a very small space, and in Tenango, you might grow up in a one-room house, but you wouldn't be sharing it with people who aren't your own family

But basically, we got along okay in this house. You could say pretty much what you liked and you knew how the other person was going to respond. And when we would go out to play soccer in the park, even if you were playing with guys from other countries, you'd still be okay, because everyone who was playing understood what we were doing there in the park. Also, if we went out to a bar, we'd go to a bar where we'd be with a lot of other Mexicans, so there wouldn't be any trouble.

Luis's strategy makes me think of Javier, a 17-year-old from Puebla I visited in the Berkshire County House of Correction in July 2003. Through his migratory network, it was Javier's good fortune to end up in one of the most beautiful and tranquil corners of rural America. But it was his misfortune that he was then only one of a dozen or so Mexican migrants to settle in all of Berkshire County, which stretches along the western edge of Massachusetts from Con-

necticut in the south to Vermont in the north. Under the circumstances, when Javier went out drinking on a Saturday night with his
cousin, unlike Luis, it was not in a bar filled with other men from
Puebla, or other men from Mexico, or even other immigrants from
Latin America. It was a local bar, filled with local men, and when Javier
got drunk, came on to the barmaid, and got into a fistfight with her
boyfriend, the police were called and Javier was charged not only with
assault but with attempted rape. When I last saw him, he had been con-
victed and was being sent off to serve a seven- to nine-year sentence in
the state prison in Bridgewater, Massachusetts, in the area of the facility reserved for sexual offenders.

When I told Luis about Javier's experience, he said,

Sure, in Mexico you wouldn't have a woman working as a
barmaid in a place where only men come to drink unless she
was—you know—there *for* those guys, I mean, unless she
was available to them. I feel sorry for this guy because he just
didn't understand what the picture was. If a guy like that
made a mistake like that in the places I go in Queens or
Brooklyn, then the worst thing that would happen is that the
boyfriend or his friends would have punched him around
and thrown his ass out on the street and that would have
been the end of it. No one would have thought to call the police. And prison? He would never have ended up in prison.

This, Luis insists, is the best reason for him to stay in New York,
even if the rents are higher and the neighborhood is dangerous and
you have to work out how to get along with African Americans who
might not be crazy about living among Mexicans, and with other
people who have come as immigrants from places you couldn't even
find on the map if you tried. He says he feels safer if he can live among
people from his own country, people whose behavior he can understand and who can understand him.

Before you get to New York, or Los Angeles, or wherever it is
you end up, you have a picture of yourself in "gringoland"
wandering around a place full of tall blond people. From TV

and from videos you get this idea that you're going to be surrounded by *güeros* and the boss is going to be someone who squints at you through cold blue eyes like in a film.

But when you get here the boss turns out to be an Italian or a Greek, or an Armenian, or a Chinese or a Korean, or maybe someone from the Middle East or from Pakistan. And some of these people like to talk about how they're immigrants just like you or how their father was an immigrant just like you. And some treat the workers very well, and others are real sons-of-bitches. But, none of them are gringos, I mean they're not gringo gringos, like we think they're going to be before we actually get here. They might have U.S. citizenship, but they're not real gringos. And even the guys who have worked in places like Atlanta in construction or Kansas in meatpacking—guys I met the different times I was crossing the border—told me that even in these places where there aren't so many Mexicans or Latinos or immigrants, even there, they hardly have contact with employers or supervisors who are actually gringos.

"But what about the customers?" I ask him.

Well, in the restaurant I'm mostly in the back, so I have no contact with the customers. But the fourth year I was in New York, we had a kitchen fire and the restaurant closed for three months and this guy I know from Tenango got me a job as a stock boy in a small supermarket on upper Broadway, and there you mostly get Jewish people, not gringos, not *americanos*. And some of these people would speak to me in Spanish—not great Spanish, but Spanish that they had learned in high school maybe forty years ago plus a few words they had picked up from the Dominican doorman in their building. It was nice. For some it was just "*¿Dónde está la leche?*" and that was what they could say. But there were people who would come into the market who worked in hospitals or schools or places where they couldn't do their job if they couldn't speak some Spanish, and you could have a real conversation with them: "Where are you from?" "How long have you been here?" "Do you have children?" "Are they in school?" Stuff like that.

I ask Luis, "Weren't you worried that some of these chatty people might actually be the migra working undercover?

Luis says,

It sounds strange, but by the time I came to New York in the 1990s, once you got past the bus station or the airport, you really didn't worry anymore, at least not after the first few days when you might be looking over your shoulder all the time. After the first couple of times I went out into the street with my brothers and I saw how they weren't nervous, I got over it, and never looked over my shoulder again.

Older guys who were here in the 1970s told us that in those days, the place was crawling with immigration agents and they would raid your apartment, your workplace, the movie house. They'd hear about a fiesta and come around and bust it. They would pick you up on the street just for looking Mexican. But by the time I got to New York, the place was crawling with Mexicans and Central Americans, and it was clear that the migra had pretty much given up on the whole deal.

To be sure, it's not just the absence of the migra that makes New York an attractive destination for Mexican migrants. Even though New York City and the New York metropolitan area are a thousand miles farther from the border and much less like Mexico in physical appearance or climate than traditional migratory destinations like California and Texas, migration to New York offers real advantages over the alternatives. One is entirely practical. An extensive and dense network of public transportation makes it largely unnecessary to own a car or drive with a fake license or with no license at all. The very grave risks borne by Mexican immigrants all over the country, but particularly in rural areas and in urban metropolitan areas like Los Angeles or Atlanta, which lack adequate public transportation, are not faced by immigrants to New York City, with its trains, buses, and more than six hundred miles of subway lines.

The other great advantage is the culture of celebration of the immigrant past that is a central part of what we might call the collective identity of New Yorkers. The widespread recognition of the immigrant origins of nearly everyone who lives in the city and its surrounding suburbs is both a public and a personal myth that finds expression in the politics of the city, where candidates for public office often proudly cite their immigrant parents or grandparents as the models for their own lives and as the basis of their claim to understand and connect with those they hope will vote them into office. The physical presence in New York Harbor of icons like the immigrant reception buildings on Ellis Island and the Statue of Liberty, which calls out to the "tired and poor" and the "huddled masses yearning to breathe free," contribute to the defining sense of New York as the "city of immigrants." As we will see when looking at the lives of migrants to Los Angeles, this is in stark contrast to the anti-immigrant, nativist politics that compete with and, historically, have often overwhelmed progressive tendencies in California state politics.

A significant result of these differences is that, while New York's mayor, Edward Koch (1978–1989), directed city employees never to turn immigration information over to federal agents, Governor Pete Wilson rode to office in California only two years after Koch's term ended, pushing for teachers, health-care providers, and other social-service workers to be required to denounce to state and federal authorities anyone they might suspect of lacking legal status. In 1994, 59 percent of the electorate in California voted for Proposition 187, which—until struck down in federal appeals court—denied access to public schools, health care, and social services to anyone in the state who lacked proper documents. Yet, in the same year, back in New York, Mayor Rudolph Giuliani (1994–2001) signed an executive order that prohibited city agencies from reporting to federal authorities any information on the immigration status of the people they served. And even when, in 2003, federal legislation and court decisions undermined the ability of New York's public officials to provide such blanket protection to undocumented immigrants, Mayor Michael Bloomberg issued a new executive order that carefully limited the latitude of city employees to ask anyone anything. Bloomberg's order directed city employees to ask no questions about legal status unless the information were required by law to distinguish those eligible for a benefit, like federally subsidized housing, from those who are not. And in cases where city employees must elicit this information, they may not enter it into a data bank of any kind.

In short, the philosophy in New York that guides public officials in their dealings with people who may or may not have legal status is the assumption that society as a whole suffers when those without documents are afraid to report a crime to police or cooperate as witnesses or enroll their children in public school. The broader community suffers if undocumented people are afraid to go to a public health-care facility although they may be carriers of contagious disease or suffer from a health problem that may impact on the well-being of others. As Bloomberg and his predecessors have asserted time and again, the New York City police department (NYPD) was never an arm of the Immigration and Naturalization Service, INS, and is not in a position to assist the agency that succeeded it in March 2003, the Bureau of Immigration and Customs Enforcement (ICE), which reports to the Department of Homeland Security. In essence, the NYPD has no time, resources, or interest in acting on behalf of or in place of the migra.

While this climate of official tolerance is a boon to undocumented migrants in New York, those settled in California can rely on a different source of strength. California has the largest concentration of undocumented migrants anywhere in the United States and its vast economy is even more reliant on their labor than is the case in any other region of the country. Even as the massive influx of migrants to California in the 1970s and 1980s began to call forth angry nativist responses, the ferocity of the hostility against them stirred migrants to collective action.

In fact, labor organizers have had far more success among workers in California, including those without papers, than anywhere else in the country. Targeting industries where the newest arrivals cluster— home-care services, janitorial work, the hotel and restaurant industries, construction, textile and apparel manufacturing, and, of course, agricultural labor—progressive unions have been active in energizing migrants to claim and expand their rights. These campaigns have focused on better pay and working conditions. But they have also provided leadership for mobilizations to overturn Proposition 187 and to encourage all who qualify to take the formal steps to gain citizenship and to vote their interests in local, state, and national politics.

Thus, in both California and New York, unlike newer migrant reception areas across the United States, undocumented migrants find safety in numbers. Luis himself says that he is about as secure in New York, dwelling among an estimated 750,000 Mexicans in the greater metropolitan area, as he could be living without documents anywhere else in the United States. He also feels more rooted since the day, in 2001, when he emerged from the number 2 train at 110th Street and Lenox Avenue and his eye fell on Juanita, who was leaning against a railing, quietly waiting for a friend. It was, for Luis, a true case of love at first sight, although it would take him another six months to convince Juanita, a primary school teacher who had only recently arrived in New York from a village not far from Tenango, to marry him. And he feels more rooted, but in other ways more anxious, since his two little girls, Paty and Katy, were born on 185th Street in upper Manhattan. At this point, his main concern is that Paty will soon turn 5 and will be ready to begin kindergarten next September at PS 28 in Washington Heights, and before this happens, he and Juanita feel that they need to decide definitively if they want to return to Puebla with their little girls or make their life in New York.

The World of Mexican Migrants

Introduction

American officials were also angered this week when the Mexican government announced that it would distribute maps of the Arizona desert to migrants, showing where water stations and other aid could be found. The homeland security secretary, Michael Chertoff, strongly condemned the idea, saying it was "a bad idea to encourage migrants to undertake this highly dangerous and ultimately futile effort."

—*The New York Times*, January 27, 2006

Highly Dangerous? Yes. Futile? No.

Michael Chertoff insists that the efforts of millions of Mexicans to enter the United States by crossing the Arizona desert are futile. Has he visited an orchard in Washington State recently? A construction site in Atlanta? A sweatshop in Los Angeles? A hotel in Las Vegas? A tobacco field in North Carolina? Has he stopped by a restaurant kitchen, a dry cleaners, a car wash, a janitorial or landscaping service anywhere in the country? Has he stood on a street corner in Manhattan and wondered who are the young men, baseball caps pulled down firmly on their heads, who race by on their bicycles carrying pizzas, panini, pitas, wraps, rotis, gyros, Vietnamese spring rolls, or moo shu pork? If he had, then he would see what the rest of us see: Mexicans, with or without documents, are now everywhere to be found in the United States.

Exactly how many undocumented Mexicans mind children, pick fruit, trim lawns, wash dishes, bus tables, iron shirts, clean offices, roll sushi, pour cement, paint trim, sell tamales, deliver menus, stitch apparel, or repair auto tires in the United States? Some authorities say the number of undocumented Mexicans may have reached 5 to 6 million, or roughly half the estimated 12 million undocumented people who live and work in the United States in 2007.

While the trickle of documented and the flood of undocumented migrants to the United States includes people from every country in the Americas, and, indeed, every part of the world, it is Mexicans who are by far the largest national group. According to the *Pew Hispanic Center Report*, one-third of all foreign-born residents of the United States come from Mexico, and people of Mexican origin—both documented and undocumented—now represent two-thirds of all Hispanics in the United States.[1] In fact some estimates put the total of undocumented Mexicans at somewhere between 10 and 15 million, even if the Pew figures are the ones most frequently cited.[2]

The History of Migration

With Mexicans heading north in such huge numbers, we might be tempted to think of this mass migration as an altogether new phenomenon. But poor Mexicans have been in motion for a long time, and the recent increased movement of Mexicans across the U.S. border is only the latest chapter in an ongoing tale of physical—if not always social—mobility.

From the 1940s to the 1960s, the massive migration of rural people to the Federal District—that is, Mexico City—quadrupled the population of the capital. In the course of the 1970s, as peasants poured into the capital city at a rate of more than half a million a year, an average of 1,370 rural people arrived each day, either taking shelter with relatives in the squalid slums of the center city or building rough dwellings from bits of scrap wood, corrugated metal, mud, and hammered-out tin cans, thus creating the 452 *ciudades perdidas*, or lost cities, that sprang up on every open piece of land in the capital. Squatter communities developed along the railroad right-of-way, under high-tension electric towers, perched at the edge of deep ravines, and along drainage ditches. They even appeared in exclusive upper-class neighborhoods; shantytowns mushroomed on beds of volcanic rock or wherever some space had been left open because the terrain was too rocky, hilly, swampy or unstable to construct the architect-designed homes of the rich.

Yet, in this epoch of large-scale rural exodus, the Federal District was only eighth among Mexican urban centers in its rate of expansion. Secondary cities like Guadalajara, Monterey, Puebla, and Veracruz, as well as the oil boom towns on the Gulf coast, drew millions of economic refugees from the countryside, particularly from impoverished indigenous communities. And while the desert region at the U.S.-Mexican border has water resources to support only a sparse population in this same period, the border began to attract first, tens of thousands, and eventually millions of poor, mostly rural Mexicans who sought work in the assembly plants or *maquiladoras* in the newly formed industrial export zone.

The 1990s was the decade in which migration within Mexico gave way to international migration to the United States. This new phase corresponds to the push by the Mexican president, Carlos Salinas de Gotari (1988–1994), to negotiate a North American Free Trade Agreement (NAFTA) with the United States and Canada. In line with Salinas's commitment to free-market neoliberalism, among the many transformative aspects of this trilateral accord, NAFTA required changes in Mexican agrarian reform legislation that brought about an effective end to the *ejido*, the land grant held by small peasant farmers. The distribution of family-sized parcels of land to *ejidatarios* had been the Mexican Revolution's legacy to the peasants who had fought from 1910 into the early 1920s for "land and justice." Article 27 of the Mexican Constitution of 1917 provided for the distribution of small allotments to peasants who were thus given "use" of their ejido plot and the right to pass along this *parcela* to their heirs, but no rights to rent or sell—that is, to treat their ejido land as private property.

In anticipation of the need to "harmonize" Mexican peasant agriculture with the private enterprise of large-scale U.S. and Canadian farmers, Article 27 was amended in 1991. The amendment ended the

Mexican government's constitutional obligation to distribute land to landless peasant petitioners, and it opened the way to the privatization of all ejido land. Under the reign of the free market that NAFTA would usher in, ejidatarios would now have the right to sell, rent, sharecrop, or mortgage their parcels. Ironically, subsidies to commercial farmers, both large and small, would continue to sustain the so-called family farm in the United States and Canada. But given its weak bargaining position vis-à-vis the other "*dos amigos*"—as Salinas liked to call the relationship with the other two NAFTA partners—major concessions were demanded of the Mexican negotiators. In the name of harmonization with its NAFTA partners, Mexico was required to withdraw almost all state support to peasant agriculture, including subsidies, low-interest or interest-free loans, the use of marketing boards to stabilize prices, and low-cost, state-produced agricultural inputs like fertilizer and insecticides. The Mexican negotiators did win the right to continue some support for the cultivation of corn, which is the staff of life in both the countryside and the city. But the agreement called for state involvement in corn production to be phased out over time.

Taken together, these measures created greater poverty in rural Mexico, intensifying the "push factors" that had long stimulated the exodus of rural people from their villages. Once NAFTA was in place, the proportion of Mexicans earning a living from the soil was cut in half. Ejidatarios often had no recourse but to sell their ejido lands, which now, some seventy-five years after the triumph of the revolution, had been converted from a resource held in trust for one's descendants to private property that could be unloaded for cash.

And so, in the 1990s, as successive economic downturns threw peasant production into crisis, rural Mexicans responded, as they had for decades, by moving to the cities. But when they arrived in the cities, they found a job market that was already inadequate to absorb the labor power of urban youth, let alone would-be workers from the countryside.

Ironically, much of the opposition to NAFTA that had been mounted by organized labor in the United States was based on fear that "good American jobs" would all go south to Mexico. To Mexican anti-NAFTA activists it was clear from the very start that this was unlikely to occur.[3] Unfortunately, their most pessimistic predictions have proved to be accurate: one study after another has shown that in Mexico,

NAFTA has produced only the tiniest gain in employment opportunities, and these increases have been outstripped by the growth of the Mexican population from 87.6 million in 1994 when NAFTA came into effect, to 107 million a dozen years later. This poor economic showing in post-NAFTA Mexico is largely the result of competition from cheap imports from Asia and the United States, which has pushed less efficient domestic producers out of business, creating a loss of manufacturing jobs.[4] At the same time, the *maquila* sector on the border has a declining rate of growth because export zones in Asia, Central America, and the Caribbean are able to offer investors even lower wage workers than Mexico can provide.

With agriculture in decline, and urban and border job markets saturated, rural Mexicans have responded since the mid-1990s by setting out for the traditional immigrant receiving areas of the United States: California, Texas, and Chicago. But they also began to move to new destinations, particularly Georgia and the Carolinas, the Pacific Northwest, the New York metropolitan area and neighboring states, onward into New England, and even as far as Alaska. By now it would be difficult to find any corner of the United States, however remote, that has no population of Mexican migrants.

So almost a half century ago—long before anyone had ever uttered the word "globalization"—harsh conditions in rural Mexico, especially the declining prices of agricultural goods, led people to leave the rural areas for nearby towns and cities. In succeeding decades the continued deterioration of conditions in the countryside has pushed increasing numbers of rural Mexicans to travel farther afield to seek their fortunes, or at least to provide for their family's survival. In addition, rural migrants have been joined in their international peregrinations by their urban compatriots, people from the cities who are often the children or grandchildren of the peasants whose rural exodus in the 1950s and 1960s shifted the demographic profile of Mexico from a largely rural to an urban society.

Mexicans in the United States

Of course, Mexicans have long lived in the Southwest of the United States. Until 1848, all of modern-day Texas, Arizona, and New Mexico and parts of California, Nevada, Utah, Colorado, and Wyoming were in fact the northern provinces of Mexico. Following its defeat in the Mexican-American War, Mexico was forced to cede almost half of its national territory to the United States—a vast area of half a million square miles that was home to an estimated eight thousand Mexican families. But, even if we don't count the descendants of these northern Mexicans—who often, and correctly, say that they did not cross the border, the border crossed them—we can trace a steady flow of Mexicans into the United States from the middle of the nineteenth through the twentieth century.

Poverty has always played a role in bringing Mexicans north into the United States. But so, too, has simple proximity, and Mexicans have a long history of working out their problems by slipping across the border. The move to the "other side" is a central theme in music and folklore, and all forms of Mexican popular culture are filled with stories of journeys *al otro lado*—framed as escape strategies to deal with personal or collective problems. Romantic disappointments, jealousies of every description, family feuds, community disputes, and personal rivalries have always found expression, if not any kind of resolution, in flight *al otro lado*, which represents for Mexicans the quintessential place to lay low and ride out a period of trouble. Tellingly, because the trip *al norte* has always been embedded in the collective Mexican imagination, it is no accident that the radical intellectual precursors of the Mexican Revolution—the Flores Magón brothers and their comrades—found refuge in California, where they published their anarcho-communist newspaper and contributed to fomenting the uprisings that led up to the Revolution of 1910.

Settlement of Mexicans in the United States has been characteristic of every period in the twentieth century. First came the refugees who fled the violence and destruction of the Mexican Revolution, which ravaged the Mexican countryside for more than a decade, killing an estimated 1.5 million combatants and civilians. By the 1920 census, a total of eight thousand villages had been wiped right off the map as a direct result of the battles and the pillage of *pueblos* and an indirect result of conscription, the loss of crops, and the spread of disease.[5]

The revolution's refugees were followed by Mexicans who crossed the border in the 1920s and 1930s looking for work in agriculture. In these decades, Mexican workers moved quietly across the Rio Grande in a continuous ebb and flow that fluctuated according to economic and social conditions on either side of the border. Some crossed back into Mexico at the end of the growing season or the termination of their contracts, while others never returned to their country of birth.

Then, in 1942, with the Temporary Worker or *bracero* Program, conceived by the Roosevelt administration as a way to cope with severe wartime labor shortages in the United States, the flow of Mexican workers into the United States became organized, regulated, and massive. Finally, in 1964, under pressure from organized labor in the United States, the bracero program was terminated by bilateral agreement. But in the course of the decades that the program was in place, an estimated 9 million men had worked as braceros, some returning to the United States for a few months each year over a period of ten to twenty years.[6]

The termination of the bracero program did not bring an end to the steady movement of Mexicans across the border. A large number of former braceros who had established work and social connections in the United States continued their pattern of circular migration in an atmosphere in which both the authorities and the general public were ready to look the other way as long as the fields continued to be sown with vegetables and cotton, and the lettuce, peaches, grapes, and cherries continued to be picked. The estimates of the number of these workers who managed to stay on permanently in the United States, combined with the modest total of Mexicans permitted to cross the border with legal documents, puts the number of Mexicans living in the United States at over half a million in the 1960s and roughly three-quarters of a million in the 1970s.[7]

The population of Mexicans resident in the United States, with and without papers, grew slowly but steadily through the early 1980s. Then, in November 1986, to the astonishment of many, including most undocumented migrants themselves, President Ronald Reagan signed the Immigration Reform and Control Act (IRCA). This legislative initiative responded to that part of the Reagan's Republican base comprised of small-business owners who required a pool of cheap, seasonal, nonunionized labor. The law established a time period of one year during which all undocumented immigrants who could prove that they had lived and worked in the United States before January 1, 1982, would be granted an amnesty for their illegal entry into the country. The act also provided strict penalties for employers who knowingly hired illegal immigrants, and it poured resources into Border Patrol enforcement activities.

Under IRCA the lives of almost 3 million people living in the United States without papers were transformed as they emerged from hiding and gained legal status either as permanent residents or as "special agricultural workers." Moreover, once legalized, the beneficiaries of IRCA qualified to set in motion a process by which they could gain full citizenship. IRCA also provided the opportunity for newly legalized immigrants to sponsor relatives, a provision that opened the door to "family unification" and the legalization of another million and a half people. But it quickly became clear that whatever expectations may have been regarding the effect of criminalizing employers for hiring undocumented workers, or increasing the staff and resources at the principal border-crossing points, these measures did little to halt the continued entry of undocumented migrants from around the world, and particularly from Mexico.

The Big Questions

As we have seen, for the better part of a century Mexicans have been engaged in what we have come to call circular migration, crossing the border and returning to their homeland, or, in other cases, staying on in the United States, putting down roots, and gaining citizenship. However, with the acceleration of the process in the 1990s, the mass movement has reached the point where one in every ten Mexicans now lives in the United States, with possibly as many as half a million Mexicans crossing their northern border each year. Thus, the magnitude of this phenomenon is indeed something new, while the panicky and hostile reaction to it, although, sadly, not new, is a situation that has taken on central importance in both countries.

Of course, some U.S. citizens are deeply dismayed and, indeed, frightened by the number of foreigners in general, and Mexicans in particular, whom they see all around. In some, this perception stirs nativist sentiment; it has even inspired the formation of vigilante groups.

These self-styled guardians of the border and of "America" may be numerically insignificant, but they have received a great amount of coverage in the media, granting them an importance in public life well beyond their narrow field of activity.

At the same time, other Americans recognize that they find themselves "surrounded" by Mexicans precisely because Mexicans have, in fact, become indispensable to the successful functioning of the U.S. service economy, to the production of food, and increasingly to the manufacturing economy as well. The immigrant rights organizers who, for many years, have encouraged Mexicans to take off work on December 12 to celebrate the Day of the Virgin of Guadalupe, have pushed for this mass observance in large part to drive home the point that "a day without Mexicans" is a day in which a large number of important—if not to say crucial—services and economic activities would come to a halt. Indeed, those who argued for a "day without immigrants" in the form of mass mobilizations on May 1, 2006, were extending this logic to embrace undocumented migrants from every corner of the world.

While both the Clinton and Bush administrations produced plans to stem the flow of undocumented migrants into the United States by tightening the border, building higher fences, assigning more officers to the job, installing more sensitive surveillance equipment and, most recently, in 2006, diverting National Guardsmen to the border zone, the everyday experience of Americans across the country tells them that despite the posturing of their leaders on the subject, and the hundreds of millions of dollars of their tax money that has been poured into "securing" the border, in fact, Mexicans are everywhere in the United States. It is clear that despite the increased expense and danger of the crossing, hundreds of thousands of Mexicans manage to enter the country every year, where they join millions more who are already hard at work. Taking this reality into consideration, it is obvious that if any effort is "futile," it is surely the official program to stanch the migratory flow by squeezing Mexican migrants into an ever narrower and more dangerous channel.

Given the centrality of the issue, it is crucial to explore some of the basic questions that anyone witnessing the increasing flow of Mexicans north into the United States would want to understand. And it seems useful to begin by going beyond a perspective that places the United States at the epicenter of all inquiry, as when we find ourselves asking, "What are those people doing *here*?" Rather, we need to look at this remarkable mass movement in a more comprehensive way.

Who migrates? Why do they migrate? Why would two people who live in the same town come to very different decisions as to whether to try their luck in the United States or stay in the village? Why would one woman determine to join her husband in the North and another remain at home in Mexico? Why do some Mexican parents take great risks to bring their children across the border rather than leaving them behind in the care of relatives? Why do young people cross? Why are more young unmarried women crossing? Why do migrants end up in the places they do? How do migrants find work and housing, and how do they avoid detection?

What happens to the people who stay behind? How are small towns transformed by migration? What do those who remain do with the money, that is, the "remittances" that are sent down to them by family who live and work in the United States?

Do the migrants come to stay? Are they really determined—as so much of the policy discussion in the United States presupposes—to realize the American Dream? Or is there another dream, perhaps a Mexican Dream, that looks quite different from the aspirations so often attributed to the Mexicans we encounter in the United States?

To answer these questions, I began by carrying out lengthy, open-ended interviews with Mexicans in "the rock," that is, the sending communities, looking at the conditions that lead migrants to risk their lives, and often the sum total of their fortunes, to cross into the United States to work. To research and write Part 1, I traveled to five different sending areas of Mexico: Jalisco and Zacatecas, which have extensive histories of migration dating back to the 1970s, and Puebla, Morelos, and Veracruz, which are more recent migrant-sending states.

Later, in the course of my research in Los Angeles and New York, I also encountered and ended up interviewing numerous Mexicans from the Federal District; from Chiapas, Guerrero, Oaxaca, and other states; along with many Central Americans and some South Americans who were working in construction and restaurants with the Mexicans I came to know. As I discovered at a later stage of my research, the great advantage of encountering people from outside the original five new and old sending areas was the comparative perspective I was able to gain on how alike and how different might be the experiences of people of different regions of Mexico and different nationalities.

At the sending end, I concentrated on villages and small towns that are powerfully influenced by all aspects of migration, in most cases places where more than half the population now lives outside the community. Although migration from urban zones has become numerically more significant in the overall flow of migrants, and, indeed, even though, without actually looking for them, I met many people from Mexico City in the course of the study, the presence or absence of these migrants from the capital has not transformed the face of a city of 20 million people. In contrast, the departure of migrants from the major sending regions has a huge impact. This is why I chose to concentrate my interviews in settings where the issue is central and the effect of migration on the community is determinant.

In Part 2 of the study, "The Journey," I collected travel tales from dozens of men and women who had left Mexico and returned home, and from many more who were still living in the United States. To research this section, I was particularly keen to record the striking changes over time in the techniques employed by those who have made their way across the border. I was also interested in exploring what the migrants report they felt at the time and the way they think about the experience years later. This section of the book covers both the standard and some of the more extraordinary ways that Mexicans manage to cross the border.

Interestingly, accounts of the journey proved to be one of the aspects of the migratory experience that the people I interviewed were most ready to share, and I covered the topic in both the Mexico- and the United States–based interviews. I also spent weeks in the Tucson-Nogales-Sasabe and the San Diego–Tijuana border zones to capture the story of the transformation of border crossing since the Clinton administration closed off the well-traveled routes, forcing migrants into the desert. In the chapters in this section of the book, I am able to present the perspectives of the migrants themselves, but also those of the border patrol, the coyotes, the Mexican consul, the local ranchers, and the organized groups of Samaritans dedicated to rescuing migrants who become lost or injured in the desert.

In Part 3, "The Hard Place," we come at last to the case studies of individuals that provide a picture of the way Mexicans work, transfer money home, find housing, learn English, enroll their children in school, worship, play, and avoid detection. These are the chapters that focus on survival strategies immigrants develop to meet the demands of exceedingly difficult circumstances, and these accounts lead, inevitably, to Part 4, which is the section of the book in which migrants share their thinking on whether they hope to remain in the United States or to return to their homeland.

In gathering material that would highlight the world of Mexican migrants in the "hard place"—which is to say, the receiving or host community, as it is euphemistically called—I sought to capture the experience of immigrants to Los Angeles, a "traditional" destination, and New York, which, from the point of view of Mexican migrants, is a relatively new destination. In addition, I interviewed Mexicans in towns in upstate New York and rural Massachusetts, in suburban New Jersey and Staten Island, which is formally a borough of the city of New York but could be a Republican-voting suburb in the Midwest for all it resembles the rest of the city. The final section, "To Stay or to Return Home," is also drawn from these same research sites.

In my original conception of this study, I planned to follow immigrants to a series of nontraditional destinations in New England, the South, and the Midwest of the United States, focusing in these cases on migrants working in agriculture but also in industries such as meatpacking, where the contribution of undocumented and documented migrants has become crucial. But accelerated migration has outrun my most ambitious plans as new clusters of Mexican migrant settlement have sprung to life in what might previously have been considered the most unlikely places. So it is that I have set aside for the next phase of this work the research on Mexican migrant life in small-town and rural America and concentrated, for the present, on the urban experience.

At the end of the book, I give a detailed explanation of the methods I used to find the people whose stories would provide insights into the experiences of Mexicans on both sides of the border, people whose lives would illustrate a range of possible outcomes of the migration process.

It might be logical to imagine that a study that focuses on people who have been pushed by forces outside their control to abandon their hometown and their country and to live among strangers in an often hostile environment would be a depressing undertaking. In reality, I have to confess that I have had a wonderful time carrying out this work. In part, the fun came from the humor of the people I interviewed whose experience in two contrasting societies often had the effect of sharpening their perceptions of the bizarre characteristics of each. In part, it was the unaccustomed circumstance of finding myself relating to Mexicans in the society where I was born and raised and where, in contrast to my usual situation as a researcher in Mexico, I actually have knowledge and resources to be able to help people—often very directly. After forty years of work in Mexico in which the most I was ever able to offer research subjects was the promise that I would write about them so that "all the world would know," I now found myself in a very different position. While carrying out the interviews in Mexico, I was able to offer information and clarification on a wide range of questions that people had about the United States and how things work in that country. In the United States, I was able to help people locate social services and health care, recover back wages, find English instruction, and make decisions about their children's schooling. I could show people how to use the public library, how to get around on the subway (when they weren't showing me), and how to fill in forms and job applications. I could make phone calls for them, and I even had the satisfaction of finding more permanent jobs for a couple of day laborers.

Still, apart from the unprecedented pleasure of finding I could be of some use to the people who were so helpful to me, there was another sustaining satisfaction to be found in this particular study. This came from a number of people who explicitly enjoyed their interviews and who said things to me similar to these words expressed by a migrant I met in the garment district in New York, a person who had a chilling tale to tell of how he reached New York as a young boy in the 1980s. Andrés said:

> The questions you've asked me? Honestly, I haven't talked about any of this for longer than I can remember. I mean, everyone has their own story and so it doesn't make sense to go on and on about your own crossing and your own hardships. But I'm glad we're talking about this now because it's really good to remember these things, and also to realize how far I've come.

Part I

The Rock

1

Beto: Those Not with Us

When Don Beto describes working in his cornfield he gropes for words to describe his satisfaction.

> For me it's absolutely essential. It's the most important thing I do. I've always liked to be out working in my fields. That's where I feel tranquil, because in the *campo* I work completely alone and I don't think about my problems, I don't think about conflicts with anyone, I don't worry about anything. I just like being there.

Beto's love for his *milpa* is striking in part because the cultivation of corn in Mexico is an age-old activity; it was already an ancient practice when the Aztecs conquered central Mexico. And yet, since the implementation of NAFTA brought U.S and Canadian corn into the Mexican market, growing *mais* has become unsustainable as an economic enterprise. Grinding the dark imported corn originally bred to fatten cattle on the North American prairies, the *tortillaria* on the main street of Beto's village stamps out gray, rubbery tortillas that are pressed and baked on an assembly line and available to the consumer at roughly three pesos a dozen. Or, at least they were until, in the first months of 2007, the rush to grow corn to convert into ethanol took hold in the United States. It was then that the price of the low-grade U.S. and Canadian corn that had been feeding the Mexican market suddenly jumped from 2,400 to 4,000 pesos per ton.*

But even as the price of imported corn climbed, homegrown, domestic corn remained by far the more expensive choice for the Mexican consumer. If a small producer like Beto were to harvest enough to satisfy his family's needs and have a surplus to sell in the covered market behind the church, he would still need to charge more for his sacks of corn than the tortilleria charges for the finished product. Even if Beto does not figure into his calculations the value of his own labor, the costs of production in his *milpa* are still so high that they put his Mexican-grown corn well out of reach of the poor, who customarily rely on the mass-produced tortillas from the tortilleria. When the price of imported corn spiraled upward in 2007, the tortillerias were forced to hike their prices and genuine panic spread among the poorest Mexicans who have little to eat other than tortillas and beans. And, even so, the manufactured tortillas on sale at the tortilleria remain the bargain option, available at a fraction of the cost of hand-shaped tortillas made from local white corn, which, when available, can cost as much as three for a peso.

Under the circumstances, the cultivation of corn is not economically rational either as a product to sell in the market or as a subsistence crop to feed oneself and family. However, the hard work seems worthwhile to Beto because it means he and his wife, Rosa, will have access to the flavorful, nutritious, traditional white-corn tortilla that puffs up when heated and gives off an aroma that fills Beto and Rosa with a feeling of well-being, that reminds them of their mothers and grandmothers grinding corn, shaping tortillas, and tossing them on a hot *comal* to cook.

When I ask Beto why he works so hard in his fields, he speaks—as do all people who still cultivate their cornfields—of the importance of having something to fall back on, of guaranteeing survival for himself and his loved ones. He goes on about the quality of the tortilla that

---

*Throughout the period of research, the peso was valued at roughly 10 to the dollar. Thus, all conversions from one currency to the other are most easily calculated by adding or subtracting a zero from the sum. For example, in this case, 4,000 pesos is best understood as $400 per ton.

Rosa can make from his corn. Yet, as is the case for other peasants who continue to grow corn and who think of it as their "insurance," the reality is that, in its own modest way, Beto and Rosa's use of white corn in their tortillas and tamales and tacos is a luxury that people with a little economic margin can permit themselves. But Beto also says,

> I'm a man, so I plant corn. That's what my father did, that's what my grandfather did, and if my sons now prefer to migrate *al norte* than to do this work, then I can understand. Times have changed. But I haven't changed, and I don't feel right if I'm not planting and harvesting.

The question of his sons' departure for New York, and later his daughters' migration, is a sore subject for Beto, who makes no secret that he disapproved of what he regarded as their abandonment of everyone and everything that really counts in life. Now, twenty-five years after his oldest son set out—without his father's blessing—for a life of struggle in Brooklyn, Beto assures me that he has come to understand the need of young people to leave. Yet, even as he describes his acceptance of the inevitable, he scans the living room where we are seated and with a sweeping gesture points to a small TV and a modest stereo tape deck and record player combination that, together with an altar to the Virgin of Guadalupe and large, elaborately framed family photos, dominate one side of the room.

> There you have it. In order to have televisions and stereos and other things of that kind, men leave their wives, their sons and daughters. They abandon their aging parents. They leave their friends, their barrio, their village, and their soccer team, to live among strangers and make money and buy things.

I am not surprised by Beto's rejection of the migratory strategy. My friend Blanca Cordero Díaz, who had studied Beto's village, brought me to meet him precisely because he is one of the very few men in "San Jerónimo" who had never migrated, even though international migration of *padres de familia*, male heads of households, has marked the town since the first bold migrants set out in the 1940s as braceros, followed in the 1950s and 1960s by others who worked each year picking cotton in Texas and fruit in California. Indeed, San Jerónimo is only one of dozens of small towns at the foot of the volcano, Popocatéptl, in the states of Puebla and Morelos, where cyclical downturns in the cultivation of a commercial crop, sugarcane, regularly stimulated out-migration, first to Mexico City in the 1930s and 1940s, and later to the United States. In fact, I had come looking for Don Beto, as he is respectfully called by his neighbors in the custom of rural Mexico, precisely because he is known for his rejection of migration as a survival strategy for himself and those he loves.

But strikingly, Beto, who is a man of many parts, is better known and respected for something other than his implacable resistance to migration. Trained as a tinsmith by his father, Beto receives remittances from his children, but also lives from what he earns mending pots large and small in a metalworking shop. But like his father, even as a boy, he turned his skill to the creation of religious objects, fashioned from tin and brightly colored—objects that now fill the shelves in his workshop, are suspended from the ceiling, and occupy every square foot of space on the earthen floor. Angels and saints and birds and sheep and fish and goats and donkeys and wise men and elaborate candelabra and the baby Jesus, and every imaginable flower and tree are all crowded into his work space and stand ready to take their places in an immense altar that Beto builds each year for the November celebrations of Todos Santos and the Day of the Dead.

The altar fills a space significantly larger than Beto's living room, a space built onto his house with remittances sent by his children, and it is here, beginning on October 31, on All Hallow's Eve, that Beto receives—with food and drink—dozens and dozens of neighbors whose celebration of the holy day centers on worship at Beto's altar. Indeed, the importance of this religious and artistic display is so great that for decades, strangers from the city of Atitlán and even Puebla have traveled to San Jerónimo to light a candle at Beto's altar. More recently, after a pair of backpacking Dutchmen described their visit to the altar to a journalist, tourists from Europe have traveled to this small town to mark the day, forcing the municipal government of San Jerónimo to turn out a tourist guide to the principal sights of the village, which includes a map that indicates the path to Don Beto's door.

Prompted by my friend Blanca, Beto retells the story of the invitation that he received from the Museum of Anthropology of the state of Puebla to create an altar for the permanent collection. Together with his brother-in-law, with whom he often collaborates in artisanal work, he traveled to the state capital from San Jerónimo with tools and tin.

> When we got to the museum, we found all these important people standing around: professors, engineers, people who kept referring to each other as "Doctor." And there we were, in our sombreros and our *huaraches*, looking like just what we are, two peasants from the countryside, from a little *rancho*.

> But we set to work building and decorating the altar, and these people were just looking at us as if we were crazy. But after a while they began to understand what we were making and how it was all going to turn out, and they started addressing us as "*maestro*." "Maestro, can I help? Maestro, what can I do to assist you?"

Beto now shows us some of the concepts he hopes to put into play in this year's altar: new forms and shapes, new combinations of colors and, in particular more use of candles than in last year's display. Above all, Beto says, the altar will be bigger and more elaborate than ever. Indeed, many people in migrant-sending communities have mentioned to me that the intensity of the celebrations around the Day of the Dead has grown every year, with more time and money committed to the creation of altars and the preparation of foods to take to the cemeteries to set on the graves of the deceased. This is a holiday that has always connected people to those who are no longer with them, and, in this respect, it seems entirely reasonable that in towns and villages where so many loved ones are not physically present, the migrants, as well as the dead, should be remembered and celebrated on this day.

As Don Beto excuses himself to return to his work on the altar for the Day of the Dead celebrations two months hence, his rejection of the material rewards of migration becomes more comprehensible. I begin to understand better why Beto is known—and in his own way, much respected—for his refusal to leave San Jerónimo and for his insistence on dedicating himself to artistic work and cultivating his cornfield. But it is also the case that his freedom to pursue the activities that are meaningful to him rests on his continued receipt of remittances from those same sons and daughters who disappointed him when they decided to seek their fortunes *al otro lado*.

2

Nopal Verde: The Life of a Town

Zacatecas lies in the parched northern desert of Mexico and has a population of only 1.3 million. But the number of people who could be said to call it home is much higher because proportionally it is the most active immigrant-sending state in Mexico, with more than half of the population living outside of the state. Indeed, those Zacatecans who still live in Mexico are connected through their migratory networks to communities all over the southwest of the United States. And in "Nopal Verde," a town in the driest region of Zacatecas, we can see what out-migration means for those who remain in a place where the greater part of population now resides *al otro lado*.

How large is Nopal Verde? As is the case for all of rural Zacatecas—or, indeed, for every part of the state outside the capital city, Ciudad Zacatecas—it all depends on whether you count only the people who live in the town at any given moment or those who emigrated early enough to have had the chance for amnesty in 1986 and who come and go regularly between Nopal Verde and Tulsa, Oklahoma—or whether you include as well those with no papers who would like to return regularly but do not dare to do so since September 11 made the return crossing into the United States so dangerous and expensive that they just stay put in the United States, skipping the festival of Santa Cruz and denying themselves the company of friends, brothers and sisters, aging parents, and even their own children.

At the health clinic in Nopal Verde, Silvia, the nurse-practitioner, describes the logistical problems she faces in trying to keep track of the shifting population of the town. "In Nopal Verde," Silvia says, "children, as well as teenagers and adults, migrate back and forth," and the nurse confesses that at any moment she has no idea how much vaccine to order for children's inoculations because until they actually show up at the clinic, she cannot guess whether she will be vaccinating the same thirty children who were brought to the clinic last year, or whether twenty-five of those kids are now in Tulsa and only five or six will show up for their shots. My friend, Gonzalo Llamas Bernal, who has brought me here to his hometown, says, "Well, there really can't be more than two thousand of the five thousand who supposedly live here." Silvia, however, differs in her calculations and thinks the population may have fallen to just over eight hundred. "Look, it's got to be a lot less than one thousand," she says. "Forty-four men migrated this month alone, and these are just the people we can think of. I mean just the people who, between us, we know personally and can count!"

Both Gonzalo and Silvia agree that Nopal Verde has long been a migrant-sending town and that even before the Mexican Revolution of 1910 to 1917, men from Nopal would cross the border to work in agriculture, rustle horses, or ride with bandits like Pancho Villa. And dozens of men in Nopal Verde can still recall their adventures and misadventures as braceros in the United States during World War II and in the postwar period. "There's always been out-migration from Nopal," Gonzalo says, "but this kind of 'contagion,' as we call it, began in the early 1990s. And after 1995 it accelerated rapidly with the crisis in agriculture, which left us with no productive base at all in the town. It's become a place that survives, basically, on remittances."

Silvia adds, "And it's not just that Nopal is now totally dependent on the money the migrants send down, but there's a point that a town like Nopal Verde can reach when you no longer have the critical mass you need to have a real community."

So many people have left that it becomes difficult for those who remain behind to sustain any kind of activity. At a certain point you don't have enough children for the school, and in fact our school is about to close. Attendance at Mass drops off and the church withdraws the priest and sends him elsewhere. The best you can hope for is a priest who serves a lot of different communities and who shows up occasionally, and once that happens, religious practice just becomes the celebration of the major fiestas.

"More and more, the people who remain in Nopal Verde feel that they have been abandoned," Silvia says, "and the children find there's no one left to play with because all their friends are in Tulsa."

But when they, themselves, get to Tulsa, it's not as if they find their little friends living around the corner or accessible in any way, given that *Nopaleños* are spread all over the city and people need cars to get around and both the parents are working and they want the children in the house, not wandering around the neighborhood. It's not like here, where kids pretty much run free.

The worst, though, is that teenagers finish secondary school and rather than even think about carrying on with their studies, like going to the *prepa* to prepare for college or going to technical school or teachers' training, they're all racing to get to the other side. And the parents don't do much to stop them because in place of the old dream that their children will study and have a brighter future, the parents begin to dream that their kids will migrate and start sending remittances! It used to be that the only conceivable reason anyone ever had to sell land would be for the education of a son or daughter, which would be understood as an investment in the future. Now people sell their parcel to raise the funds for the coyote fees.

Taken together these changes in attitudes toward schooling lead to what Mexican educational experts increasingly describe as "deschooling," the *descolarización* of Mexico, that is, the decline in the average number of years of study attained by the population. It is one of the most measurable and chilling indications of the changes that migration produces in the sending communities. While ever larger numbers of people seeking and attaining more years of schooling is taken as clear measure of development anywhere in the world, the migration process in Mexico has reversed decades of growth in school attendance and the length of students' academic careers. Young people look around, and they talk to those who have been to the other side and returned, and they can see that the pursuit of any kind of higher degree in Mexico is *less* likely to pay off in monetary or material terms than making their way to the United States and finding work in even the most poorly paid unskilled job.

Indeed, Silvia's assessment coincides perfectly with what I had heard from Esteban, a university student I met in a small town in Veracruz, who was the only one of his entire cohort of friends who still lives in Mexico. "Because of the lack of good jobs here in Mexico, people my age feel that higher education is just a ticket to nowhere," he told me.

> Young people think it's a waste of time to go to *prepa* and university. These are not qualifications that amount to anything in the U.S. job market, where no one's interested in you because you earned a diploma or a degree or because you can do advanced math. They couldn't care less. They're interested in your ability to push a broom, and you'll come away with a lot more money if you push a broom for a few years, than if you had spent the same time studying in Mexico. So why bother? That's what people say.

I ask Esteban why he has stayed behind. "That's simple," he says. "I'm in love. I've got my *novia* here. She's still in high school and I don't want to leave her."

> But I can't say that I won't go. The fact is some young people go just for the pure adventure of crossing and seeing what life is like on the other side. I actually know guys who went

to the United States because they love hip-hop music or a particular sound of a particular band.

You can't blame them. People come back and they drop English words into the conversation as if they can't think of the word in Spanish. And they drop the names of places they've been and you haven't, and I don't mean the Empire State Building, which is a name that anyone could know without ever crossing, but places like Bensonhurst, Elmhurst, Sunset Park, and Jackson Heights! Places that sound wonderful.

Esteban says that even in the case of his closest friends he is constantly taken by surprise.

The strange thing is that one day you're talking to a buddy who is dead set against migrating and who really gets worked up when you mention that you might consider taking off. Then a month later you hear from a cousin in Brooklyn that your friend is living with him and eight other guys at Bushwick Avenue and Decatur Street!

The truth is, you never know. A person's plans can change from one day to the next. Maybe his girlfriend breaks up with him. Maybe he comes up with an interesting idea he wants to fund—something like an Internet service he wants to set up in the front room of his parents' house, something like that. Or maybe he just gets lonely. Right now, of the thirty-two kids in my class in the *prepa*, thirty-one are on the other side. I'm the only one who's still here.

Silvia's observations were also confirmed for me by Maestro Isaac, a schoolteacher in "Tepec" in the Mixteca region of Puebla, who told me that he had always counseled his high school students to stay in their town. "Just like our parish priest, I always emphasized to these young people the importance of building their lives here, the dangers they would face on the other side, how much their families would miss them—all the reasons a teacher would give to a student to stay and struggle here."

But then Isaac's own baby son bit through an electric cord, severely burning his mouth. If the boy was not to live his whole life with a disfigured face, it was clear he would need complex reconstructive surgery. So the teacher packed his bag, hired his coyote, and made his way to the other side to earn the money to bring his child to New York for the operation. As Isaac notes:

> The ironic thing was that my former students, who were now spread from Brooklyn to Queens, became an indispensable lifeline for me when I arrived. They really pitched in to support me in every way they could. They helped me find work and learn my way around, and not one of them *ever* spoke the words that were often in my mind, which was how was it that I had not followed my own advice?

The "contagion" of out-migration also frustrates the optimistic plans of people who have worked so hard in the United States with the expectation that they will return to their hometown and use their savings to start up some kind of business. Silvia explains the problem.

> What are you going to do?—set up a little grocery store? There aren't enough people around to be regular customers. What's more, nowadays, on Wednesdays the weekly *tianguis* comes to Nopal, that is, the street market with fresh fruit, vegetables, meat, and all kinds of dry goods and clothing and household wares. This kind of market moves from place to place. Every day these merchants set up along the main street of a different community. Nopaleños really prefer to buy in the *tianguis* than to shop at the grocery on the corner because the once-a-week street market is like a fiesta, and maybe the prices are a little bit lower, but most of all it's a moment to walk out in the street and see it crowded with people, just as if Nopal Verde were still a real town rather than totally depopulated.

It is telling that no small grocery does well in Nopal Verde, but in "Piedras Blancas," a neighboring town, Don Chucho, who returned after twenty years in Los Angeles, runs an operation that is part mini-market, part tortilleria, part video-rental store, and part sandwich shop and café. It is also the headquarters of Chucho's Minivan Service, a single vehicle that plies the road between the Zacatecas airport and the village. Its driver, Don Chucho, meets the flights of returning migrants by prearrangement and undercuts the fare of the licensed taxis and limousine service by posing as the personal friend or relative of the returnees—a fiction which, in the case of Piedras Blancas, is almost always the truth. Don Chucho is diversified in these ways, but, he tells me: "Just for insurance, I keep pigs, I keep honeybees, and, of course, I have my little *milpa* where I grow my corn and my beans, because in life, you never know."

Silvia confirms that, in fact, Chucho's survival as a businessman is the exception; most of the enterprises that returnees hope to establish falter for lack of customers. Indeed, my friend Gonzalo, who comes from a peasant background, is one of the few people in Nopal who manages to live in a modest degree of economic security even though he receives no remittances. Like Don Chucho in Piedras Blancas, Gonzalo accomplishes this by pursuing a diverse range of activities. Apart from teaching classes in economics in the university, he is in demand as an electrician and a carpenter, and he has worked as a cobbler since childhood. In addition, Gonzalo keeps pigs and he speculates in dry chile and beans, buying at one price, and storing the crop in a warehouse he built for this purpose until the price of these unstable commodities rises. He also changes dollars to pesos when the banks are closed on weekends or for people who don't wish to travel all the way to the city to change money, and he sells phone cards and hamburgers right out of his kitchen window, as I was able to observe while enjoying a delicious *comida* with his family.

To provide me with an answer to my question, who can make it in Nopal Verde and who cannot? Gonzalo introduced me to Samuel and Vicente, two brothers, both recently returned from a stint painting houses in Tulsa, Oklahoma. The brothers, who look very much alike, are nonetheless a study in contrasts. Vicente, the older by two years,

was an unenthusiastic student who completed only primary school
plus two years of middle school before joining the exodus of men from
his town to Oklahoma. His brother, Samuel, stuck it out in middle
school, completed *prepa,* and went on to the faculty of medicine, surgery, and orthodontia at the State University of Zacatecas. There he
graduated in dentistry, the least expensive of the three concentrations
offered in the faculty, and as such, more in line with his very limited financial resources. In dentistry, Samuel explains, all that students need
to purchase in the way of equipment is their own drill. Moreover, the
period of course work is shorter than that required to qualify as a medical doctor. So with some help from his older brothers, Samuel was able
to get through the program, and he graduated in 2003.

But, of course, Samuel could hardly set up a practice with only a
drill in his hand. He would need to build a clinic in Nopal Verde and
outfit it with equipment. So he traveled to Tulsa, where Vicente was
able to find him in a job as a housepainter in a crew in which he himself had worked for some years.

I ask whether it is unusual for someone from Nopal who has sac-
rificed to study and earned a university degree to find himself working
in the United States in construction or landscaping or painting—the
areas of concentration of Nopaleño migrants.

"Not really," says Vicente. "I can think of a bunch of people besides my brother."

> There's a friend of ours who qualified as an agronomist, and
> he worked with me in construction, but at the lowest end,
> which is where you sift through piles of rubbish at the dump
> sorting waste materials from salvageable building materials
> like wood and bricks. Then there was a couple, both teach-
> ers, who managed to regularize their status in the United
> States because her father had gotten citizenship under
> IRCA, and both of them found jobs as teachers in a primary
> school in Oklahoma. But he left to do housepainting be-
> cause he could earn more than double the salary he received
> as a teacher in rural Oklahoma, and the *maestra* gave up her
> post at the school and started cleaning houses because, if

you're a hard worker, that kind of job also pays better than elementary school teaching.

Like these neighbors from Nopal, Samuel was soon earning $10 an hour and clearing $400 a week painting houses. The work was steady and every week he grew closer to his goal. That goal was the purchase of a dentist chair, basin, console, light fixture, a drill mount, the sterilizer, the shaker to mix the fillings, and the standard array of tools, along with the construction material to erect a one-room clinic, with a second room alongside where he planned to open a sandwich shop, just in case his dental practice didn't take off.

"Did your boss in Tulsa understand that he had in his employ a person who had completed medical training at a university?" I asked Samuel.

"Sure," he replied. "In fact he proposed to become my silent partner. He wanted to invest in my practice, lending me the money to get set up. But what he couldn't imagine was how few patients I would have and how little I would earn."

Indeed, even though Samuel is the only dentist practicing in Nopal—or in any of the four surrounding communities—business is slow. This is not only because of the depopulation of the zone produced by migration. It is also because of a lack of confidence in dentistry on the part of local people, and a culture of neglect of dental hygiene that, Samuel says, is very hard to overcome.

It's not only that people don't get information on prevention of tooth decay. No one ever comes to me to say, "Doc, I feel like I'm getting a cavity. What should we do about it?" They won't turn to the dentist until the tooth is so far gone and the pain is so intense that the only remedy is to yank it out.

I charge one hundred pesos—ten dollars—to fill a cavity and the same price for an extraction. I know how to make bridges, both permanent and removable. I can make crowns and cap teeth with materials as expensive and elaborate as the patient might wish. The latest thing in this work is not the gold or silver tooth, but initials set in a white tooth. But 95 percent of the patients come to me too late to think about any remedy but extraction. People just burst in here shouting, "Get this tooth out! Out!!" And that's pretty much what I get to do. So my practice is almost pure mutilation, not restoration or prevention. It's a shame, really.

Samuel needed only a year and a half to put together the basics for his practice, in part because a friend who was putting in new drop ceilings in a medical building in Tulsa tipped Samuel off that he had met a dentist who was carrying out a total renovation of his office and Samuel was able to buy all the fixtures and equipment, including the chair, for just over $1,000. Another friend with a small truck and the papers to cross the border drove down to Nopal Verde with Samuel and all the secondhand equipment, so now that Vicente and Samuel have finished building the one-room clinic, Samuel says he's all set.

But what about Vicente? At age 28 he has his wife and his children all waiting for him in the house to which he has added a new roof, new windows, and a modern kitchen and bathroom. But when I inquire, he says that what he hasn't figured out is any way to earn a living in Nopal.

There's no point in buying land—and there's plenty for sale, too, because it doesn't provide income. The wells around here are all dried up. Moreover, there's no one around to work it for you. The only people you can hire around here are the least capable, the people who don't have the imagination and ability to haul their asses over to the other side.

Basically, the people who are still around here are not the best workers, they're not energetic people and they're in such demand that they see no reason to work hard on any one job because they can always get someone else to hire them.

Dissatisfaction with the existing labor pool—if not to say contempt for the men left behind—was a constant theme in my conversations with returned migrants. Don Chucho had also voiced the same complaint, that precisely the people who might be available to work as *jornaleros*, day workers, are "next to useless" because there are so few left and they are in such intense demand that they can command 100 to 150 pesos a day. What's more, they often "knock off early and don't work very hard" because they know that work will come their way whether or not they have a reputation as hard workers.

Thus, to the extent that Vicente's projections involve hiring others, his prospects are not encouraging. Moreover, the kind of jobs that Vicente has held in the United States have not given him the work experience that he could translate into a well-paying occupation or business in Nopal. Indeed, researchers, like my friend Saul Macías, have asked an important question: What do people learn in the United States that they can bring back with them and put to use? Saul has been following closely the case of a pizzeria in the state of Puebla that was set up by a couple of migrants who have returned to their hometown of Atlixco. This small city on the slopes of Popocatéptl has a permanent population of 86,000 and a weekend population that is swelled by the presence of hundreds of upper-middle-class people from Mexico City who have built vacation homes on the edge of the town. The pizzeria, Saul says, is identical in every detail to the pizza parlor where the two migrants worked in Brooklyn. The tables are the same, the ovens are the same, and the array of toppings are the same. The two partners have even purchased a motorbike so they can make speedy deliveries to customers' homes, just like Domino Pizza. But so far it is not clear that the concept will catch on.

So, Vicente tells me, the only thing he can think of that might work is to raise sheep. But he knows that he needs more than one activity to really make a go of life in Nopal Verde. Thus, in a statement that certainly closes the subject for the time being, he tells me, "You know, you were lucky to catch me today, because tomorrow I'm heading back to Tulsa with a couple of other guys who also know how to cross."

3

San Rafael: A Life of Cooperation

"San Rafael," in the state of Puebla, is smaller than Nopal Verde and is, if anything, in an even more advanced stage of abandonment. As my friend Maru D'Aubeterre Buznego and I approach the town, bouncing along a dirt road in her ancient Volkswagen Beetle, we see an important visual clue that tells us this is a migrant-sending town. San Rafael may not have a well-paved road, but it has telephone lines. In fact, it has high-speed telephone service that carries the voices of migrants in California back to their loved ones in the pueblo. Indeed, well before San Rafael had decent drainage or potable water or paved sidewalks and streets, the state governor acceded to the demands of the remittance-sending migrants that, first and foremost, the village needed telephone poles and phone lines.

The most recent, massive migration of *Rafaeleños* to the United States is only the latest chapter of a longer history of physical mobility driven by poverty. Apart from growing their corn, people in San Rafael have long been famous for their woven baskets and sleeping mats, which they would haul all the way to the city of Puebla on the back of a burro or to the Federal District on the third-class bus. Through the first half of the twentieth century, Rafaeleños would sell these hand-crafted wares to urban poor people, who had plenty of use for straw goods but no access to these products in the city. In the 1960s and

1970s, men from the village expanded their range of sales, traveling all the way to the capital, where they did a brisk business in *morongo*, blood sausage, which they sold in the street. But even this far-flung activity was eclipsed when, in the 1970s, men from the community started crossing the border as "wetbacks," *mojados*, as they themselves express it, and finally settled in California, where they worked in agriculture and later in construction, and eventually, in disproportionate numbers, as street vendors.

The Rafaeleños who dwell two thousand miles north of their village are, in fact, the ones who have had the most to do with shaping the appearance of San Rafael. Certainly, all the cinder-block and brick houses in the pueblo belong to the migrants, while the adobe and the wood and thatch houses in the village and just outside of town belong to those who have never been to the other side. But the most dramatic transformations in the pueblo have been the fruit, not of individual striving, but of the collaborative efforts of the "hometown association"— comprised of Rafaeleños who are spread from East Los Angeles to San Bernardino and El Monte, in California, along with a small group that followed a relative who had somehow made his way to Utah.

With funding from the hometown association, the church in the *zócalo*, the main square, has been elaborately painted in bright blue, white, and gold, and the interior frescoes depicting scenes from the life of San Rafael have been artfully restored.

The zócalo itself has also received careful attention and renovation with collective remittances sent down by the migrants, although here the results are somewhat less happy. The main plaza of a village like San Rafael is often filled with broadleaf shade trees with huge boughs and limbs that form a canopy over the benches. Typically, local people may use the term *jardin*, that is, garden, interchangeably with "zócalo" to denote the main square. But the plaza in San Rafael looks quite stark, if not to say naked, having been stripped of its mature shade trees in the restoration project that seems to have been dominated by a faction of the hometown association that felt that insofar as the trees were not the kind that grow in California, the plaza would look much better if the ancient Mexican shade trees were cut down and replaced with little saplings brought in from Los Angeles.

Given the lack of greenery, the feature of the renovated square most likely to catch the eye is the large plaque that lists the names of the migrants who participated in these projects, together with the names of the municipal officers who administered the funds once the money reached San Rafael. Another plaque across the street acknowledges the role of the hometown association in the construction of the clinic, the only health-care facility in the village.

But the main square and clinic projects are by no means the full sum of the amenities that have been given to the village by the hometown association. Logically, we would anticipate that some branch of government, whether federal, state, or local, would take responsibility for building or renovating a schoolhouse, digging drainage ditches, paving the roads, securing potable water, or extending the electric current to every street. However, given the official neglect of rural infrastructure in marginal zones like this one, these services are actually supplied by the migrants who are in California and Utah, even as they individually send money so that their own families will have enough to eat. In San Rafael, and, indeed, all over Mexico in migrant-sending communities, it is the migrants working in minimum-wage jobs on the other side who have made these basic services available to their own families, and by definition, to the community as a whole.

Of course, for Rafaeleños, the custom of *cooperación*, as it is called, is deeply embedded and has its origins not simply in the period before out-migration was common, but in pre-Hispanic Mexico and later in colonial times. For hundreds of years, members of small, relatively closed communities like San Rafael have always "cooperated" to sponsor the festivals that honor their saints and to maintain the church and public spaces. Chipping in is an obligatory social responsibility and failure to do so for lack of personal or family funds is a source of humiliation to those who cannot meet the quota set by the community for contributions in cash or labor power.

Some of these community responsibilities are civic duties, as in the case of the development of physical infrastructure like digging ditches for drainpipes or serving in municipal government. Other responsibilities are religious, such as taking charge of the worship of a saint, a task—and an honor—that in San Rafael, as elsewhere, involves bringing the statue of the saint into one's home for a year, receiving with food and drink all who might come to worship there, and organizing and underwriting the fiesta associated with that saint's day celebrations. Indeed, before taking on such a responsibility, the person chosen, the *mayordomo*, must nail down commitments from both his blood relatives and his "fictive kin," that is, those friends who have accepted the duties of ritual co-parenthood and have become his *comadres* and *compadres*. Any and all of these friends and relations may be called upon to pitch in to help the *mayordomo* properly meet the social obligations associated with the care and worship of the saint.

Thus, the activities of the hometown associations or clubs based in the United States are only the modern-day expression of very old traditions that bind people together, even as these duties burden the very poorest people in a community.

Take, for example, Don Claudio, whom Maru and I met on the road as we approached the village. Claudio, a peasant in his midforties, is one of the rare people we could find who is still trying to earn a living from his land. With little prompting, he gave us a breakdown of his economic situation, which, as for all other peasants in the parched and underfunded region, starts with the fact that he has land, but no water available for irrigation. Thus, he depends entirely on rain to water his crops—rainfall that may be abundant or sparse, or may not come at all. Generally, Claudio plants corn and beans that he hopes to sell on the local market, but his fixed costs are high: the rental of a tractor to prepare the land for sowing, bags of fertilizer to enrich the soil, and insecticide to deal with grasshoppers, among other inputs. He explains:

> In a good year I can grow four tons of corn and a maybe three and a half of beans. But with the sparse rainfall we had this year, I harvested less than a ton of each. Six months of work, plowing, sowing, weeding, fumigating, and that was all I brought in.

> Of course I could raise animals. But without water, I would have to spend two hours every morning herding them to a stream to water the cattle and then another two hours to

bring them back in the evening. When I grew up, this would have been the work of a young boy. But today we want our children to study, and right now I have all four of my children in school.

To make up for the shortfall, Claudio is working as an assistant to a housebuilder, an *albañil*, in Puebla, but the bus fare alone comes to 20 pesos and he takes home, at best, 80 pesos for a twelve-hour day. Apart from this effort to supplement his income, Claudio is in line to receive a federal grant of 1,000 pesos a year for each of his four hectares of land through a program called Procampo. He explains:

The other day a federal deputy arrived and he was going on about how he was going to make sure we all received money from Procampo. But what good is that going to do me? The government doesn't give the *campesino* this money. It turns the funds over to a "promoter," an animator, from the Ministry of Cattle, Agriculture, and Fisheries. This guy is supposed to administer the money but he only hands it over to you specifically to buy sheep or goats, and only after you have purchased these animals and you can produce a receipt. In reality, you never receive a *centavo* of this in your own hands. They don't trust you with the money. And if you buy animals and they die for lack of water, it isn't as if Procampo is going to come along and reimburse you. It's like they think you caused the drought and lost your herd on purpose!

It's the same with the program they have for mothers, Progresa. They give the mothers 300 pesos every two months, but only if they bring the children to the clinic. But we don't have a clinic here, so my wife has to take the children to town, and with what it costs to take the bus or minivan, the Progresa payment doesn't come close to covering the trip. I think we'd be better off if the government would just leave us alone and forget about giving us anything.

Claudio's current drama is that in the midst of his personal economic crisis, neighbors have come to him to say that his share of the cost of digging a well is 350 pesos, which is a sum that he will have to come up with or face social isolation. This, then, is the problem with the system of "cooperation." It falls equally on everyone in the pueblo regardless of his or her capacity to chip in for the common projects that should, in any event, be the responsibility of government.

With such an impoverished local resource base, the potential of migrants to accumulate capital in California becomes the answer to every problem, strikingly enough, not only for people in San Rafael who have remained behind in the village, but for official Mexico as well. Although the migrants' associations are largely nonpartisan, the efforts of the hometown clubs have been recognized by the governors of those Mexican states that have the highest rates of out-migration: Durango, Guanajuato, Guerrero, Jalisco, Michoacán, Oaxaca, Puebla, and San Luis Potosí. The state governors bring their own political campaigns north to the United States, meeting frequently with the club members and leaders to press the migrants to invest in their hometowns.

Thus, in addition to all the other projects they undertake with the fruits of hard labor in the United States, the migrants and their hometown associations are increasingly viewed by politicians in Mexico as the answer to the problem of stimulating economic development. As it is, individual and collective remittances sent by migrants working abroad to their families in Mexico—which the Bank of Mexico estimated at $23 billion in 2006—have become the mainstay of the economy of countless villages, towns, and cities. Indeed, there are innumerable towns, villages, and *ranchitos* that, as Maru says, "you can't even imagine without their remittances. They simply could not survive."

But not only do migrant workers push themselves to make up for the lack of government spending that would make the lives of those left behind more bearable. In addition, policymakers in Mexico assume that collective and individual remittances will be productively invested in the migrants' hometown—particularly in the development of infrastructure. The official expectation is that this investment will make up for the shortfall in public spending, and to stimulate this process, programs of matching funds have been promoted. Since 1992, for example, every dollar contributed by Zacatecas hometown associations to the funding of projects back home has been matched by the Zacatecas state and the Mexican federal governments, each adding a dollar in a so-called Two-for-One Program. In 1998, the addition of a dollar from the *municipio* turned the program into Three-for-One, and in 2000, the Vicente Fox government made this a nationwide policy under the Citizens' Initiative Program.

The perversity of this growing dependence of government upon the downtrodden individual is all the more shocking when we consider that the funds collected by the hometown associations are largely contributed by people who are not merely poor, but who have often earned these dollars under conditions of extreme exploitation and personal risk to themselves.

All this helps to explain why, in 2003, when the San Rafael hometown association collected $15,000 from its members, the association elected to spend the money to sponsor the largest carnival and rodeo ever witnessed in the village, with all rides, prizes, cotton candy, and other treats offered free to the children of San Rafael. Later in Los Angeles, I came to know Dario, one of the principal organizers of the carnival, and I asked him why the club had elected to sponsor the carnival and rodeo rather than invest the money in some infrastructural project. He said:

> You know, everyone turns to the migrants for everything. Your own relatives and the pueblo as a whole. This puts a lot of weight on the shoulders of the migrants, who just give and give because there's no public funds to fix anything—not the school, not the roads, not even the cemetery. You could end up sitting in Los Angeles thinking about nothing but all the souls who cannot find rest because the gravestones are crumbling and the weeds have taken the place over.

Dario explains that having your name on a bench in the zócalo, having a plaque with your name on the list of donors to the health clinic, marks you as one of the important people of the pueblo. Even a person who was a nobody at the bottom of the heap before he left for Los Angeles can turn into a somebody. "So, yes," he says, "there's a lot of satisfaction in sponsoring a project. But we got to thinking that there's more to it than paying for drainage ditches and then putting up a plaque. We thought that we could also contribute by cheering people up." This is why Dario's committee came up with the plan to sponsor something different for the festival of San Ysidro.

> All of us here in L.A., we all remembered that when we were kids there would be carnivals with rides and prizes and candy for the people who could afford these things, and we never had the money to buy even a ticket for one ride. For us there was no Ferris wheel, no bumper cars, no nothing. We could all remember standing outside the fence and watching other people enjoy themselves inside. So we decided that the Rafaeleños of California would pay for everything, and that way every child in the village could have everything for free.

I would have to guess that the children and parents in San Rafael were happy with this gift from the hometown association, but clearly no one was happier than the donors themselves, as I could see when, months later, I was invited to a *comida* at a bungalow in East Los Angeles where the video shot at the carnival was being screened and enjoyed—and not for the first time—by the crowd of Rafaeleños who filled the room.

The clamorous success of the carnival was followed, in 2004, with the importation—direct from Los Angeles—of a famous *grupera* band that played typical *ranchera* music from the state of Sinaloa, updated with the use of trumpets, trombones, drums, and electric bass. For this concert, the hometown association determined to sponsor the admission of every adult and child in the village. However, the committee counted on recouping some of the $15,000 they had spent to fly the band and all its equipment down to Mexico and transport them three hours from the airport to the pueblo. They planned to sell tickets to people from neighboring towns, even as everyone from San Rafael would be admitted for free. But Dario says,

> What we didn't take into account was that when the band set up with all its equipment, it was so loud that people in the neighboring villages could enjoy the music without going to

the trouble of traveling to San Rafael, let alone buying a ticket. So people had a very good time, but we didn't recover the money we laid out. Still, it was worth it just to pull this off. To bring a band to San Rafael that's known to *hispanicos*, to *latinos* everywhere in the United States! It was really worth it. It can't be sewers and cemeteries *all* the time.

4

Marta: The Tyranny of In-Laws

Until I met Marta, I believed, as so many experts insist, that migration is driven by a combination of the lack of land, falling prices for agricultural products on the national and world markets and, especially in the case of migration from urban areas, the failure of those who hold political power in Mexico to come up with economic policies that would create jobs for young people as they entered the workforce.

Until my friend, Nancy Churchill, brought me to "Pantla" and Marta described to me her sufferings under the rule of her husband's mother, I didn't understand that some migration is prompted not by economic but by cultural forces. Specifically it is caused by the tyranny of a mother-in-law over the young woman her son brings home to live in his parents' house in accordance with the tradition of "patrilocal" residence for a young couple, that is, the obligation of the bride to take up residence in the home of the parents of the groom.

Marta was typical of the majority of women in the countryside of Puebla who had gone straight from their wedding ceremony to live in the household of their in-laws. When she talked to me, however, we were not in the home of her in-laws. We were close by in the nearly completed two-story house that Marta's father, Don Nacho, had built for her with the remittances sent from Brooklyn by Marta's husband,

José. We were in a cinder-block structure with a tile roof and four ample bedrooms, a kitchen, and a living room that dominated a knoll on
a piece of land that had previously been part of Don Nacho's allotment
of ejido land. Marta says:

> Of course my dad has hung onto three hectares of his ejido
> parcel because, you know, he's one of those men who is
> really uncomfortable if he isn't producing corn. It's this big
> thing with him because he really thinks the corn he grows is
> better than what everyone else grows in their *milpa*—not to
> speak of the imported corn that they use in the tortilleria.
>
> So he still wants to plant his *parcela*. But he gave each one of
> us kids a house lot out of the other two hectares of land that
> he inherited from his father, who was one of the original eji-
> datarios here in Pantla. But the deal is that, in return, we
> girls have to go out and help him in his *milpa* when it's time
> to turn over the soil and plant or harvest because there's
> really no one you can hire to do that for you. It costs too
> much because there are hardly any men around.

So it was that, even before Marta married, she knew that if she
and her novio, José, could raise the funds to construct a house, they
would have a piece of land on which to build. But it would take eight
years of hard labor in casual construction jobs that José found in New
York, and eight years of physical separation for the two before the
house project was even underway. And in the first months of those
eight years, Marta lived with José's parents. Indeed, José and Marta had
lived together at his parents', but only for a week before José left his
bride behind to set out for New York. Marta explains,

> José and I met on a *combi*, of course. That's where all my
> friends ended up meeting the men who became their hus-
> bands. You stand at the bus stop waiting for the combi, the
> van that's going to take you into Puebla to wash and iron or,
> in my case, to clean someone's house, and you look around at
> the young men and you don't say a word because some of

these are unmarried men in their mid- or late twenties whom you wouldn't know, unless they're friends of an older brother. But the combi arrives and you pile on and you're all squashed in together for an hour-long ride into the city, and by the time you get off, you've got to know each other pretty well.

Only a month or so after meeting Marta on the combi, José "declared himself," as the expression goes, and Marta became his *novia*. They married a year later, at which point he brought her to his parents' to live and took off with his brother and a coyote to a job on a construction site in Brooklyn.

In a town like Pantla, the mother-in-law, the *suegra*, has total authority over the daughter-in-law, the *nuera*. When Marta joined the household of her in-laws, she was one of three young women, all new wives of three brothers, all living in the house of their husbands' parents' while their husbands were living together alongside the Gowanus Expressway near Greenwood Cemetery in Brooklyn.

The patrilocal arrangement, as Marta explained it, is supposed to serve as a kind of apprenticeship for married life.

The idea is that your *suegra* is going to teach you the proper way to look after your husband, how to cook food the way he likes it, how to wash his clothing. But with all the husbands in the United States, we were just an unpaid workforce for his parents, who had no children left at home. We washed and cleaned under the orders of my *suegra*. We were marched out to the *milpa*, which was a two-hour walk from the village, and there we were set to work with hoes, turning over the soil, planting, and later weeding and carrying out all the labor involved in raising corn. My mother-in-law was in charge of the whole operation, and she wouldn't allow us to sit down to rest. We had no water to drink, and often we went for hours without so much as a tortilla with *frijoles*. My mother-in law just supervised, she didn't do any work other than keeping an eye on us and telling us how useless we were. Once I became so thirsty that I drank water from a puddle and, of course, I became very sick.

But this, Marta tells me, wasn't the worst of her situation The worst was that her *suegra* would not allow Marta, or any of the other daughters-in-law, to leave the house, not even to visit their own parents in the village.

> Your *suegra* would keep you home saying that every time you left the house the family was at risk of scandal because you might stop to talk to a man as you walked across the plaza! In fact, sometimes the problem was not that you *might* speak to a man along the way. Sometimes your *suegra* would accuse you directly of plotting an affair with another man and claim that the visit you wanted to make to your own parents was just a cover for your betrayal of her son.

"And there was always the threat," Marta says, "that when your husband would call on Sundays from New York, your mother-in-law would spin all kinds of lies about you: that you were disobeying her and your *suegro*, that you were creating a scandal in the village with your loose behavior, that you were unfaithful to him."

This was how Marta described her situation in the mid-1990s and I couldn't help but think that what she had depicted was a case of extreme pathology. I asked her if this life wasn't somehow extraordinary.

"Talk to any of my friends," she said. "They'll tell you the same stories from their own experience." And indeed I did interview many other women, in Pantla and other villages, who reported leading lives of total subordination no better and sometimes even worse than what Marta had described. Marta was ill-used, but she was not beaten by her in-laws, as other women reported they had been.

And thus, I learned that this remarkable residue of the past, the absolute submission of young married women to their husband's parents, and the availability of daughters-in-law as unpaid, forced labor, was still widespread and common practice in rural communities— above all, but by no means exclusively, in indigenous communities. What has happened, though, is that this custom has been transformed by migration so that the mediating influence of the husband, who might normally intervene with his parents to protect his bride from exploitation and abuse, is removed from the equation to the extreme disadvantage of the young wife a male migrant would leave behind.

Still, it seemed astonishing to me that in the twenty-first century, with all the changes brought to the countryside by migration and remittances, such oppressive conditions could persist. When carrying out a joint interview with Marta and Margarita, one of her friends, I asked them if there were no examples of mothers-in-law who were caring and understanding of their daughters-in-law. They thought for a while, discussed the question between themselves, and then Marta turned to me and said, "There are actually two modern *suegras* here in Pantla." This was the exact terminology she used: "modern mothers-in-law." And when I asked what accounted for their "modernity," which I understood to mean their empathetic capacity and kindness, Marta explained that both of these women had married early, and their sons had also married young, and that both, as a consequence, were women in their mid-thirties who constituted a new generation of *suegras*.

And so, Marta's experience should be understood as typical, not exceptional. Yet, the outcome of her tale was strikingly different from the standard scenario. Perhaps because she was a young woman who had completed secondary school and had more personal confidence; perhaps because she was in her early twenties, not a teenager, when she married, perhaps because she had such a close relationship with her own parents—after several months of living under the arbitrary command of her mother-in-law, on an occasion when she had, once again, been denied permission to cross the village to visit her parents, she simply walked out.

> I went to my parents' house and I got down on my knees in front of my father and I lowered my eyes and I begged him to allow me to come back to live with him and my mother. I think he didn't know what to say, and for sure he didn't know the trouble that he would bring upon himself, but he just made me promise that I would help my mother in all her tasks and he said, yes, I could come home.

The trouble that would come to Don Nacho amounted to being shunned by the majority of his neighbors for having broken with tradition. Taking his daughter back had undermined the authority of her in-laws—and, by extension, the entire system of patrilocal residence—and it shook the patriarchal foundations of village life more vigorously than an earthquake. Marta says,

> My dad paid a heavy price for taking me in. He's a man who was very respected in our pueblo. He'd been on the school committee and people knew him as an *albañil* and he depended on their goodwill to get himself work. So when people stopped speaking to him, it was very hard.

Effectively, Don Nacho was shunned until his son-in-law returned to Pantla and took up residence, first in Don Nacho's house with Marta, and eventually in the house that Don Nacho had built with the remittances that José had sent down from New York. When José chose his wife over his parents, when he accepted her word over the calumny spread by his parents, when he agreed to live temporarily in a matrilocal setting, that is, with Marta's parents, until the construction of their own house was complete, the public shunning mostly ended. And in some sense, a new era began in Pantla

While Marta escaped the oppressive control of her in-laws, most of her contemporaries have no alternative but to submit unless and until their husbands send remittances sufficient to construct their own home. In the meanwhile, in the struggle between daughters-in-law and mothers-in-law to receive and control the remittances that are sent back to the village, extravagant lies are often told by the parents to the son. The son, for his part, would need a very firm level of commitment to a young women he may scarcely know and with whom he may have lived only briefly, to take her word over that of his mother. Marta explains:

> You can't believe some of the things the mothers say when the son phones on Sundays. They say, "Your wife is running around wearing pants instead of a skirt. She's cut off her braids and is wearing her hair short!" And these are just the *indirectas*, as we call them. Sometimes the mother just plain says to the son, "Your wife is fooling around."

All that Marta had described of her life with her mother-in-law and the ill feeling between them came back to me when I returned to a village in Morelos where I had lived in the 1990s. Here I visited a former neighbor, Celia, whose husband I had never met because he had been off working in Houston the entire time that I had lived in this small town. Now Héctor was back.

Celia told me that only one week after Héctor returned from Houston, at a dinner at his parents' house with his brothers, their wives, and children, Héctor's older brother suddenly piped up and announced to him that Celia had been having an affair with a taxi driver with whom she had been seen every day riding off in the direction of Cuautla.

"Just like that," Celia said. "Out of nowhere, in front of the children and my in-laws and everyone!" And, evidently, Héctor, rather than thrashing his brother and defending his wife, turned to Celia—in front of everyone—and asked, "Is this true?"

Celia says that she knew from the start that her brother-in-law was hoping to make trouble and ruin any pleasure that Héctor might be enjoying upon his return.

It was plain to me that my *cuñado* was just trying to hurt Héctor, because he's always resented Héctor's success in Houston and he's jealous that we now have a real house and he's still living with his family in an adobe house. But he hurt me and he hurt our marriage because instead of defending me and being angry at his brother for his lies, Héctor was angry with me for giving people cause to gossip. He was furious and he said, "People see you walking about the village!"—as if I had any choice. What did he expect? If I didn't leave the house, how did he think I could get to the market to buy food to put on the table for his children?.

So after this he forbade me to leave the house at all. Try to imagine this: I am a 40-year-old woman who lives in a new two-story house, but I am really alone because my daughter is married and my son is in Mexico City studying. I have a husband who comes and goes to Houston when he chooses

and I am forbidden by him to leave the house. I'm a prisoner, but I haven't committed any crime.

When I recounted Celia's story to Marta, she was unsurprised.
"Sure," she said.

The same thing happens all the time here in Pantla. The
husband doesn't want his wife to leave the house, not even to
buy food. And if, say, she wants to do something useful where
she can make a little money, something like preparing and selling tamales in the market, or selling clothing in the weekly
tianguis, her *suegros* won't let her. Why not? Because it will
suggest that her husband doesn't send enough money home
and is a failure, and this will expose the family to ridicule.

Marta goes on:

And it's bad enough that your friend Celia is a prisoner in
her own house, but, it could also work out that when her
husband goes back to Houston, she will really *need* to sell
tamales because it might be that she relies completely on her
suegros to pass along to her some part of the remittances that
her husband sends back to the village. Here in Pantla you get
suegros who never pass the wife and grandchildren their
share. They just hang onto all the money, and it's too bad for
the wife.

This, Marta says, is why many women begin to campaign to join
their husbands in the United States to "help" them "get ahead," as they
frame it. They explain to their husbands that, working together, they
can accumulate capital twice as fast without doubling the expenses.
Marta says there are a lot of pressures that push women to join their
husbands up north.

There's always talk in the village and lots of women feel they
have to justify to everyone why they *haven't* migrated with
their husband. Mostly, they say that they don't want to raise

their children in a place like the United States. But, then there are also the wives who are more ambitious than their husbands, and who push their husbands to migrate in order to send remittances and give them a future. Then there are men who don't want to migrate but they feel they're not *macho* if they don't. And then there are the really sad cases— men who migrate and cannot return home because things didn't go well for them in the United States and they would be coming home with nothing, so they're stuck there.

Of course I have friends who have followed their husbands to New York. But it's not a great situation. Either you have to leave your children behind in the village to be brought up by their grandparents, which is great if the *abuelos* are loving people, but you see cases like my friend Margarita, where the *abuelos* use the grandchildren to get more money from their son and daughter-in-law, and then they spend it on themselves, not on the kids. Or you take your children with you— but that means you have to cross at the border with a coyote, which means coming up with at least $7,000 for the wife plus the children because coyotes charge more for the kids, and anyway, do you really want to take these risks with your children?

As these women's experiences reveal, despite the rapid pace of change in the Mexican economy and in its political life as a multiparty system begins to take hold, many social aspects have changed slowly or not at all. In a word, patriarchy lives, and nowhere more so than in the kinds of small towns where these interviews were carried out: that is, precisely in the places in Mexico most likely to be migrant-sending communities.

The persistence of patriarchal attitudes, even among those who have spent half a lifetime in the United States, was clear in a chance conversation I had with Don Juanito under a gigantic eucalyptus tree in the central plaza in Tepec in the Mixteca region of Puebla. Juanito had emigrated thirty years earlier. He had regularized his status under IRCA and brought his wife to live with him in Dover, New Jersey, where they had raised six sons. Juanito tells me that only the second oldest is married, but "luckily," this young man listened to his parents and traveled down to Tepec to find a wife. That this young woman is from Tepec is very much a point in her favor in the eyes of her father-in-law who, despite thirty long and seemingly satisfactory years spent in New Jersey, desperately hopes that all his sons will find an "unspoiled village girl" for a wife.

The persistence of patriarchy was clear as well in the ways that land is held and regarded. As we have noted, Article 27 of the Mexican Constitution was reformed to harmonize Mexican property law with that of the United States and Canada in preparation for the negotiation of NAFTA. At that time, many specialists in rural development assumed that soon all the peasants would lose their land. But in countless cases, ejidatarios have held onto their land. In part this may be because, like Don Beto, they value the land as a way of life. But it is also the case that ejido land is no longer worth much as a productive resource, and unless it has some value as real estate, it is unlikely that anyone will step forward to make an attractive offer that might induce an ejidatario to sell out.

In the end, migration has had some remarkable effects on land use. In many villages, men who migrated precisely because they had *not* inherited land and would have been condemned to a life of working the fields of others as *jornaleros*, ended up earning enough in the United States to buy land from neighbors who had lost interest in cultivating their *parcela* because of the high risk and low prices in agriculture. Thus, in a strange turnabout, in many rural areas in Mexico, those who were previously the poorest villagers with the most limited education and prospects have acquired land and even concentrated fairly large amounts of it. Correspondingly, those previously advantaged by their possession of at least a small ejido plot have preferred to sell land that they now regard as unproductive or that is now impractical to cultivate because they have no sons on hand to help and the price of day labor is so high. Having sold their land, these former ejidatarios may open a small business or build a house with the proceeds of their sales. Alternatively, they may simply live on the remittances sent by their children. Or they may sell some part and hang on to the rest, as we have seen in the case of Don Beto, whose continued cultivation of his cornfield is, in effect, a luxury that he can afford because his children migrated long ago and they continue to send him remittances.

But even as so many villages have witnessed a great shuffle and shifting of ownership of land, either as a potentially productive resource or a source of prestige or security, some ejidatarios have started to put their allotment to an entirely new use. This has been to parcel it out and assign it as house lots for migrant sons and daughters, as was the case for Marta's father, Don Nacho. In this way the father enjoys a big boost in authority. He might be an old peasant in *huaraches* and a straw sombrero that frames a weathered face, but he is the one who controls the land and decides who among his children will be given a plot on which to build. In some cases, the father's retention of his ejido land produces a family compound. Each son and daughter builds a house in what becomes a cul-de-sac of immigrant dream homes constructed by a group of siblings—a great source of satisfaction to a father who may hope to keep his family together in spite of the centrifugal tendencies of migration.

Accordingly, the enhancement of Don Nacho's patriarchal authority was evident in the deal he struck with Marta when he said to her, "I'm giving you a nice lot for your house and the same for your sisters, and I will help each of you to build a house if your husband will send the money. But you have to work with me to plant my corn."

And so, Marta, whose bitter memories of her life with her in-laws centers on performing forced labor in their cornfield, very willingly works in her father's *milpa* at much the same tasks: hoeing, planting, weeding, and harvesting. In this way, Marta now ends up with a two-story house and a living room large enough to furnish with a couch, two chairs, a television, and a stereo player—but also an entire corner piled high with sacks of corn from her father's *milpa*.

5

Dolores: "We Only Speak on Sundays"

In the kitchen of a new house in Veracruz, Dolores is frying eggs and toasting fresh tortillas on a *comal*, a metal surface heated from below by a brazier filled with charcoal. "This is the old way of doing these things," Dolores admits, but she insisted, when Antonio returned to build their modest house, that she had to have a proper setup to cook traditional foods in the traditional way.

Dolores confides that she is not entirely comfortable with a good number of the consumer products that Antonio's remittances have permitted her to buy over the years he has been working in the United States, not to mention the appliances, like the microwave, that he brought down to "San Pedro" when he last made the return trip from the other side. "Antonio is used to these kind of machines," Dolores says, "and he wants to have them in the house he has built for us here. But he's been living in another world all these years and it's hard for me to get used to some of the things that have been in his life in New York." Dolores explains:

> When my sister-in-law reached New York in 1997, she moved into the room that Antonio had been sharing with her husband, Chuy, and Antonio moved into the living room with his cousins. Two years later, when she returned,

she told me how amazed she was to find that, living without women, these men had divided among themselves all the household tasks like shopping, cleaning, and cooking. As it turned out, it was Antonio's job to clean the bathroom, and he actually did clean the bathroom, every day with a damp rag and once a week with bleach. Of course, I didn't say it straight out, but it was hard for me even to picture because it was so far from anything that I had ever seen a man do— let alone Antonio, whose mother and sisters did everything for him and for his brothers in their home.

I was astonished that Dolores was so surprised, and I asked her if Antonio had never described his living arrangements or how he managed his food and laundry. She said:

To be honest, I didn't ask. It wasn't that I wasn't curious, but in a way I didn't want to know too much. Maybe it was my fear that he was being looked after by some other woman, maybe a *dominicana* or a *puertoriqueña* who could get him his papers. All the stories you heard were about loose women who were all Dominicans or Puerto Ricans who were like sorceresses who would bewitch your husband and steal him from you. So what I knew was that he was living with his brother and cousins, but I never asked any details about how they got by.

"But did he talk to you about his work?" I asked.

Well, he would tell me each time he got a new job—or he'd say something like, "Don't look for any money this week because the auto body shop closed and I have to find something else." But I didn't know a lot of the details because we only speak on Sundays. When he would call, I would just say a few words, and then I would put each of the kids on the phone to tell Antonio everything that they were doing in school so that they would know that their father cared about them and their schoolwork and that he was still in their lives

and that he had expectations for them—that he was not just
a stranger who sends money and toys.

Dolores says that this kind of routine was also crucial in terms of
shifting to Antonio some of the burden of discipline that falls on the
shoulders of a woman who, in effect, is raising her children as a single parent. "What I do," she says, "is to take the phone and to say to Antonio—
loud, so the boys could hear—'Your sons are not obeying me.' Then I
would call them to the phone and Antonio would say, 'I'm your father and
I'm telling you that you have to listen to your mother!'"

It was for this reason that Dolores, like many other women I interviewed, had only a very approximate idea of where her husband
lived and how he earned the remittances that arrived every two weeks
via Western Union. To be sure, as Dolores attests, part of not knowing
is not wanting to know because of the fear that a husband who has
gone off to New York on his own may find another woman and may
start a new life and a new family, abandoning the one he already has in
Mexico.

When our conversation came around to this most intimate and
sensitive subject, I found that many of the women left behind held a
view similar to the one expressed by Dolores when she stated bluntly:
"Men have their needs, so I would understand if Antonio went with a
prostitute." Recourse to paid sex, in the eyes of the women left behind,
constitutes the lesser evil when compared to the possibility that their
husbands could establish an enduring relationship with someone else.

This response is noteworthy in light of the very sketchy level of
knowledge that people in rural Mexico have about HIV/AIDS. In the
United States, migrants find themselves bombarded with information.
Back in the village there are posters, but rarely any health educators
capable of explaining the full implication of the "Get yourself tested"
exhortations to the figures—all male—who are depicted on the in-
structional drawings posted on the door of the health clinic.

When I point to one of these posters as Dolores and I pass the
clinic in San Pedro, she shrugs and says, "That's another thing I try not
to think about. Sometimes I ask myself: How well do I really know the
father of my children?"

"After so many years apart," Dolores says, "your husband can become a stranger to you. It sounds terrible to say, but I can tell you for certain that there are women in the village who would be just as happy if their husbands never came back, as long as they continued to send money for the children."

"Is this because the women have found someone else?" I ask. She replies:

> People always joke and say, "Well, there aren't many men left in the village," but those who are still around are really kept hopping. It's hard for me to know because I try not to listen to this kind of gossip, let alone join in, because I'm sure that people who enjoy telling me these kinds of rumors will be talking behind my back the next day.

> But when you consider that many of the wives left behind are still teenagers, and even though these young women are supposed to be under the supervision of their in-laws, there are high school boys around who are basically their age and haven't left yet for the other side and who knows what might go on? One thing's for sure, even if the lover is a teenager himself, he would know enough to keep his mouth shut and not brag to his friends, because the husband could return and hear the rumors and you don't even want to think about what could happen!

But Dolores doesn't think that some wives dread their husband's return because they've taken up with someone else. On the contrary, these women are just not used to living with a man.

> A woman can wait and wait for her husband's return, but in the meantime, if he has sent the money for her to be living in her own house, she gets used to managing the household on her own. Then he comes home for a few weeks or months, but he's very overbearing in his behavior. And he keeps talking about his sacrifices, but doesn't appreciate hers, and he expects to be waited on like a king to make up for all he's done without.

Dolores says, "You've got to remember that a lot of these wives met their husbands when they were, say, fourteen years old, and they accepted this young man as a *novio* when they were fifteen. Then they married at sixteen and a few days or weeks later he takes off and they've never really lived together as a married couple."

> They don't really know each other well, even though they have children together. And you've got these husbands who phone up every Sunday and say, "Tell me about my children. Tell me about my parents." But they don't say a word about her. He doesn't really know her, so he doesn't care about her. He cares about his parents, of course, and *his* children, because they are part of him. But she is like a stranger to him.

And sometimes, as I learned from my friend Celia, fathers really don't know their own children. Celia says that her husband left for Houston when her son had just turned 9 and her daughter was 13. Somehow Héctor grasped that in the course of his absence, his daughter had grown to womanhood. But he always retained the image of his son as a boy. Thus, when Héctor returned seven years after leaving Morelos, Celia traveled with her two children to the international airport in Mexico City to welcome him home. But when he emerged from the baggage claim and saw the three of them waiting, Héctor assumed that the tall, muscular young man standing next to his daughter was her *novio*, and he became enraged that his son had been so disrespectful to have missed the welcome party at the airport.

When I relate this experience to Dolores, she is not surprised. "Listen, I have a neighbor named Gregorio," she says, "who is sixteen years old and the father of a newborn son. But he's never once seen his own father, who has never stopped sending money, even though he hasn't been back to San Pedro since Gregorio was born."

"It's always hard," says Dolores.

> My husband sent money for Oscar's birthday and he also sent money when Oscar graduated from primary school, which was an especially proud day for his father because Antonio himself had never made it past third grade. But Oscar

just looked at the money and he went into the bedroom, closed the door, and I could hear him crying. You never really get to accept the absence of this person, although it brings you many benefits.

In the end, women worry about losing their husbands and being abandoned. Both wives and parents worry that the remittances will stop flowing if their sons and daughters meet someone "up north" and form a family with that person. Indeed, part of what makes the relationship between women and their *suegros* so bitter is that everyone is living on the edge, in extreme insecurity and totally dependent on remittances that may or may not come.

Dolores has had plenty of time in her life to think these things through. She says:

You live your life like a widow, you see your children grow up without a father, you depend on someone thousands of miles away, your in-laws dump on you, you have people gossiping about you and passing rumors that you've been unfaithful to your husband. You see your own friends migrate while you stay behind. These are painful things to endure.

Part II

The Journey

6

Tomás: Traveling in Style

Tomás is standing on the curb in front of his house with his arms crossed over his chest looking ruefully at the van parked at his door. This small, rusted-out Ford was not in his homecoming plans three months earlier when he decided it had been too long since he'd been back to see his wife, daughters, and grandchildren in Trancoso, a town of twenty thousand, some ten kilometers from the capital of the state of Zacatecas. The vehicle that he intended to drive to Mexico was an eight-year-old Chevy pickup truck with a cabin, four-wheel drive, extra-heavy suspension, and only 180,000 miles on the odometer. The truck—which Tomás referred to in our conversation in Spanish not as a *camioneta*, but as a *troca*, and at times more affectionately as *mi troquilla*, was the key element that for years had held together his life in the United States, allowing him to move between East Los Angeles, where he lived with his three brothers, and his work as a plumber and electrician on construction sites on the west side of the city and out beyond the Hollywood Hills in the San Fernando Valley.

This truck also figured in his plans to stretch his time at home in Zacatecas to months, rather than his usual stay of a few weeks. Tomás was calculating that with all the immigrants from Trancoso sending remittances back to build their dream homes, there would be plenty of work for a skilled electrician and plumber who also knows carpentry, plastering, painting, and roofing, and how to pour a foundation and lay brick, cinder block, or even adobe—not that anyone in Trancoso still wants adobe, even if, he tells me, "this is what rich people in Beverly Hills and North Hollywood sometimes require to achieve a 'hacienda effect.' And, you know, they're not wrong to want adobe, because it's a lot cooler in the summer."

With the truck to haul materials, Tomás could make a reasonable living in Trancoso, where the demand for skilled and unskilled builders—*albañiles*—greatly outstrips the supply. Indeed this is the situation to be found in any city, town, or village in Mexico where the people who hope to build houses and have the resources to do so are thousands of miles away in the United States bussing tables, delivering pizzas, or cleaning offices to earn the remittances to underwrite the construction project back home.

Thus Tomás, after nearly thirty years of construction work in California, was much in demand in Trancoso and could actually make himself a modest living in his hometown. True, his earnings as an *albañil* in Trancoso represent only a fraction of what he was accustomed to earning even as an *unlicensed* plumber and electrician in California. And there were many occasions when Tomás's take-home pay would triple if a friend would lend him his certification number or an associate would "rent" his number to him so that Tomás could charge the $50 an hour that a licensed workman can command.

So Tomás's long-anticipated return journey to his family in Mexico was scheduled to be made in the truck. But the plan was halted at the off-ramp of the Golden State Freeway when, according to the police officer involved, Tomás failed to come to a complete stop before turning right onto César Chávez Avenue.

> It's almost thirty years that I have been driving in the United States without a license and nothing's ever happened to me. I've never even been stopped. I've never been given a ticket. Not for anything. So now this cop says that I didn't stop at the corner—which wasn't true. But even if I had a thousand witnesses who had seen me stop, I can't show up in traffic court to argue with the guy because I don't have any papers.

What's more, when the cop stopped me, I had the registration for the truck but no driver's license, so he tells me he's going to impound the truck. So now I'm supposed to pay the cost of towing, the ticket for failing to stop, the infraction for driving without a license, and the whole deal is going to cost me $1,800, and that's if I chase over to the pound to get my truck right away and I don't end up paying an extra $800 a month as a storage fee.

I've got to say, I really liked that truck. But without a driver's license there was no way that I could just pay a fine and drive away in my truck. Besides, I knew I could buy something like this Ford van I have here for about $700.

"So you just stood there," I ask Tomás, "while they hauled away your truck?"

It was worse than that. I had all my tools in the back—like, everything I own and use on the job—stuff that's worth maybe a couple of thousand dollars if I had to buy it all again. And this son-of-a-bitch is telling me he's going to impound the truck with all the tools in it. This cop was really arrogant. He was a real gringo kind of gringo, and he was pretending that he didn't know a word of Spanish—which I seriously doubt.

But I got lucky because the guy driving the tow truck was a Chicano, and he figured out what was going on and told the cop, "I don't want to lift the rear end of this truck with all that shit rolling around in the back." So the cop relented and he let me unload my tools from the truck. But there I was at the foot of the off-ramp with no truck and just about everything I own in the United States piled around me on the pavement.

After a quick cell phone call, Tomás's brother came to pick him up. The next day, Tomás bought the $700 van and he moved his departure for Zacatecas forward without waiting to see if the cop would make good on his threat to get a warrant for his arrest for driving without a license. "It could have been a lot worse," Tomás says. "I was planning a trip home in any case. But it's real sweet and easy to come home. It's another thing to try to get back to L.A."

Tomás should know. He is a walking compendium of audacious border-crossing techniques. In his first crossing in 1977, for example, he rode for six hours from Ciudad Acuña, in the northern state of Coahuila, to San Antonio, Texas, suspended from the undercarriage of a train.

> The way it works is that you have to make your way to Ciudad Acuña, which is the border town across from Del Rio, Texas, and you wait around until the northbound train stops—which it's going to do for about two minutes—and that's all the time you have to scramble underneath the train where you find a kind of a shelf, which is actually part of the wheel well. You can crawl into this space over the wheel and lie down on this shelf. We joke that it's as if the people who designed the train knew that guys like us were going to need a comfortable place to stretch out while riding to the other side.

> So once you insert yourself into this space, you look for some kind of hole so that you can thread your belt or a cord or whatever you've brought along for this purpose, through the hole to strap yourself in place because, the truth is, once the train starts to move and the sparks start to fly off the tracks and the wheels kick pebbles up at you, you could really lose it. You could get so frightened that you let go when you really need to hang on. The sparks and the stones aren't really dangerous. What's dangerous is if you get scared or inattentive, and that's when you can fall down under the wheels and get your feet cut off, or worse.

Tomás explains that this border crossing was organized by a coyote who received $250 from each of the migrants to deliver them to a factory in Houston that contracted him to supply unskilled workers. So the coyote was earning at both ends.

> But I'll tell you, the guy earned his pay, because he was right there with the rest of us, and this was something that this coyote did at least a couple of times a week: the trip from Ciudad Acuña to San Antonio under the train. Once we got to San Antonio, the coyote lowered himself down and ran up and down the train banging on the side of the cars and shouting for us to untie ourselves and crawl out and follow him.

The coyote took all eighteen men he had brought across the border to a McDonald's, where he bought everyone a Big Mac. They then returned to the rail yard and waited until dark for the train that would take them straight through to Houston and the factory that had contracted their labor. "But this time," Tomás explains, "we weren't riding under the train. We were riding in style."

> The coyote put us on a train that was carrying brand-new cars and we just opened the car doors, climbed in—one guy sitting behind the wheel, his *compadre* next to him riding shotgun—and we just rumbled along on this train. You could even sleep in the back seat of the car if you wanted to, but no one wanted to because these cars had keys in their ignition, so you could listen to the radio. And they had cassette players, too. I said to my *compadre*, "Too bad you didn't think to bring along cassette tapes. We could be listening to *rancheras* right now!"

Tomás says that in spite of the danger of riding under a train, this first crossing was one of the best he would make, in large part because the coyote was very professional and because the coyote worked alone, guiding the migrants from the Mexican side and personally delivering them to their destination. Tomás would not always be that lucky.

For example, in 1990, after spending several weeks with his family in Zacatecas, Tomás traveled by bus to Tijuana, was picked up by a coyote in the bus station who inserted him into a group of more than fifty men and women who would move across the *linea* in a pack. Massing at the border crossing into the United States, the group ran north in the southbound lane of Interstate 5, while southbound cars swerved to avoid hitting them and the INS agents captured only the slowest of the group. This was a technique so starkly simple in its conception that Tomás wondered, even as he ran along, why he had bothered to contract a coyote to take him across. It was so easy to run in a pack, and there was no shortage of women and *gorditos*, and women who were themselves rather *gorda* who would inevitably fall behind, thus opening the way for more fleet-footed migrants like himself to make it to San Ysidro on the California side. In fact, Tomás says that at first he made the mistake of trying to help a small, Guatemalan woman who was making very slow progress up the southbound lane of I-5 when he came within an inch of being grabbed by an INS agent.

> The migra got hold of the señora and was trying to grab me as well. But she struggled with him, and meanwhile I slipped out of his grasp, and I didn't stop running until I got to the parking lot of the 7-Eleven in San Ysidro. That's where the coyote told me he would pick me up along with the others who had contracted with him and he would transport us all to East LA.

But this is where Tomás's serious problems would begin. As I myself learned years earlier from Pedro, a coyote I interviewed in Tijuana in 1992, the work of people smugglers is increasingly differentiated and specialized. Pedro was a specialist in "jumping the fence," passing people over or, more frequently, under the sixteen-foot fence that ran along "El Bordo," the borderline separating Tijuana from the stretch of no-man's-land between Tijuana and its twin city, San Ysidro, twenty miles south of San Diego. Pedro's part of the operation required him to deliver his group of migrants to a prearranged spot on the U.S. side. There his "associates," the people with whom he coordinated his work, would pay him $100 a head as an advance on the $300 that, in those days, was the sum they contracted to receive from the migrants' "sponsors," that is, the friends or relations who were waiting for them in East

Los Angeles and who had committed to paying the coyote fees. In those days, Pedro had explained, his team contracted to deliver the migrant, as they put it, COD—cash on delivery.

Back when Tomás crossed, the coyote's fees were even lower, but today, in 2007, the sums that change hands may easily run ten times the standard fees that Pedro charged in 1992. But the fundamental division of labor is the same and, except when business is very slow, a coyote like Pedro is likely to take charge of recruiting migrants, hiding them in a safe house on the Mexican side, and bringing them over the border. Meanwhile his associates on the U.S. side—typically people who have proper credentials to live and circulate in the United States—"buy" the migrants from the coyote who has brought them across and take charge of transporting the migrants to their final destination. That destination could be a border city, it could be Los Angeles, or it could be the airport or bus station from which they will catch a flight to Chicago, New York, or even Juneau, Alaska. It all depends on where their friends and relations are waiting for them.

But there's a problem, Tomás says.

> You may have an excellent coyote who looks after you on the Mexican side, who comes recommended by people in your hometown, or maybe the coyote is someone you don't know but who inspired confidence when he presented himself to you at the bus station, someone who seems to know what he's doing. But once he takes you across to the other side— whatever method he uses to take you across—this first guy is going to disappear. He heads back to Mexico to bring an- other group across and you're left with his *cuates*, his pals, and you have to hope they are capable and honest and won't rob you or rape you or rip you off in some way.

In the crossing that Tomás made in 1990 the relief he felt in arriv- ing safely in San Ysidro was short-lived. The coyote to whom he was "sold" set out with his group of seven migrants in a van driven by a friend. But the group could only travel up Interstate 5 to a point just south of San Clemente, roughly halfway between San Diego and Los Angeles, where the INS maintained what look like tollbooths that stretch across I-5 and allow for surveillance of every car and truck that passes. At this juncture, it fell to the coyote to lead his charges around the checkpoint by cutting a wide swath through the mountains east of the highway. However, the coyote became disoriented and lost his way.

> Pretty soon it was clear that this coyote didn't know where he was or what he was doing, and even the most obvious strategy—like you need to walk along keeping the noise and lights of the cars to your left—was something he couldn't figure out.

> And the worst was that all the other guys were from the city, and I was the only campesino in the group. I was the only one who had ever spent a night in the desert, or climbed a *cerro*, or knew how to get water from a cactus, or how *not* to step on a snake. The other guys—well, they knew that a rattlesnake rattles. But that was about it.

> So I had to lead the group. I had to tell these city guys what to do. I should have left that son-of-a-whore coyote in the desert running around in circles and collected the coyote's fee for myself. But we needed the coyote to pass us along to his friend with the van who was waiting for us north of the San Clemente checkpoint.

But Tomás acknowledges that, on balance, it is a big advantage to cross the border in the company of urban people—above all, Chilangos, that is, people from Mexico City, from the Federal District, the DF, as it is called.

> When you have to do something like cross the border, it's great to do that with a Chilango. The Chilangos are the smartest people that exist in Mexico. Life in the DF is very difficult and very dangerous and people who grow up there really have to learn to figure things out very quickly in order to defend themselves. They're very sharp, very astute. They know every trick anyone can pull.

Tomás has never been to the capital of Mexico, and all the Chilangos he knows are people he has met in Los Angeles or in the process of crossing the border. But, he says, "to be the *compañero* of a Chilango—now, that's a real advantage in life!"

Tomás offers as an example another crossing he made years earlier in the company of two men from Durango and a Chilango.

> Once we crossed into the United States, we were passed along to a pair of coyotes who were totally spaced out on drugs. These guys were smoking marijuana and popping pills and, I can tell you, they had a lot more energy to walk across the desert than we did, given that we were running on pure *tacos*, not drugs.

The original group, Tomás explains, numbered ten, but the coyotes abandoned the people who fell behind, and when anyone protested, one of the coyotes whipped out a gun and started waving it around.

> So we shut up and did what we were told, and the two coyotes led us to a van, and they drove us to East L.A. to an area that I actually knew quite well because when I first came to L.A., on my way to work, I used to ride a bus that passed through there. The coyotes had us phone our relatives and tell them to get the money ready, and then they locked us in the back room of a bungalow in what I realized—from the sound—had to be a street close to the Santa Ana Freeway. They figured on holding us there until the next day, and meanwhile they're sitting on the veranda at the front of the house smoking pot.
>
> So the Chilango pulls a nail clipper out of his backpack—the kind with the tiny knife that swings around to form the top of the clipper. Then, very patiently, he digs around the window of the room where we're locked in. And finally it gives way and he can push the window out by its frame. He wakes the other two guys, and we step outside, climb over the fence

at the back of the yard, slip into the alleyway behind, and we just walk over to the bus stop and wait for the bus that runs all night.

Tomás says that his advantage was that he knew the numbers and routes of lots of buses in L.A. "You know, you can get people who've lived their whole lives in L.A., but always driving around in cars, and they haven't got a clue how to get around the city on a bus."

I put the two guys from Durango off the bus at Olympic and Doyle and I pointed out where they needed to go so that they could get to their relatives on foot. The Chilango needed to get to Chicago, so I put him off at the corner where he could pick up the bus to the airport.

Tomás notes that in a challenging situation, you don't need to be with a Chilango as such. You just need to be with people who are smart, preferably people who have been across to the other side before and who can figure things out. Sometimes the crossing can go very well.

One time in the 1990s when I crossed at Tijuana, I just attached myself to a group of five guys at the fence—two guys from Sinaloa, another from Durango, and two more, like me, from Zacatecas.

We all had some experience crossing in the past and among the six of us, it worked fine. We waited for the right moment, we ran across a stretch of no-man's-land, we waded the Tijuana River—which was more mud than water at the time—using big green garbage bags over our shoes and pants so that the mud wouldn't give us away later on when we got to the other side. We ran across I-5, and then we just walked to the terminus of the trolley, waited for the right moment, and bought a ticket from the machine to ride the trolley from San Ysidro to San Diego. Once we were in San Diego, we bought another ticket from another machine to ride the

Metrolink to Union Station. And that's it. Next thing we're in L.A. with no coyote, no nothing.

Tomás allows that they had to be very careful at Union Station, which is one of the few places in Los Angeles where he or anyone of his acquaintance has even *heard* of anyone being intercepted by the migra. He says, "Of course you can't stand around gawking like you've never set foot in L.A. before. You've got to look like you know your way around. That's why you could only use this method—the trolley to the train to the bus or airport—once you know how things work on the other side."

As we talk, sitting under the shrine to the Virgin of Guadalupe that hangs from the wall in the front room of his house in Trancoso, Tomás is frankly worried about how he will get back to L.A. Many of the methods he used in the past no longer work for anyone. "What's worse," he says, "is that I'm getting old and it gets harder every time."

Tomás missed his chance for amnesty in 1986 because he was back in Zacatecas during the window of opportunity that would have allowed him to declare his undocumented status without penalty and set in motion the procedures to become a United States citizen. His problem now is that he is in his late fifties and lacks the stamina he would need to employ some of his favorite crossing strategies of the past. In essence, the physical options for crossing the border are narrowing for him at the same time that border crossing options are narrowing for Tomás and for everyone else.

7

Elena: "Absolutely Still"

Elena, a woman from Puebla who lives only a few blocks from Tomás and his brothers in East Los Angeles, also cites this narrowing of options as the reason she could not return to her village, San Rafael, when her mother, Doña Lupe, was dying.

> When I first came to Los Angeles in 1992, I could still go back and forth, but now I don't even think about it, not even when my mother grew ill. When my mother died, of all of us kids, only my brother Freddy, who got his papers in 1986 under the amnesty, could be at her side. It was a terrible, terrible thing.

Elena came to Los Angeles when she was 18 and she was, as she puts it, "one hundred percent clear" in her mind about one thing. She was clear in her thinking about it probably from the age of 10, when she was one of six children of an absent immigrant father. And she only became more certain as the years passed and her father's annual visit, in the week of the festival of San Ysidro, produced another three sisters and two brothers in the household, along with two more rooms made of cinder block built onto the single one-room adobe in which she had been born.

Elena was so certain about her wishes for the life she wanted when she grew up, that when Diego began to come around from a neighboring village when she was only 14, and pressed her to become his *novia*, Elena could tell him straight up that she would never, *never*, marry anyone who planned to migrate to Los Angeles, like the other men in San Rafael, without taking her with him. She was plain about it: she didn't care how difficult it would be to cross the border, or how dangerous or expensive. She didn't care how precarious her life in Los Angeles might be. She didn't care how homesick she might become, or how much she would miss her mother and sisters. She planned to live as a family here, there, she didn't care where. But they had to live together as husband and wife. *And* Diego had to stop drinking, another thing that she wasn't going to tolerate.

It wasn't going to be easy for Diego to quit drinking; his father and his older brothers were all alcoholics. And it wasn't going to be easy for the two of them to live together in East L.A. or even to get to East L.A. But Elena had a plan.

Diego crossed first and found work in construction, and later in a factory. Elena was to follow Diego, but by now she had Caterina, her 18-month-old daughter, and to pay for her journey, Elena had only the $700 that her mother had managed to set aside from the remittances sent by her husband. In 1990 this sum would cover Elena's travel expenses from the village to the border and the crossing at Tijuana. But the coyotes wanted more money to bring a child across, and in any case, Elena was frightened at the prospect of carrying a child through the desert and the mountains.

So Elena devised a strategy. She explains:

> My brother Freddy—the one who has papers—has a son, Federico, who was born in Los Angeles just about the same time that I gave birth in San Rafael. Freddy could cross the border anytime he liked because he's a U.S. citizen, and in those days, all you needed to bring your child back and forth between Mexico and the United States was a birth certificate. Freddy even brought Federico down to San Rafael to visit my mother, and this is what gave me the idea of how I could get my baby safely to L.A.

On the appointed day, with Caterina wrapped in her *rebozo*, Elena took the bus from San Rafael to the city of Puebla, and then a direct flight from Puebla to Tijuana. In the meantime, Freddy caught the bus from East Los Angeles to Tijuana, where he met his sister at the airport. Elena had removed the little gold earrings from Caterina's ears, pulled a soft, snug blue hat down over her head, and—dressed in a Los Angeles Dodgers pajama that her uncle had brought down for the occasion—the baby was carried across the border in the arms of her Uncle Freddy, who presented Federico's birth certificate to the border officials. Elena says:

> The funny thing was that my father was dead against my coming to join my husband in Los Angeles. He couldn't see any reason for a wife to join her husband up here. I mean, given the way he had lived his whole life, he was kind of offended that I had a different idea. That's why he didn't offer to pay my coyote fee, as he had done for my brothers.

> But in the end, he was the one who gave me instructions, who told me to do whatever I could to keep the baby awake all through the trip from San Rafael to Tijuana so that she would be exhausted when the moment came to pass by the border officials and she would fall asleep on her uncle's shoulder. My dad knew a lot of ways to cross, and he was always a great person to give advice on crossing—even for babies.

Having resolved the problem of getting her child across the border, Elena still had to get herself to East Los Angeles, and this she accomplished with the help of Don Teo, a trusted coyote from San Rafael, someone who had already "passed" her uncles, her elder siblings, her cousins, and some of her girlhood schoolfriends.

> Back when I crossed, the coyote was always someone you knew, like the uncle or the cousin or the father of people you knew from home, if not your own blood relation. You would hear stories about women who had been violated or migrants who had been robbed—but always by bandits, never

by their own coyote. The coyote would take big personal risks to rescue you if you fell behind. If he abandoned you in the desert or the *cerro*, how would he ever face people back home in the village?

"Were you afraid of the migra?" I asked.

No. I was afraid that we'd be set upon by bandits who would rape us. I was really afraid to walk in the mountains because even though San Rafael is surrounded by mountains, they're covered with spiny cactus and I would never have had any reason to walk there, let alone at night. But the migra? No. I knew from my father that they don't mistreat you, they just take your name and bus you back to the border and dump you on the Mexican side. My father had told me: "The migra won't do anything to you. Just do as they tell you. If they shout, '*¡Parate!*' you stop. If they tell you to put your hands above your head, you put your hands above your head. You do as they say, then they expel you, and the next day you try again."

Elena says that her father had once explained how he would keep up his spirits while crossing. He would tell himself: "Hey, we're probably only one of—maybe a hundred, maybe two hundred—little groups walking around in the desert south of San Diego tonight. How many little bunches of people can the migra grab and send back? Maybe ten in a whole evening. All the rest of us are going to make it."

"And that," says Elena, "is what I repeated to myself and that's what happened in our crossing."

The coyote had dug a hole under the fence, and we crawled through. We only walked for eight hours, and that was moving pretty slowly, because most of the group that night were women. It was cold because this was January, and it snowed on us as we crossed the higher elevations. But, overall, it wasn't too bad.

For Elena's group, the most difficult part came when they reached their "safe house" just north of the San Clemente checkpoint,

> This was a very tiny two-bedroom house, like the one I live in here in L.A., but it had a huge tree in the front yard that covered the whole house. We were altogether thirty-five people waiting in that house, and when we were all loaded into one small van, you can imagine that we were basically stacked like cords of wood, one on top of the other, on the floor of the van. Fifteen minutes later this van stopped at a car dealership, where we were transferred to a couple of other vans, and after a twenty-minute ride, to a pickup truck with a camper on the back.

Elena explains that the camper was air-conditioned, outfitted with a bed and a little kitchen, and was empty during the journey north. Rather than ride in the camper and risk discovery at a checkpoint, Elena and seven others lay stretched out behind the driver's seat in the cabin of the pickup, covered by a tarp.

> The driver made us discard any gold chains or watches or anything made of metal that could set off an alarm. He told us that as we approached a checkpoint he would turn off the air-conditioning and that's how we would know to keep absolutely still, not a move, not a cough, not a sound, while they checked the truck. Twice, he shut off the air-conditioning, and we were absolutely still. And that's how I made it to Los Angeles.

8

Angel: Cat and Mouse

Oftentimes, as both Elena and Tomás indicate, a well-organized crossing can go very smoothly. It is also interesting how rarely the migra figures in migrants' tales as a sinister or violent force. Even today, when the crossing has become far more difficult and dangerous, the migra is more often described not so much as an enemy than as an opponent in a contest where one side has all the equipment and material resources and the other side has the advantage of numbers and quick wit. The sense of being caught up in a game of cat and mouse, a phrase I first heard from Pedro, the coyote I interviewed in 1992, was repeated to me by a great number of the people I spoke with in 2006.

One of them was Angel, who had been a bartender in a hotel in Mexico, a landscape worker in Chicago, and later a deliveryman and *saladero* in a sandwich shop in lower Manhattan, which is where I met him and where he described to me the crossing he made in 1988 with Martín, a friend from a small town in the state of Morelos.

> First we traveled twenty-eight hours in a bus from Mexico City to Ciudad Juárez, on the Texas border at El Paso. Everything was prearranged by a coyote from our town who lives in Chicago, but that coyote had his guy, Paco, right there at the border. Well, Paco was Mexican from Juárez, but he had

lived in El Paso and he had U.S. citizenship and he was the person who took care of us from start to finish. All we had to do was check in at a certain hotel in Juárez and Paco would get a call from the hotel clerk and he would drive down from El Paso to pick us up at the hotel to take us across.

Both Angel and Martín knew from friends of the relative ease of crossing at the places along the Texas border where the Rio Grande is narrow and there is no strong current that could sweep a person downstream.

Paco had it all figured out. He had a helper whose only job was to push us across the river in two large inner tubes, so we wouldn't get wet and look like *mojados* when we got to the other side. Once on the other bank, we were to walk along the street until Paco swung by in his car, opened the door, and called, "Jump in!" Then Paco drove us to his house where he put us up as if we were his personal friends: food, cots, everything you could want.

The next day he took us, and a third guy named Arturo who had crossed from Juárez to El Paso the day before, to the local Kmart and bought us clothing that he said would make us look "more presentable." Then he took us to a barber to get haircuts that would make us look like *tejanos*, not *mexicanos*. He even showed us how to walk so no one would pick us out as Mexicans. The key, he said, was to swing our arms and not to put our hands in our pockets.

Angel and Martín changed into their Kmart rig in the bathroom of a gas station. Arturo didn't have to change; he just added a pair of sunglasses to his ensemble. Paco handed them their airline tickets for Chicago, and he dropped them a little ways outside the entrance to the airport in El Paso.

Paco explained everything we needed to know. Neither Martín nor I had ever been in an airport before so he was very clear about how to get on and off an escalator, where to walk, how the metal detector is a machine that checks for metal, not immigration status, so we had to focus our minds on walking through it without getting nervous and if the machine beeped we should just take our change out of our pockets and put it in the tray and how we should turn right and walk along a long corridor and how to time our arrival at the gate just as our flight was called for boarding, at which point we should go to the counter with our tickets and get whatever seats they would give us.

"And so you boarded the plane and flew to Chicago?" I asked.

No. Arturo, who was wearing a pair of shorts and a Mexican T-shirt with an Aztec calendar on the front, got on the plane and flew to Chicago. We were in line to board when we were spotted by the migra. The agent stepped forward, and he said, "Well, guys, it looks like today is not your day. I know you'll try again, and I know you're going to make it sooner or later. But not today."

And that was it. The agent handcuffed Angel and Martín and took them to the detention center, where their airline tickets were confiscated. Then the two of them were deposited on the Mexican side, not as they might have wished, near the International Bridge, but across from the airport in a particularly sleazy part of Juárez. The two had no idea where they were, but they found themselves standing around in their white shirts, ties, and jackets in an area of Juárez full of drug dealers, pimps, and prostitutes.

At this point Angel phoned the number that Paco had given him in Juárez, and Paco's mother answered. Much concerned when she learned exactly where they had been "repatriated," she enlisted the help of a neighbor, who picked them up while Paco himself drove down from El Paso to arrange a second attempt. Angel says,

It was those white shirts and ties and jackets, and the new shoes that gave us away. Paco had decided that Arturo needed only a pair of sunglasses on the top of his head to complete his outfit. And that's all he bought for Arturo at the Kmart. But he tried too hard with Martín and me. He thought that with the clothes and the haircuts he could make us look like businessmen, because we were older than Arturo. But he ended up making us look like two Mormon missionaries, with the little black ties. Later on in Chicago we heard stories about Paco: how he had dressed one guy up in a Hawaiian shirt and Bermuda shorts to make him look less conspicuous!

In fact, the migra had a lot of fun with us. The first time this guy caught us, he kept joking about Martín's brand-new penny loafers and kept saying he wanted to trade shoes with him. The second time he caught us—I mean the very same officer, the very next day, as we lined up for the same flight— he started in again with us: "What? You two again! At least you guys could have switched clothes with each other." Then he turns to me and says, "Can't you see those loafers are killing his feet? If you were a decent friend, you would have traded with him for a few hours! You know what you guys look like?" he says. "You look like two *chambelanos*."

You know the *chambelán* is the boy who escorts a fifteen-year-old girl to her *quinceañera*, her fifteenth birthday party. So the migra says to us: "Yup. A pair of *chambelanos*! People don't go around like that in Chicago, I can tell you."

The next day, using the same routine, but arriving just as the gate was closing, Angel and Martín caught their flight for Chicago, still dressed like *chambelanos*.

9

Fernando: "A Snake's Breakfast"

While Angel and Martín's 1988 crossing had the playful air of cat and mouse, in the course of both the Clinton and the Bush administrations, crossing the border has become an ever more dangerous and expensive undertaking for anyone like Angel or Martín, or for Tomás, who is determined to pursue work in the United States as his survival strategy, or someone like Elena, who insists that she wants to live with her husband and children in the same place at the same time.

Since the early 1990s, successive U.S. administrations have responded to the pressure of domestic critics who, even before September 11, 2001, charged that the country had lost control of its borders. The response has been to strengthen border security with the construction of higher fences, the installation of floodlights, the use of helicopter surveillance by day and infrared cameras by night, and the purchase and deployment of more sophisticated and effective detection equipment like hidden electronic sensors. With the institution, in 1993, of El Paso's Operation Blockade—which would be hastily renamed Operation Hold the Line—followed in 1994 by Operation Gatekeeper in the Tijuana–San Diego Sector of the border and Operation Rio Grande in south Texas, spending on border enforcement grew year by year until, by 2000, it had tripled and by 2004 it had increased fivefold over a ten-year period. By 2006, defense contractors like Boeing, Lockheed Martín, Raytheon, and Northrop Grumman, all active in Afghanistan and Iraq, were also bidding on multibillion-dollar federal contracts to construct a "virtual fence" along the border that will combine ground surveillance satellites and motion-detection video equipment with unmanned aircraft. In addition to all the new technology that has been and will be applied to intercepting those who cross from Mexico, a key part of reinforcing the border is a threefold expansion in the size of the Border Patrol, which is projected to reach eighteen thousand agents by 2008.

Thus more agents have been assigned to the task of patrolling the most heavily utilized border-crossing points, particularly at Tijuana, where both Elena and Tomás crossed so many times, and along the Texas border, where it was once so easy to cross that day workers would simply remove their shoes and wade the river, dry off, and walk down the street to their place of employment, or would-be migrants, like Angel and Martín, were floated across the river on inner tubes to keep their clothing dry.

The unintended outcome of the intensification of enforcement at traditional crossing points has been to push migrants away from those points of entry into the Arizona-Sonora desert, a zone where the border used to be marked only by a three-string cattle fence because it was an area where no sensible person would ever have thought to attempt a crossing. Strikingly, while there were only a handful of *recorded* migrant deaths in the Arizona desert before 1994, since intensified surveillance closed off alternative routes, more than three thousand migrants have died along the border—the greatest share of them in the Arizona-Sonora desert and the El Centro Sector along the southeastern edge of California. And not only the number, but the causes of death have altered dramatically. Before the crackdown at urban border crossings, the would-be migrants who lost their lives on the journey generally died in vehicular accidents, drowned in the Tijuana River or the Rio Grande when they were carried by currents in unusually swollen streams, or suffocated as they hid in railroad boxcars, container trucks, or car trunks.

Today, however, all this has changed as more migrants feel constrained to make their crossing attempts along new routes through the desert. Marked by extremes of heat and cold, rough terrain, and a total lack of water, the Arizona route requires those who cross to spend days walking through one of the least habitable environments in the hemisphere. Here migrants risk death by dehydration, the bite of poisonous snakes and insects, or at the hands of bandits or vigilantes. Where Tomás's stories of his many crossings involve walking "for hours" through the mountains south of San Clemente, those who cross today in the 280-mile stretch of the Arizona border that the U.S. Border Patrol refers to as the "Tucson Sector" have to figure on walking through the desert for days.

For example, Fernando, a Chilango who presses pants in a Korean-owned dry cleaners on the Upper East Side of Manhattan, told me that although his father and all of his uncles used to cross easily along the Texas border, by the time he crossed in 2000, he had to take the desert route.

> My compadre and I flew to Nogales and went to the hotel where we were supposed to be picked up by our coyote. The friend, who had crossed with this coyote the year before, said the guy was very capable and would brief us carefully ahead of time on how we were going to cross and what to expect.

> Well, the guy arrives, he shouts, "Jump into the truck and crouch down," and he drives off with us and four other guys in the back of this truck. We traveled for about two hours crouched down like that, and then he shouts at us to get out of the truck and start walking, and we didn't have a clue where we were, other than the obvious—which was that we were in the mountains.

> So there we are with no food, no heavy clothing, no water, and some pal of the guy who brought us in his truck is now set to lead us through the mountains. Luckily, it was a clear night, which was just as well, because there were a lot of snakes, but I mean *a lot*!

Fernando noticed that his new "guide" had a big pack on his back, and since he wasn't pulling any food or water out of this pack, Fernando began to think he was probably carrying drugs. "So I'm thinking," says Fernando, "this is all I need. I'm going to end up as a snake's breakfast or I'm going to be picked up as a *narcotraficante!*"

Fernando knew that the group was supposed to walk north toward a highway, where a van was waiting to take them to Phoenix. But it was increasingly clear that the group was lost and the coyote had no more idea than anyone else what to do. On the second day of their march northward they were out of both water and food and it was obvious that they were in big trouble.

> A couple of the guys had blood running out of their nostrils and two of the others were like *medio loco*, I mean they really made no sense at all. Like one of them spent a lot of energy killing a rattlesnake that we had come upon, instead of just walking around it. By now it was two days since we had any water, and I said to my compadre, "I think this is it. I think we're going to die."

At this point Fernando's friend began to collect whatever brush he could find. He also found some pieces of old auto tires, which was a stroke of luck because burning tires would send up a nice black plume of smoke into what was a totally clear sky. So they built a fire and waited for the Border Patrol to spot them.

> Once we made this decision, we started to feel better as we sat there waiting for the migra to close in. But no one came. Later on we found out that it was the Fourth of July, so probably the migra wasn't even on patrol. So we had no choice but to start walking again, and after a couple of hours we came on some rusted auto parts and some oil drums where water had collected, and we drank that filthy water and it gave us the strength to walk another few hours. It was close to dark when, out of nowhere, we stumbled onto a paved road where we were picked up by another coyote who was waiting for a completely different bunch of guys. Strange, isn't it?

Fernando's brush with death by exposure and dehydration is the kind of experience that has become increasingly common since the implementation of the new policies that close off the traditional routes and funnel migrants into the desert. It is telling that by 2005, the number of dead brought to the Pima County morgue had exceeded the facility's 120-cadaver capacity and the county medical examiner had to rent a refrigerated tractor trailer to serve as a temporary morgue to store another 60 to 70 bodies. Given the far greater risk involved in walking for days, rather than hours, it is not surprising that the number of deaths of migrants on their journey has increased to an average of more than four hundred a year, if we count only those cases where, rather than being devoured by scavenger animals, the remains are actually recovered by the Mexican police or the U.S. Border Patrol.

10

The Tucson Consulate

Given the danger of the desert crossing, the Mexican consulate in Tucson, Arizona, has become an anomaly. Unlike any of the other forty-seven consular posts in the United States, a full third of the Tucson staff is assigned to the consulate's Department of Protection. This unit includes three staff members who focus on the daily reports of those detained by the Border Patrol, one concerned with children who are separated from their parents in the desert crossing or who must be repatriated when their parents are arrested, one who deals with would-be migrants who are hospitalized after their ordeal in the desert, and two who, very tellingly, have evolved into experts in forensic science. To be sure, every Mexican consulate in the United States has the task of protecting Mexican nationals in the geographic area for which it has responsibility. But the challenges facing the Mexican consulate in Tucson are particularly dramatic: 124 Mexicans were found dead in 2004 in the Tucson Sector. In 2005 the number reached 151, and in just the first three months of 2006, 30 Mexicans had died in the desert even though the temperatures in January, February, and March are moderate compared to the extreme heat of summer and fall.

The focus on death at the Tucson consulate is striking to anyone who is familiar with the Mexican consulate in Manhattan; there the burgeoning population of Mexican nationals has rendered a building on East 39th Street entirely inadequate to meet the needs of an ever-expanding number of expatriate Mexicans. The New York consulate, originally designed to promote trade between the two countries and to showcase Mexican culture in its second-floor art gallery, now struggles to provide conventional consular services—passports, birth certificates, and other official documents—to masses of Mexican citizens who begin to line up between two and three in the morning in the hope that when the consulate opens at 9:00 A.M., they will receive one of the coveted 250 slips that guarantee that the bearer will be received by consular personnel at some point in the course of the day. It is telling that one of the consular functions where the New York staff habitually runs months behind the demand for services is in the registration of babies born to Mexican nationals in the tristate area, and particularly in New York City, where Mexicans—depending on whether we count both documented and undocumented people—have one of the highest, if not the highest, birthrates of any national group in the city.

In contrast to the early-morning line around the block that is a permanent feature of the Mexican consulate in Manhattan, the Tucson consulate is a quiet place, housed in what looks like a family home on the South Side of the city. A bungalow in the Arts and Crafts style, the house has a welcoming front porch and a living room that has been redesigned to serve as a waiting room, where, on the morning in April 2006 that I came to interview the consul, I found myself completely alone.

When I asked how it was possible that none of the twenty seats were taken by Mexican nationals seeking consular services, the receptionist suggested that some might have been put off by an incident the previous day, in which a right-wing group calling itself the Border Guardians recited the Pledge of Allegiance, shouted "Long live George Washington!" and "God Bless America!" and then set fire to a Mexican flag they had brought along for the purpose, burning it to a cinder on the sidewalk in front of the consulate.

On the other hand, she allowed, it could be the case that there are no lines around the block as in New York because the resident population of Mexicans in Tucson is very small. To be sure, thousands of Mexicans pass through Tucson every month on their clandestine migratory journey. Moreover, Tucson has an established community of Mexicans who became United States citizens with the amnesty in 1986. In addition, there are thousands of Tucsonians of Mexican parentage who were born in the United States, as well as a historic community of Mexican Americans who became United States citizens when Mexico lost its northern provinces to the United States in 1848. But apart from these people, there is virtually no community of undocumented or documented Mexicans comparable to the great masses in other cities in the United States, particularly Los Angeles, Chicago, and more recently, New York, Las Vegas, Houston, Atlanta, Seattle, and rural areas like North Carolina and Kansas. Consequently, the staff at the Tucson consulate serves only one thousand to fifteen hundred people a month, a figure that also includes all U.S. citizens who are seeking visas and residence permits for Mexico.

In conversation, Juan Calderón-Jaimes, a career diplomat who is the consul in Tucson, is quick to emphasize the positive aspects of his work: every year 25 million visitors, largely from Sonora and Sinaloa, cross the border into Arizona, where they spend an estimated $1 billion on goods and services. Trade and tourism from Mexico is so important, he says, that the city of Tucson has just opened an office in Hermosillo, the capital of Sonora, to promote this kind of cross-border traffic.

But the consul was clear that much, if not most, of his time was taken up with the perils of migration, and, indeed, his concern had intensified as he received predictions from meteorologists that the summer of 2006 would be particularly hot. That likelihood, combined with increased activity of the Border Patrol at the crossing points in California and Texas that are preferred by migrants, along with greater vigilance at all the "twin city" crossings, like Nogales, Arizona, and Nogales, Sonora, or Agua Prieta, Sonora, and Douglas, Arizona, meant that the consulate had to anticipate larger numbers of people attempting to cross the desert in the most dangerous months of the summer when daytime temperatures can rise as high as 120 degrees. Indeed, in response to this challenge, the consulate prepared public-service advertisements to run on Mexican radio and television warning would-be migrants not to attempt the crossing in the summer, a preventative campaign focused on the most intense migrant-sending areas. Calderón explained:

In spite of all we do, people continue to use the desert route because they believe it is the only one where they stand a chance of evading interception by the Border Patrol. Thus, we have two people at the consulate whose work is dedicated to the identification of the bodies found in the desert and the notification of their families. Sometimes it is the Tohono Nation police on the Tohono O'Odham Reservation who find the bodies and they are always very helpful. But more than 90 percent of the bodies are found by the Border Patrol, and then they contact us here at the consulate.

When we receive word that remains have been found, our colleagues go through the belongings that were collected with the bodies to try to find a telephone number, anything that would enable us to locate the friend or family member who had sponsored the trip to the United States and who might still be waiting to receive a call from the coyote. Other times we find the telephone number of the family back in Mexico. The difficult part, as you can imagine, is to find the words to tell a father and mother that their son or daughter is dead, to tell a wife that her husband perished in the desert.

In the garage-like annex to the little house that serves as the consulate, a team is at work plotting on a map the spot where bodies have been found. Oscar Angulo, a 25-year-old graduate of the University of Arizona who was born in Nogales, Sonora, and is perfectly bilingual, shares this responsibility with Jerónimo García, another consular officer. Oscar says:

My colleague and I have no medical background, no special training for this work. We just make an appointment with the medical examiner, and we go over the belongings that have been found with the bodies to see if the migrant had a secret hiding place of some kind and, in fact, we often find addresses or a photo ID card with a thumbprint inside their belt, under the insole of their shoes, or sewn into their garments. When we find nothing that gives us a clue, we take photographs of everything and then we see if the computer can match up the possessions we found and the body itself with a missing-person report filed in Mexico.

When all we have to work with is bones, we have the medical examiner's office send a sample to the University at Baylor, Texas, where DNA testing can be carried out. Basically we are working with DNA, but also more straightforward information like height, weight, the shape of the face, scars, and tattoos. If we can associate a name with the body, then we can contact a family member, and if we can't come up with a name, we send the information that we do have to Mexico, and then if a family member files a report, we can just pull up the information, make the match, and start the process of repatriating the remains.

11

No More Deaths

In fact, it is not only the Mexican consular staff in Tucson who concern themselves with the perils of the desert crossing. Only a few blocks from the consulate, in the oldest part of Tucson, is the shrine of El Tiradito, which became the rallying point in the 1970s for grassroots opposition to the construction of an expressway that would have destroyed the last remnants of Spanish colonial and Mexican Tucson. It is at this very small and emotionally affecting adobe building, with its votive candles and its *retablos*, that No More Deaths (NMD), an umbrella group that describes itself as "a coalition of individuals, faith communities, human rights advocates, and grassroots organizers," has pitched a small tent and set out a table. Here volunteers provide public information and a point of communication for all local people who share a preoccupation with the rising death toll, and with border policy in general.

Founded in 2004, NMD began as a small, if passionate, local movement of Samaritans who were prepared to camp out in the desert in the hottest part of summer to provide aid to anyone they might encounter staggering along, with no water or food, bruised, injured, or too sick to go on. Maryada Vallet, a twenty-three-year-old volunteer from Phoenix, explained that the group in the camp is composed mostly of young people, although it includes some retired women and men and an assortment of pastors, priests, and religious leaders like Brother David, a monk with a long white beard who goes about the desert in his Franciscan robes—no doubt a striking sight for anyone he encounters on the migrant trails.

The volunteers set up camp in an area well known for migrant traffic. Every morning at sunrise, taking advantage of the cooler early hours of the day, they set out in "patrols" that walk along well-trodden routes through dry riverbeds, looking for trash and other evidence that the trail is in active use. The groups hike out for a couple of hours along the washes, and if they don't encounter anyone, they leave bottles of water under trees and what they call "migrant packs" of fresh socks, crackers, apple sauce, granola, sports drinks, canned tuna or chicken, and Vienna sausage for protein—all things that people in churches back in Tucson assemble, supplies that can be quickly consumed by anyone who comes along. Maryada explains,

> We always try to remember that even when we don't see any-one on our hike, it doesn't mean that no one sees us. We are not so much hoping to encounter migrants on the march as we are trying to be there when someone really needs help. We move along talking, singing, making noise because we don't want to sneak up on people. We figure they will come out and get help if they need it.

In addition, Maryada says that, whatever else they do on a patrol, they always pick up trash because they have come to understand that "it's not just human life that is endangered by the border policy. Forcing migrants into the desert has compromised the entire desert environment."

> Of course we are concerned with the environmental dam-age, but we also clean up the trash because we really want to develop positive relations with the ranchers and the other permanent population that lives out there around the town of Arivaca. A lot of these folks feel deeply aggrieved that the migrants, the Border Patrol, and humanitarian workers like

us are trespassing on their land and trooping up and down
in ever larger numbers.

Some of the ranchers, Maryada says, are more welcoming to the
Samaritans and have offered them showers and the chance to refill water jugs from their well. Others, she explains, are more ambivalent:
"They don't like people crossing their land, but they also don't want
their ranch to be the place where migrants get sick and drop dead."

My own trip to Arivaca, with a nice side trip to the Arivaca Café,
confirmed for me what I had learned from Maryada of the range of attitudes among the local people toward the migrants, the Border Patrol
and the Samaritans. The only restaurant in a town with a population of
917, the café is a place where ranchers with pistols on both hips might
share one of the large tables with some of the artists and aging hippies
who decided, in the 1970s, to make the desert their home. When I
joined others at a table and explained I was writing on immigration,
this disclosure elicited opinions as ferociously strong and as diametri-
cally opposed as any expressed on the topic anywhere in the United
States. The only difference was that, in the case of Arivaca café society,
the views are expressed by people who are neighbors and are going to
have to keep on sharing tables at the café for a long time to come. To
the extent that they agreed on anything, they agreed passionately that
responsibility for a totally unacceptable situation lay with the policies
of the federal government, which they roundly denounced as contradictory, vacillating, and injurious to the country as a whole and to Arivaca in particular.

More reticent than my lunch companions at the Arivaca Café
were the Border Patrol officers I sought out at their post on the Arivaca
road. When I asked questions, they all referred me to the public relations officer for the Tucson Sector. But when I asked if I could sit a
while in the shade with them, their innate good manners, or perhaps
the tedium of their duty that afternoon, prompted them to offer me a
seat and one agent in particular, whom I shall call Bob, opened up.

In terms of law enforcement, this job is pretty much at the
bottom of the heap. We got guys here who were recruited
straight from jobs at Taco Bell. This is the only federal force

where you don't need a college degree. All you need is high school or high school equivalency. We always say, if they thought you had any brains they would of sent you to the FBI, not to the border.

The pay is good, though; you start at about $40,000 and you can make $50,000 with all the overtime. Straight out of high school. The training is physically demanding, and everyone has to learn Spanish, but for guys like me who already speak Spanish, it's like the only advantage you ever got in life!

But right now they're recruiting like crazy and sending people out as quickly as they can because it's all political now. The politicians want to look like they're doing something to seal the border. So they want more troops sitting out here in the desert. And at this point they're talking about sending in the National Guard, which is a total joke, because these people aren't trained as law enforcement officers, although I don't doubt that there are guys who joined the Guard who will be very happy to sit out here with us rather than getting their asses blown up in Iraq.

Indeed, only a month after we talked, in May 2006, the first of what would become six thousand National Guard troops were dispatched to the border. Under this new program, Operation Jump-Start, Guardsmen were assigned to staff observation posts, maintain and repair vehicles, and generally to stand about with M-16 rifles on their shoulders. The weapons, however, are officially intended only for self-defense against armed bandits or drug runners because Guardsmen can only alert the Border Patrol to crossing attempts they might observe; they may take no direct role in apprehensions.

In addition to vehicle maintenance and other chores, the National Guard has been put to work constructing the infamous fence—370 miles long, according to the defense bill that passed the Senate in 2006, and a full 700 miles in the House of Representatives' proposed legislation. So we now have an answer to the question put by many: in the absence of the cheap, unprotected labor of undocumented Mexican workers, who will actually build the wall that the politicians insist is key to the defense of America and all its values and for which Congress overwhelmingly approved an expenditure of $1.2 billion?

In 2006, with the construction of this wall finally underway, I could not help but think of Bob, the Border Patrol officer, who had assured me:

> The wall is totally for show. There's no wall that's going to keep anyone out who's determined to cross. They'll go over, they'll go under, or they'll go around.

> What would help is better detection equipment of every kind. But it has to be coordinated, which isn't likely to happen as long as the politicians are driving the policy. Like there's no use in spending millions on unmanned infrared cameras planted in the desert that can detect five guys walking along a wash five miles away if you don't have the equipment to keep tracking them while you close in and you haven't got the vehicles or the roads that get you to the spot where the infrared camera picked them up. The whole thing is a lot more complicated than building walls or doubling the number of patrols on the ground.

Tellingly, Bob's views dovetailed perfectly with those expressed by Steve Johnson, a man in his early sixties who had spent the previous two summers in the NMD desert camp. Steve insists that the flow across the border can't be halted and all the money and energy devoted to trying is simply a show that politicians want to put on for the folks back in their home district.

Born and raised in Huntsville, Alabama, in a Southern Baptist evangelical family of Goldwater Republicans, Steve went to college in Tennessee, became a civil rights activist with the Southern Christian Leadership Council in the 1960s, and heard Martin Luther King Jr. address the striking Memphis sanitation workers the night before he was assassinated. Steve explains that his involvement with NMD is a kind of natural outgrowth of the work he had been doing in a soup kitchen since retiring in Tucson.

I love the desert. I've got to admit that I'd be walking out in the desert even if there wasn't any good reason to be there. I don't speak much Spanish and I don't have any medical or legal experience, but when I got to the camp, I realized that what they really need is people with enthusiasm, people who are willing to get up at four-thirty in the morning and make coffee for everybody.

I asked Steve if he and the others in the camp are concerned about vigilante groups such as the Minutemen, the Civil Homeland Defense, Ranch Rescue, and the American Border Patrol (a group that hopes to be confused with the U.S. Border Patrol). These people have taken advantage of Arizona state law, which allows individuals to carry concealed firearms, and they have set themselves up as vigilantes to "guard" the border from "invasion" from Mexico.

"Honestly," Steve says, " I got to tell you these people are really not worth discussing."

They say that there are hundreds of them, but there are actually just dozens, and they say that they're doing something, but they're actually just sitting around in picnic chairs drinking beer on the hillside. They're not really a player; it's the press that makes them into a player. People who have attended a Minuteman confab have looked around and realized that there are a lot more press than Minutemen there.

In any case, Steve says, there's no need for the Samaritans to worry about the vigilantes because the NMD activists have a lot of company out there in the camp. The Border Patrol have the Samaritans' camp under surveillance twenty-four hours a day: "But it makes no difference because everything we do is transparent. That's one of our protocols, that we are not hiding anything, that everything we do is out in the open."

The problem is that most of the front-line workers on the Border Patrol are very inexperienced and young. They just love riding around in their SUVs and riding around on horses chasing people through the desert. Let's face it, if you double your manpower every two years—which is what the federal government has done—then half of the people you have working for you are going to have no experience at all.

But Steve emphasizes his feeling that the Border Patrol is not the enemy.

We had an agreement with them that lasted for several years, but then they got a new sector chief when the Border Patrol became part of Homeland Security, and the number two man for this sector, a fella named General Robert Rule—he's a general in the Border Patrol—he said at a meeting we attended in Arivaca one time, that economic migrants are just the clutter that we need to brush away so we can get at the really bad guys, the really dangerous guys, meaning the dope smugglers and the people smugglers.

Well, when you have that kind of mind-set, that the migrants are just "clutter" in your way, it dehumanizes them. So it's from the top down that the migrants are dehumanized, not from the bottom up. The people who actually work in the field in the Border Patrol, they see what's going on and they realize what the story is. They start out as young kids, real gung-ho, ready to capture all these lawbreakers. But after a few years they grow up, and they realize *why* people are crossing the desert, and then they try to be as helpful to the migrants as they're allowed to be.

Maryada, Steve, and the other volunteers made it through two scorching summers in which they carried on their humanitarian work under the agreements they had established with David Aguilar, the sector chief of the Border Patrol. But when Aguilar was transferred to Washington to head Immigration and Customs Enforcement and was replaced by Michael Nicely, surveillance of the camp intensified and harassment of the Samaritans increased. Maryada relates that the agents would sit in their diesel vehicles with the engine running day and night and their exhaust wafting into the camp. "We started calculating how many agents and how many hours were dedicated to sitting in SUVs with the air-conditioning running just watching a bunch of folks go about their lives in the camp, and it turned out to be hundreds of man-hours."

> I once led a group of high school kids from Tucson on a garbage pickup hike, and suddenly, as we were resting under a tree with our garbage bags, Border Patrolmen on horseback thundered down on us from two sides pretending that they thought we were a group of Mexicans they were supposed to apprehend. "*¡Sientate! ¡Sientate!*" they yelled, even though we were already seated and no one was going anywhere. It was frightening, but probably it was a good learning experience for the high school kids.

"Some of these guys just get off on having power over us and over the migrants," Maryada says. "But, on the other hand, they all carry emergency medical supplies, water, ice, and food just as we do, and many of them are genuinely humane to the migrants they catch. What's more, some of the border agents really *do* understand why we're here."

For example, she says, the previous summer she and two other Samaritans were trying to help an old man who had come up from Mexico to look for his daughter, who had been left behind in the desert when crossing with a group. The father knew that she was "presumed dead," but he felt he had to go out there and search until he found her.

> Well, there was this Border Patrolman, a fifteen-year veteran, who decided to help us look. We spent hours out there with the agent searching for this body, and we got separated from our vehicle and we stayed out too long and the agent started to feel sick, so we dug out our supplies and sat him down and gave him water and then we made it back to the road. But we teased him, saying we could imagine the headlines in the *Tucson Citizen*: "Border Patrol Chief Rescued by Humanitarian Group!"

12

Shanti and Daniel

For all the ups and downs in their relationship to the Border Patrol, the real sea change in relations between the NMD volunteers and the migra came on July 9, 2005, with the arrest of two Samaritans, Shanti Sellz and Daniel Strauss. Steve Johnson recalls:

> It was really hot. We got up before dawn and as soon as the sun came up, the heat became intense. We'd had probably ten days of 105 degrees or more. I like it hot, but that was probably too hot even for me. You understand that when the air temperature registers 105 degrees, the ground can be 130 degrees.

Steve explains that he was with Willy, a young man from Missouri, and the two were carrying migrant packs and were on their way to a cattle tank, which was a gathering place where migrants would spend the night because it was a protected place surrounded by trees. Steve recalls that it hadn't rained for a couple of months, so the water in the cattle tank was really green and nasty and that's how the people in the desert get sick: they run out of fresh water and have to drink the stagnant water. Then they get stomach cramps and diarrhea and vomiting, and that leads to even more dehydration.

Well, as we were cresting the hill, we were making a lot of noise, which is what we always do because we don't want to deal with drug traffickers or migrants who don't need us. Cresting the hill we saw nine people walking toward us in single file. We had surprised them because the wind was blowing toward us and they hadn't heard us coming. So we walked up to them and wished them *bien venidos*. We could see that the water that they had in their jugs was green, so we knew that they had just filled up at the tank. So we shook everyone's hand and said hello and took them under a tree for a little bit of shade, and Willy, who speaks fluent Spanish, asked them if anyone wasn't well. They said they were okay, but after passing out food and water, we saw that one of the men just couldn't hold anything down and he vomited twice.

At this point, that man took off his boot.

Of course, normally you wouldn't take your boot off in the middle of the desert with two gringos, but when he did, we realized why. He had huge blisters on his feet, but I mean the worst that I had seen in the whole summer. I had seen photographs that were worse, but not in person. So we got our moleskin and bandages and started patching both of his feet, and when we finished with him, we turned around and all the other eight had taken their boots off, and all of them had blisters, some of them almost as bad as Emil, the man we'd just been treating.

Steve and Willy didn't have sufficient medical supplies to treat them all, nor were they carrying enough water for nine seriously dehydrated people, so they patched them up as best they could with the first-aid materials they had on hand, and walked with them as far as the road. Then, while Willy sat with the migrants under a tree, Steve walked back to camp to get a pickup truck, returning with a nurse and another volunteer, Daniel Strauss, who has first-responder training.

Willy had learned that the migrants had come from Chiapas and had been traveling for a couple of weeks just to get to the border. It seems they had been moving north with a coyote, thirty of them, and the first night they were in the desert, one of the women in the group had fallen and sprained or broken her ankle. She said that it was her fate and for the others to just leave her there in the desert, and they left her with a little water. But they thought she had probably died because it was 105 degrees every day for that week.

The remaining twenty-nine migrants plus their coyote continued walking north when they were spotted by a Border Patrol helicopter and "dusted." Steve explains:

In a "dusting" a crew brings the helicopter down right on top of the group they're targeting and they motion for them to lay flat. Well, of course no one is going to lay flat with the prospect of having a helicopter land right on top of them. So what happens is that people take off and scatter in every direction. This is how migrants get into trouble, because often the group never reassembles.

It tells you something that we medically evacuated sixty-eight people last year, and well over half the people we treated had got into trouble because they had become separated from their group in the course of a dusting. It just doesn't make sense, because scattering people is against the Border Patrol's whole goal of arresting people and sending them back. It's much easier to apprehend a group than a bunch of scattered, lost people.

In this case, only nine of the twenty-nine reunited, but they didn't have a coyote with them, so they spent three days wandering. Indeed, the reason they were traveling during the day was that they were lost and desperate. When Steve returned with the nurse, she did a triage of the nine and picked the three who were in the worst shape. "We got those three back to the car, and as for the remaining six, we filled their jugs, gave them as much food as they could take, and we bid them farewell."

On returning to camp, Steve and Willy found Shanti Sellz, who had just returned from searching—unsuccessfully—for the remains of a woman who had died roughly two weeks earlier. Shanti offered to drive the three migrants to Tucson to get medical attention, and Daniel Strauss went with her, taking Shanti's car, because no other vehicle was available.

Shanti and Daniel put large eighteen-by-eighteen-inch Samaritan signs on the car so the Border Patrol would know who they were, and that they were involved in a medical evacuation. But as they headed toward Tucson, a Border Patrol vehicle followed them, then passed them, and then drove on ahead and watched Shanti and Daniel from the side of the road as the two drove by with the three migrants in the backseat. Finally, the Border Patrol gave chase, stopped the Samaritans, and arrested them and the three Mexicans, charging Daniel and Shanti with transporting undocumented immigrants in furtherance of their illegal entry, conspiracy to transport an illegal immigrant, and passing a Border Patrol checkpoint without stopping.

The agents separated Daniel and Shanti from one another and from the migrants. Two of the migrants were detained and then bussed back to the border. But they put Emil, the man who had received treatment for dehydration and blisters, in federal prison in Wilmot and kept him for two months as a material witness. Steve says:

> That was just to put pressure on Shanti and Daniel to plea-bargain. The feds were prepared to drop the charges and give the two of them one year's unsupervised probation if they would say that what they had done was against the law. Naturally, Daniel and Shanti refused to make this statement because what we're doing is not illegal. What we're doing is providing humanitarian aid, and in some places, including Arizona, you're obliged to give assistance. It's not a question of it being illegal, but rather if you fail to help someone in distress, you're breaking the law!

Steve acknowledges that the Border Patrol is equipped with medical supplies and water and ice, and that he and the other volunteers could call the nearest post and ask for an agent to pick up migrants they find who are sick or injured. But the problem, Steve explains, is:

> We can call the Border Patrol and have a car pull up in twenty minutes—or they can take two hours to show up because a dehydrated migrant who we just found on the trail may not be their highest priority at that moment. So we have to act, because if we find people who are in a real bad way, we've got to move quickly to get them medical help.

So Daniel and Shanti, having taken the responsibility to bring the sick migrants to Tucson without calling the Border Patrol and waiting for agents to show up, now found themselves in prison, first at the Ajo Detention Station for a day, and then at the federal penitentiary in Wilmot. Steve explains:

> When Shanti and Daniel were arraigned two days later, 250 people showed up at the courthouse. The two of them were marched in wearing orange jumpsuits with shackles on their arms and legs. The federal prosecutor didn't want to give them a bond because he said they were "flight risks," which has got to be the most absurd thing you ever heard in your life: these are people who are totally committed to their humanitarian work and, in fact, when they were released they went straight out to the desert to walk the migrant trails.

"You can just imagine the story from there," says Steve. "Before Shanti and Daniel were arrested, there were a couple of dozen of us who were actually out in the desert and we were supported by about 150 people back in the Tucson, who made up the migrant packs and took care of the fund-raising, and would drive out to the camp to bring us supplies and home-cooked food." After the arrests, there were hundreds of volunteers walking the trails in the desert and tens of thousands of people supporting this work with funds, and sixty thousand postcards addressed to Paul Charleton, the U.S. attorney for Arizona, all proclaiming, "Humanitarian aid is never a crime."

This is how we gained a voice that we never had before, and the Border Patrol realizes what a mistake they made, and the United States Attorney's Office realizes what a mistake they made, but these are very stubborn people, needless to say. Still, it looks as if we are going to reach an accommodation. We've been negotiating with them since August 2005, and it looks like the charges will be dropped and we'll have protocols to work with this coming summer.

Indeed, on September 1, 2006, U.S. District Judge, Raner C. Collins, dismissed all charges against Shanti and Daniel, ruling that both had made reasonable efforts to ensure that their actions were not in violation of the law.

13

"Walking Around, Living Their Lives"

As the Bush administration has played upon people's fear of terrorism—and the more generalized fear of "the other" that terrorism inspires—the notion of securing the northern and southern borders as well as the Atlantic and Pacific coasts has taken on an ever more fanciful and surreal quality. Clearly, the promise of secure borders appeals mightily to those who seek reassurance that they are safe from harm. And yet, all the evidence points to the reality that the authorities are, in fact, incapable of sealing the borders—that they have no way to stanch the flow into the United States of all kinds of people whether "good" or "bad," whether well-intentioned and hard-working or menacing.

Nevertheless, in a perverse kind of bipartisanship, politicians of both parties have pandered to the most irrational impulses in their constituents, promising forms of border enforcement that supposedly offer a guarantee of immunity from people with evil intent. When politicians attempt to reassure their constituents with higher and longer fences, and suggestions that the exclusion of Mexicans from the United States will enhance national security and well-being, they are counting on the triumph of irrational wishes over common sense.

In the process, the attempt to seal the borders has created unprecedented danger for those who feel they must pursue a life of low-wage work in the United States as their only possible family survival

strategy. And apart from the greater physical risks, heightened enforcement at the standard border crossings has forced a higher percentage of migrants to engage the services of coyotes. As a result the
new policies have quadrupled, and in some cases quintupled, the cost
of crossing.

As it turns out, the huge expenditure of financial and human resources intended to close off the border with Mexico—a policy that
costs the U.S. taxpayers more than $2 billion a year—can be said to
have had no effect whatsoever on the continued *presence* of undocumented Mexicans in the United States. Pedro, the coyote I interviewed
in 1992, described to me back then the pressures he experienced in his
"busy season" in January, when all the migrants who had returned
home for Christmas needed to cross back into the United States to re-
sume work in Los Angeles. But speaking with him today, he notes that
there is no longer a post-Christmas rush in the life of a coyote.

> Since September 11, the immigrants who used to go home at
> least once a year—sometimes for Christmas and sometimes
> for the festival of the village saint—now just stay where they
> are in the United States. They can't come up with the $2,000
> or $3,000 that it's going to cost them to get back to their jobs
> up north. Or, if they are ready to go into debt to spend that
> kind of money, it's going to be to bring their wife and their
> kids up north to live with them in the United States, because
> the annual visit home is just not in the picture anymore.

To be sure, it has long been the case that official statistics on "apprehensions" tell us little about the outcomes of programs like Operation Gatekeeper because exactly the same would-be migrants may be
caught several times in a single night, and are likely to continue their
efforts to cross until they are successful—at which point they disappear
from the statistical records of the Border Patrol. But now the government figures supplied to the public are even more contradictory and
surreal because both the Clinton and the Bush administrations have
taken any rise in the number of migrants apprehended as an indication
of the effectiveness of the Border Patrol and its detection equipment.

But when the statistics show a drop in apprehensions, the INS, and now ICE, claim that this decline should be taken as clear evidence that the border operations have worked successfully to discourage Mexican migrants, and that fewer Mexicans are actually attempting to cross.

The reality is, we don't know how many cross, just as we don't know how many undocumented Mexicans—or for that matter, how many undocumented immigrants from all countries—are living in the United States, even if the figure of 12 million, generated by the Pew Hispanic Center, has taken on the weight of fact, as it is cited more often than any other estimate. What we do know is that deaths in the course of crossing have grown precipitously, from dozens to hundreds, and that these deaths are increasingly concentrated in areas where no one would have thought to cross before the traditional entry points were closed off. In the end we can only guess what percentage of all migrants who try to cross is represented by the figure of the hundreds of bodies or skeletal remains actually found in the desert.

Yet border crossing, like the rest of life, is also a matter of unexpected circumstances and inexplicable luck. I have talked with migrants like Fernando, who described crossings so frightening that I had to remind myself, as I recorded his story, that the central figure was sitting in front of me recounting his experience and so the event must have turned out better than I might fear. On the other hand, among the day laborers I met at a shape-up on Port Richmond Avenue in Staten Island was Francisco, who had crossed in Arizona in 2005 after the border was tightened. He told me that although he had braced himself for terrible hardships, his crossing turned out to be "like a Boy Scout hike with friends," more an outing in the countryside than an ordeal.

In the end, as Tomás says when he considers another attempt to reach East Los Angeles from his home in Trancoso, Zacatecas, most people keep at it because they feel they must, and sooner or later they do find a way.

> I know of two guys from my town who didn't make it. Actually, no one knows what happened to them. Their families still don't know anything. And I know a couple of people who turned back. But they were young guys who were

mostly crossing for the adventure of it, not really to work. So when things didn't go well, they turned back.

But, just look around you. Everywhere you go in the United States you see Mexicans walking around, working, living their lives. Everywhere! What other proof do you need to know that the people who want to get to the United States are going to make it across one way or another?

Part III

The Hard Place

14

Carlos: Names and Networks

Hardly anyone he worked with in the hotel kitchen could believe that Carlos was a Mexican. He was too tall. Neither the Ecuadorians or Colombians on the pantry line preparing salads and appetizers, nor the Peruvians and Dominicans on the hot line, flipping sauteed mushrooms around in a skillet, or grilling the chicken breasts, or deep-frying the breaded shrimp, nor the Chinese busboys, nor the college students waiting tables at the "front of the house" could connect the man from Guadalajara, Jalisco, to the short, stocky men from the countryside of Puebla and Veracruz whom they had come to think of as *los mexicanos*. Yes, he looked as *mestizo* as anyone could expect a Mexican to be. But at nearly six feet, he was too tall to fit the expectations of his coworkers.

But Carlos was different from his fellow migrants in other ways as well. For starters, he had entered the United States on a student visa, which set him apart from the Mexicans who had spent anything up to $3,000 to have themselves smuggled across the border and transferred as far as the New York metropolitan area—not to mention the South Americans who were working off $10,000 debts for their chance to roll grilled zucchini and roasted red pepper wraps in a hotel kitchen in New Jersey.

Of course Carlos was not supposed to be working on a student visa, and as he would explain to me, that made his first year in the United States technically as illegal as those of any of his coworkers. But his visa was a true document, and this piece of paper allowed him to fly back to his home in Guadalajara to propose marriage to his *novia* and return a week later, an engaged man—a life-transforming moment his undocumented friends could never dream of living except over the phone. Indeed, it wasn't until Carlos had overstayed his visa in 2002 that he really became undocumented like the rest of his coworkers, and only then that he was completely accepted by the others.

> The guys took me out for a beer and said, "Okay, now you're really one of us," which surprised me, because from the time I had to pick out a new name, come up with the correct number of digits for a Social Security number, and buy myself some papers—really, from the time I started working— I already thought of myself as one of them.

With the documents he purchased in New Jersey for $100—a bargain compared to the money Carlos's friends and neighbors from Guadalajara had paid for the same kind of papers in California—Carlos became "Guillermo Pérez" and had to train himself to answer not only to Guillermo but also to "Guille," and "Mino," and even "Willy," and all the other nicknames that a real Guillermo might be called.

"Since I was in the United States on a visa, I couldn't work legally for even ten minutes as Carlos Vázquez. So I had to work up the Guillermo ID. But one new name is nothing," Carlos told me. "There are guys who take out eight, nine, ten credit cards in different names, and how is anyone going to track them down? Once you get into it, once you give up your real name and identity, it's like all the constraints fall away."

> The whole thing is unreal when you think about it. People can have two or twenty identities. They can spend and spend and never pay up. They can marry one woman as Pedro Gómez and another as José López and another with another name and then leave the country as "Carlos" and leave all their identities and mistakes behind.

And, indeed, Carlos, having worked up his "Guillermo" identity, found that one pseudonym could be insufficient to meet even his modest goals.

> Take the case of my work at Wendy's, which was one of the first jobs I held. I started out working in condiments and changing the cooking oil in the fryer, and the manager, a Puerto Rican, liked me a lot. In fact, after two weeks on the job, I became the Employee of the Month: a $25 prize and "Guillermo Pérez's" photo smiling down from the wall for all the customers to see!

The problem was that Carlos wanted to work mornings as well as afternoons because Wendy's paid only $7 per hour.

> But the manager says to me, "I can't give you two shifts because Wendy's only hires part-time and two shifts are going to put you over the limit. Get yourself another set of papers in another name," he tells me, "and you can come in as Manuel or Miguel or Daniel in the morning and Guillermo in the afternoon."

It was the same, Carlos says, when he got his job on the pantry line.

> At a certain point they needed me to work on banquets— you know, decorating the tables, ice carving, that kind of thing. So they wanted me to work at the front of the house under one name in the mornings and as Guillermo in the kitchen in the afternoons.

Carlos's cousin David was his guide in the creation of multiple identities because David, of course, was not really "David" but César. However, César was lucky enough to have the Social Security card that had actually been issued to his father, David, in the 1970s when his father picked strawberries and garbanzo beans and worked in construction in California. So César took his father's card and his father's first name and he is actually able to direct his Social Security contributions into his father's account, something that gives him pleasure because all around he sees other immigrants with fake Social Security numbers paying into a system from which they will never be able to collect a dime.

For this reason, Carlos is unsurprised when I tell him that the President's Council of Economic Advisers has reported that the United States economy receives at least $10 billion a year in Social Security contributions from people who, lacking real papers, will never be able to draw on their accounts. Happily, Carlos notes, his Uncle David is one of the lucky few. He will be turning sixty-five next year and he can actually draw money out of this account, even though he hasn't been back to the United States in thirty years.

"But how," I ask Carlos, "can your cousin César, who is—what, thirty years old?—go running around New Jersey with a Social Security card that says he is sixty-four?" Carlos replies:

> Did you ever read a story called *Dorian Gray*? We joke that we Mexicans have discovered the secret of eternal youth! The fact is that there's no way that the people in charge of immigration can keep up with any of this, and in any case, no one who is supposed to be checking your papers really cares if they are phony or real. They just want you to have some kind of papers so that *they* don't get into trouble.

I think to myself that this is just as well, since three other undocumented Mexican migrants of my acquaintance are all using the Social Security numbers issued to their sons, who were born in the United States during brief periods in which the family reunited in California before the wife and children returned to the village in Mexico. This would put three people out there in the active labor force who are—at least in terms of their credentials—5, 7, and 8 years old, respectively.

But, as Carlos says, my three friends are unlikely to be found out. Carlos himself has worked at Wendy's, two hotel restaurants, and an Italian trattoria, as well as in construction, and in none of these jobs has anyone ever asked him to confirm the validity of his papers. In fact, no one

has asked him to show a green card or produce any other form of identification or permission to work or live in the United States.

"The people who hire you couldn't care less," Carlos says. "They
don't check. They don't care." He goes on:

> An Uruguayan I worked with in the hotel, an older guy with
> a lot of experience, explained the whole thing to me. Often
> the people you work for don't show your salary as an ex-
> pense when they add up their own accounts. It's like you
> don't exist.

Carlos notes that the only workplace where he had ever heard of
an appearance by the migra was at the hotel. That raid was carried out
months before he was hired in the kitchen and the migra never returned during the full two years he worked there.

> Yeah, it's hard to believe, but the guys told me that it's like
> the hotel itself calls the migra and the migra comes in and
> carries out a big sweep, and they grab everybody in the hotel
> who doesn't have real papers and that's going to be just
> about everyone except the Puerto Ricans, the Dominicans,
> and the college kids.

> At first I couldn't see why the hotel would do that, but later I
> understood that this way the hotel doesn't have to give any-
> one a raise or pay compensation or benefits. The migra
> comes, hauls all the workers away, and—bang!—the hotel
> just hires a lot of new people without papers.

Just before Carlos started his job at the hotel the migra carried out
a targeted raid and took away two Russians who had worked there for
more than four years.

> These were guys who had been engineers in their own coun-
> try, but they were working at the hotel without papers as
> maintenance men. They did all the maintenance everywhere

in the hotel. You name it—air conditioners, elevators, esca-
lators, these two, Vladi and Boris, really knew how to do
everything.

So why, I ask, would the hotel want to get rid of them? Carlos is
careful to say that it all transpired some months before he got his job at
the hotel, so he didn't witness any of this episode firsthand. However,
he says:

The other guys told me that the two Russians began to think
that they were really important to the owner, and they were
beginning to insist on a raise and they wanted the owner to
sponsor them for green cards. And that was it! Next thing
you know the migra turns up, Boris and Vladi are hauled
away in handcuffs, and the hotel hires new people to do their
job.

At first Carlos couldn't understand how and why the hotel owners would take the risk of calling in the authorities. After all, the hotel,
at that point, would have to pay a fine for hiring people who lack
proper documents.

It's true, the hotel has to pay a fine, but figure it out: In the
kitchen they pay a Latino $6 to $8 an hour, but a gringo with
the same skills, he gets $12 to $18 to do the same job. So you
can work out what the hotel owner saves over time when he
hires us. All those hours, all those days: just add up the difference. It's nothing for the hotel to pay a fine every once in
a while, and it's really worth it for them to get rid of anyone
they begin to see as too demanding, as a troublemaker.

So the hotel management saw the Russians as troublemakers? I
ask. Carlos explains:

It's funny. It wasn't as if the two Russians were organizing a
union or something like that. They just wanted to cut a better deal for themselves because they knew that they had spe-

cial skills and they thought the hotel owners couldn't replace them so fast. Well, that's what they thought!

Carlos's Russians made me think of Graciela, a woman I met in Puebla who couldn't understand why her husband, who had washed dishes and bussed tables for twelve years in the same Chinese restaurant in "Mapleville," a rural town in upstate New York, wouldn't even approach his boss to request that he sponsor him for a green card. Graciela had told me:

> I get so angry, I get so frustrated because Alberto, who, I can tell you, is *not* a shy guy when he is back here in the village with us, is like a total wimp when he's in Mapleville. This Chinese guy completely depends on my husband because Alberto opens the restaurant in the morning and starts setting up long before the cook comes in. Alberto is the last to leave at night after he launders and folds the napkins and tablecloths, unloads the dishwasher, stacks all the chairs on the tables, and mops the floor.

> So I say to him: "Alberto, the boss can't get along without you. You need to make him sponsor you for a green card." But Alberto always says, "Believe me, the day the boss has to sponsor me for a green card is the day he'll figure out how to get along without me."

Graciela says that she and Alberto discuss this every time he comes home to Puebla, something he used to do every Christmas, although since September 11, he has only made one visit in five years. She tells me that her idea is that in upstate New York you don't have *esqineros*, day laborers standing around on every street corner (*esquina*) just waiting for work. She argues that because Mapleville is isolated, it cannot be so easy for the Chinese owner to replace Alberto the way a boss anywhere in New York City could just head for the corner where he knows the *esquineros* congregate and pick out a new worker. Graciela keeps making this argument to her husband, but this is the point in the discussion where Alberto always says:

Tell me something: How did I get my job at the restaurant? I was standing on a street corner in Brooklyn with my cousin when this Chinese guy comes up to me and asks if I want to work. So I say yes, and he hands me a bus ticket to Maple-wood, a telephone number to call when I get there, and six hours later I'm running around in a white jacket refilling water glasses in a Chinese restaurant in upstate New York.

So don't you think, that Mr. Lee can send one of his pals over to a street corner in Brooklyn to find someone else? If I had a green card, he would have to pay me minimum wage and benefits, and if he refused, I could go work somewhere else—which is why he's not busy sponsoring me for any-thing, not even after twelve years opening and closing his place seven days a week.

I tell Graciela that I have heard tales of people being sponsored by their employers and she says:

That's what I say to Alberto, but he always says that maybe a real gringo is going to feel he wants to do that for some hardworking guy from another country, that it's part of be-ing an *americano*. But a guy like Mr. Lee doesn't think that way. If he's going to sponsor somebody, he's going to spon-sor a cousin from China. When he wants someone to work a fourteen-hour day, he's going to pick up a Mexican on a street corner. He's going to pick up someone he can get rid of when he doesn't want him around anymore. He knows it wouldn't be that easy for him to dump a Chinese guy from his hometown.

I relate this story to Carlos, who confirms my sense that by now the labor market for low-wage undocumented workers has virtually no geographic limits. Job recruitment takes place not only on a day-to-day, face-to-face basis on street corners, but would-be employers in far-flung places like Mapleville are able, through intermediaries, to tap into the abundant supply of undocumented workers who are concentrated in the standard urban "receiving" areas like the greater New York metropolitan region.

Carlos himself had a brief stint as an *esquinero* in Dover, New Jersey, at a point when he thought he could earn more money if he could get work in construction.

> The problem was that on a construction site, you really have to know what you're doing, even if the work is supposedly "unskilled" and they're only going to pay you minimum wage.

> Most of the guys with me on the street corner had been *albañiles* in Mexico and even though construction here is completely different from back home, they know how to move around a work site. In Mexico you build a house from the ground up, either in adobe, brick, or cinder block. The house just rises up from the ground and when you get high enough you put in the windows and then, in the end, you top it off with a roof. In the United States you first dig and pour the foundation, then you put up a frame and a roof, and then the walls, and then everything else.

Precisely because construction is different in the two settings, Carlos says that it helps to have been around tools all your life. "I swear I spent one day on a construction job," he recounts, "when I realized that I was so bad at it that I was going to end up getting killed or killing one of my coworkers. I was going to swing around by mistake and whack someone in the head with a two-by-four. I was going to fall off a ladder because, basically, I'm scared of heights. So I quit. I didn't even stay long enough to get paid."

Instead of a street corner shape-up for a job, Carlos found his restaurant employment through his network, which, in his case, is centered on his cousin, César, that is, "David."

> David is a man with a million contacts so whatever I needed—a job, a place to live, an ID—he was able to fix me up. He gave me a room in the house he rents. He's my

cousin, so of course he's going to help me. But I'm really lucky because I happen to have a cousin who is really a smart guy and a well-liked guy and a person who knows a lot of people.

Carlos says, "You've got to have people here, brothers, cousins, friends from your hometown, because there's no way you could eat, pay rent, and buy a warm jacket unless you share with other people."

It's hard to imagine how the very first Mexicans who came here survived. You have to live with other people. I've met guys who crossed on their own and they made friends with people from other parts of Mexico who were waiting at the border to cross. And when they all got to the other side, they lived together as a family. You can't cover your expenses on your own, let alone put aside money to send home.

Of course, for a migrant like Carlos, being plugged into a network is a necessary, but not a sufficient condition to guarantee a job placement. Carlos says, "Even your own cousin can't risk his credit with an employer or a contact by saying you're a good worker and that you won't fail to turn up if in fact you can't be relied upon." This is one of the many characteristics of undocumented migrants that makes them so attractive as employees. Turnover is not a problem for employers, who can rely on their own workers to recruit friends and relations to fill any vacancy in the workplace as it comes open. And the worker who has recommended a friend or relation often takes on responsibility for training the person he brought to the workplace because he stands to lose credit, not only with his boss but also with his coworkers, if the new person he recruited cannot do the job properly.

And so David's recommendation proved crucial in every case, but only by presenting himself as eager and capable could someone like Carlos climb the well-defined job ladder that characterizes the food and restaurant sector. Carlos explains that he started out changing the frying oil at Wendy's and working across the street in the afternoons at an Italian restaurant washing pots. But with David's wealth of contacts, he was soon able to set Carlos up at the hotel as a dishwasher, which means that Carlos did not have to enter the kitchen at the very bottom of the hierarchy.

> The man in charge of washing pots, pans, and baking sheets is at the very bottom in the kitchen. This work pays the same wage as a dishwasher, but it is a lot harder than washing dishes, because all the food is cooked on. Some people say that the guys who bicycle around delivering the takeout food are a notch below the lowest guy in the kitchen, but at least they are seen as having some skills because they have to be able to read addresses and street signs and make their way around the city. They are also entrusted with something that has value: the bag full of food, which could be worth $20, $30, maybe $50. Probably the lowest level are the guys who stick restaurant menus in people's mailboxes, because that's a job where you're not carrying anything of value and you don't even have to read the name of a street. You just have be able to figure out what a mailbox looks like, or how to get yourself into the lobby of a building by ringing all the buzzers until someone lets you in.

Like the great majority of Mexicans who work in restaurants and delis, Carlos found that he could move up the ladder according to the skills he could master in food preparation and the amount of English he could acquire. For a dishwasher, a spot chopping vegetables would represent a major step up. Skill in that job could lead to a place as *saladero*, who has to compose a salad according to some preset design, or grillman, who has to cook meat, poultry, fish, or vegetables—all of it thrown on the grill at different moments—to just the right point. If he stuck with it long enough, Carlos might hope to become the cook's assistant, or even the cook, and possibly, one day, would rise to the level of chef.

While Carlos's description of the hierarchy in the kitchen is the one I have heard most often, from another migrant, Angel, I get a very different take or, at least, a more complex picture of the relative status and advantages of workers involved in food preparation and delivery. Angel is the migrant whose story we picked up as he crossed the border at Juárez with his friend Martín, and was detained twice by the same INS agent at the airport in El Paso before finally taking off for Chicago on his third try. After a stint landscaping in suburban Chicago, Angel went to New York to join friends from his hometown who found him a job in a gourmet sandwich shop in lower Manhattan. Angel says:

> I've been at the sandwich shop for eight years and basically I can do every job there is: *sandwichero, saladero, supero,* you name it. Right now, I'm the guy who comes in at 6:00 A.M. and I open the place and get going baking the muffins and the cookies and preparing the fruit salad and the "special salad"—whatever that turns out to be on any particular day. I really like the kitchen work when it's quiet and I'm working alone or with just a couple of other guys.

But the ease that Angel feels with his food preparation comes to a halt around 11:00 A.M. when the phone starts ringing, the takeout orders flood in, and the lunch rush begins. Angel explains that because this is Manhattan and the rents are so high, each square foot of space comes at a premium. Counting the women taking orders and packing the takeaway food behind the front counter and the men in the kitchen, there are twenty-three people working in an area about the size of a one-car garage.

> Once it gets busy, it doesn't matter that a whole bunch of us come from the same hometown and some are brothers and nephews and all that. Everyone is fighting for his three inches of space and elbowing the guy next to him, because if you can't clear a little piece of counter for yourself, you can't turn out the food you're responsible to prepare. And then your coworkers at the front of the shop can't fill the orders as fast as they come in. To be honest, it makes me tense.

This, Angel explains, is why he prefers delivery. After deductions for Social Security, he earns $320 a week from the kitchen work. But on the best days, he can earn a lot more per hour from his deliveries. As soon as the lunch orders begin to flow in, Angel grabs one of the ten bicycles that Veronica, the owner, supplies for this purpose, and he sets out on three hours of rounds that earn him anywhere from $20 to $80 a day. This huge variation in earnings between a good and a bad day on the job is determined mostly by the weather and by the number of deliveries to people who have no idea that the standard minimum tip on delivery is 10 percent and who, instead, offer the deliveryman the pennies, nickels, and dimes that they receive as change when they pay their bill. Angel says:

I like being out on the bike riding through the streets. If the weather's good, I really prefer to be outdoors than fighting with people for space in the kitchen.

And when the weather's bad, and especially if it snows—well, that's okay, too, because that's when you really do well with tips. You get a huge number of orders because even people who normally go out for lunch don't want to go out, and they're grateful to you for bringing their food to them. On days like that, people come to the door and see you standing there dripping water from your jacket, with water pouring off the beak of your hat, and a bag of sandwiches and hot soup in your hand, and they say to you, "Hey, take it easy out there with the ice and the snow." Or they say, "Keep warm" or "Stay dry" or "Watch out for the cabs—they're crazy." It's like the customers are worried about you personally.

Like other people who are on the receiving end of deliveries, I had imagined that the worst part of the job would be confronting traffic and foul weather. But when I ask Angel what are the biggest challenges he faces and if he has ever had ugly experiences in the course of his work, he surprises me by saying:

The worst thing is that there are doormen who are total despots. It's like they're the king of the building and you can only enter the realm by their favor. I'm not kidding. It's like they don't want to see that you're trying to earn a living, just like them. But, then, the best doormen are the Dominicans and the Puerto Ricans because they ask you where you think you are supposed to be delivering the food, and they put you in the elevator, press the button, and tell you whether to walk left or right when you get out. Then, next time you come to that building they greet you—*¿Cómo estás? ¿Qué hay?*—like a friend and a fellow worker. Someone explained to me that this is why these guys have these jobs, because they all speak English, but then they can turn around and speak to us and if there's any confusion, they can help everyone out—the customers and the delivery guys.

Really, most of the bad things happened when I first started and I didn't have two words of English and the system of intercoms just about did me in: you would ring the buzzer next to the number of the office or apartment, and then you would hear a voice, but you couldn't tell if the voice was saying that you should wait there because the person was coming down to meet you or if you were supposed to come up the stairs—but where? It's very hard when you don't even know the word for "fifth floor" in English.

This question of facility in English and the advantages it brings is a topic that comes up in almost every conversation I have with migrants. In my talk with Carlos, I ask how much difference it made that he had a smattering of English even before he came north. Carlos explains that at Wendy's he worked for a Puerto Rican and with Hondurans as coworkers, but mostly with other Mexicans. The hotel kitchen was more mixed, but the language of the workplace was always Spanish.

The waiters, the waitresses, were all gringos. They were high school and college students, but mostly they knew some Spanish. A bunch of them spoke Spanish pretty well and they really liked to speak with us: they were always asking us to teach them the kind of words you don't learn in school. How do you say "jerk" in Spanish? How do you say "asshole" in Spanish?

And they would teach us words we wanted to know as well. Basically, these people were nice, and sometimes we would all go out for a beer or to dance after work. You could be friends with these people. You could even have an argument with one of them—all in Spanish, which to me seemed like a kind of achievement, like getting to a whole new stage.

I asked Carlos what kind of argument he would have with one of his coworkers.

For example, there was a girl, about twenty years old, Emily, who was a hostess in the restaurant, and she would come into the kitchen on her break and want us to drop everything and make her some kind of dessert. Basically, she was a nice person, but kind of spoiled—her father was a friend of the owner's and that's why she had this summer job. And so she would insist and carry on, and you had to tell her, "Hey, get out of here. We've got forty orders to fill and we haven't got time for you." And you could say this to her in Spanish.

So you never really needed English? I asked.

Well, you don't absolutely need it, but of course it helps. I myself was lucky because I had more schooling than a lot of the other people I met on the job. So I had a little bit of English, and that English helped me to move up to the pantry line, where you have to bark out the orders. And when you work on the pantry line, you actually learn things. You can learn how to design appetizers, *tapas*, hors d'oeuvres and how to decorate cakes and dessert plates—like when you have to dribble the raspberry syrup around the edge of the plate and sprinkle the dark chocolate shavings along the side.

Through his cousin David, Carlos learned of a local immigrant aid center that offered English language classes at nominal cost. He attended as often as his work schedule permitted—which was not very often—but he found he made real strides. "In this respect," he said, "I was really advantaged because I had completed high school in Mexico and had some university courses as well. But there were lots of people in my class—and not just Mexicans—who basically couldn't read or write in their native language, so given the way these courses were taught, for them to make progress in English was pretty close to impossible, although they tried very hard."

> Everywhere I worked, though, it was all Spanish. My *compañeros* on the hot-food line were all Mexican. There was another guy from Guadalajara in charge of the broiler, a guy from Nayarit on pots and pans, and me working the grill. We had a really good team—very compact. We worked under a chef who was an Arab, Farid, and he respected us. He took off on vacation and he said "I'm going to leave the whole operation to you guys. I have confidence in you."

"So he spoke Spanish, too?" I asked.

> Well, he understood just about everything and certainly a lot more than he let on. But he always claimed that he had no Spanish, and in fact he would get irritated with us and he would tell us, "You're in this country now and you guys should be speaking English."

> But we were really working well together, and basically, Farid, the busboys, the college students, the owner of the hotel, everybody could see that we did our work well and that we were a team. Once the hotel owner came in and wanted us to drop everything and prepare something special for him and his friends. We just told him that we had all these orders to fill first. He was annoyed, but he just said: "I'm going to sell the hotel to you guys and retire. Then you can have all the headaches."

Unlike the work Mexicans find in construction, sweatshops, groceries, and Korean dry cleaners—the other common areas of employment for Mexicans in New York—restaurant and deli work offers some opportunity for mobility. The Mexican consulate in New York can put researchers in touch with the handful of Mexicans who have opened their own restaurants or have climbed the ladder from delivery boy to dishwasher, all the way up the food-prep line to chef.

But Carlos never saw himself rising through the restaurant ranks to realize a modern-day version of the American Dream. Carlos says he had only one goal in mind in coming to the United States, and that was to accumulate the money he would need to build a house for his recently widowed mother. His goal was to build this house in the village where she had been raised, and then to put away enough money to complete his studies and marry his girlfriend.

> Yes, I guess I was also curious to know more about life on the other side. I wanted to see the whole thing for myself. But basically I had a concrete plan that I expected to carry out in two years.

As it turned out, it took Carlos four years to put together the money he would need to realize his projects because, like almost all the migrants he encountered in the United States, he found that it was a lot more expensive to survive in the United States than he had calculated, and he had to send some money home to his mother just to make sure she had enough to live. Thus, the bigger, long-term projects simply took more time to fund, even though he was frugal. As he noted: "I only spent on the basics. No cigarettes, no heavy drinking, and I only had three changes of clothing, which, I realized, is really enough for a guy who wears uniforms at work." The guiding principle of Carlos's time in the United States was that it would be a temporary sojourn with a specific monetary goal in mind.

Now back in Jalisco, Carlos has married and become a father. He is completing his studies and building the house in the village for his mother, and also working in the Ministry of Rural Development, a job he managed to get through his network of contacts back home. As Carlos says, "If there was one thing I learned during my time in the United States it was the importance of contacts!" But he also harbors another dream.

What I really want to do is to start up a nonprofit organization to work with "pre-migrants," or "potential migrants," which is probably a better term. In this center we would address the challenges people are going to meet once they get to the other side. We can work on basic survival skills and teach them how to fill out a job application, how to budget and save the money that they will earn, and how to send remittances. We could offer some very basic English and some literacy in Spanish for people who don't even have that. Above all, we would want people to know what rights they do have in the United States, even as undocumented immigrants.

15

Sara: "Ten Words in Ten Years"

By her own account, Sara knows ten words of English, one for every year that she has lived in East Los Angeles. As she explains it, these words are the only ones she really needs to get by in a world filled with friends, relatives, customers, storekeepers, teachers, health-care workers, and even police officers, who are not likely to address her in anything other than Spanish. It could happen, she says, that an *americano* might appear at her cart to buy *elotes*, the corn on the cob that she sells piping hot and smothered in mayonnaise, rolled in Parmesan cheese, squirted with lemon juice, and sprinkled with salt and hot chile. It's not likely, but it *could* happen. And when it does, Sara is ready with her ten words:

"Onedollar."
"Corn."
"Cheese."
"Mayo."
"Mustard."
"Salt."
"Potatochips."
"More."
"Please."
"Thankyou."

"Chile," she says, doesn't count as one of the ten because, as she points out, it's the same in Spanish or English. And "lemon" is so close to *limón* that she also doesn't count it as one of her words.

The absence, the near irrelevance of English in Sara's life, is the same as that experienced by a majority of Latin American migrants who live in the language ghetto of East Los Angeles or in South Central Los Angeles. The Pew Hispanic Center survey of Mexican migrants throughout the United States in 2005 found that when asked, "How much English do you speak?" more than half said "None" or "A little," while only 44 percent could claim that they spoke "Some" or "A lot." And indeed, I can confirm that a wrong turn off the Santa Monica Freeway placed me in a monolingual Spanish world. Latino cashiers, baggers, and stock boys I encountered in a New York supermarket often seemed surprised—and sometimes even unnerved—to be addressed in Spanish by someone like me, a person they would not take for Hispanic. But in the monolingual Spanish world that lies just off the freeway in East Los Angeles, it works just fine to open any conversation in Spanish, to stop anyone and ask—as I did—for directions and help in Spanish. At the gas station–convenience store complex where I pulled in, there wasn't a word of English to be heard, and it seems likely that the 44 percent of Mexican migrants in the United States who told the Pew Hispanic Center researchers that they know "some" or "a lot" of English are not the ones living between Whittier Blvd and Olympic Avenue in East L.A.

When Sara first arrived in Los Angeles, she did, in fact, briefly attend free night school courses to learn English. But, having no children, she found no one in her world with whom she might converse in English, and she says that she quickly lost what little ground she had gained.

Sara acknowledges that if she had found work cleaning house for an *americana*, she might have ended up speaking English, at least with her employer, which she thinks would have been a good thing. Housecleaning was, indeed, the work that Sara had performed as a teenager in Mexico when, through friends in her village, she found a job sweeping and washing dishes and clothing for an urban, middle-class family in the city of Puebla. But Sara is a person who, as she expresses it, was "born to sell," and persuading passersby to buy her *elotes* in a parking lot in East Los Angeles is a perfect job for her. The work requires long hours and great energy, but it can bring in as much as $100 a day.

The workday begins for Sara, her husband Pablo, and her sister-in law, Mariluz, at 6:00 A.M. in a ten-foot-by-six-foot metal toolshed. This structure sits behind the bungalow just off Wabash Avenue in East L.A. that they rent for $1,400 a month with five other migrants from San Rafael, the same village in the state of Puebla from which Elena and Diego emigrated, indeed, the same hometown from which Dario, the organizer of carnivals and rock concerts, hails.

In selling *elotes* in the street, Sara is only carrying on the custom of San Rafael, which, as I know from my trip there with Maru, has always produced vendors, first of woven baskets and sleeping mats, and decades later of *morongo*, blood sausage, which the men sold in the street in Mexico City. The first migrants to California from the pueblo worked in agriculture in the central valley or in construction in Los Angeles, but later waves of immigrants, like Sara, reestablished the Rafaeleño tradition of street vending. By the time I met Sara, Pablo, Mariluz, and the five relatives with whom they live, many more Rafaeleños were living in East Los Angeles, pursuing this kind of work, than lived in San Rafael itself.

The workday begins early for these street vendors. At dawn, Pablo drives a minivan to a wholesale market at Olympic Boulevard and Central Avenue in East Los Angeles where corn arrives by the trailer-load from Sonora and Sinaloa in northern Mexico. Here he buys twenty dozen uncooked ears at $2.50 a dozen and hauls them back to the toolshed where, over the course of an hour, he, Sara, and Mariluz will shuck and clean the corn silk from the cobs and prepare them to boil for up to two hours, which is what it takes for this Mexican-grown corn to become tender enough to eat. Sara explains:

> While Pablo is buying the corn, Mariluz and I peel and slice the potatoes that we make into potato chips, so we really have to slice them very thin. We go through four fifty-pound sacks of potatoes each week, which Pablo picks up for us at another market where he can get them for $11.50 a sack. We

also go through four big jars of mayonnaise every week at $4.50 a jar, three bags of Parmesan cheese at $12 a bag, plus the lemon juice that we buy by the bottle, six per week, and the hot sauce, chiles, margarine, and the packages of wooden sticks to push into the bottom of the corn cobs. And apart from the potatoes these are just the supplies we need to dress the corn.

When Pablo returns, he takes charge of the giant copper pot in which the potato chips will be deep-fried over a second gas fire set up in the shed. Here the three of them will work for the next couple of hours, cooking the corn and loading it into a barrel, and frying up the potato chips and "*chicharones*," which are not really fried pork rinds as the name suggests, but rather an extruded paste of four, salt, and lard shaped to look like pork rind. These "*chicharones*"—like the potato chips—will be scooped into plastic bags to be offered as munchies at $1 a bag, along with the *elotes*, which are also priced at $1 a cob.

Once the corn, potato chips, and *chicharones* are cooked, Sara begins the painstaking process of organizing the condiments, which she buys in bulk at a nearby big-box store and scoops out into smaller containers that will fit in a small crate at the rear end of the supermarket cart, precisely the spot where a child would sit, if being pushed through a supermarket by her mother. Sara carefully arranges the wooden sticks and the aluminum foil to wrap around the base of the cob, along with the mayonnaise, chile, cheese, salt, lemon, margarine—each with its own lid with a hole cut for the spoon. "Everything has to be just so," Sara explains, because once she rolls the cart into the parking lot, sales may be brisk, and she is going to have to work fast to flavor the corn and potatoes in a variety of different ways to suit customers who, for their dollar, may want their *elotes* and their chips plain or garnished with any imaginable mix of condiments.

Once Sara has organized the condiments, Mariluz, who only works in preparation, not the vending, of this food, takes off for a factory job. With the twenty dozen ears of corn in a barrel, and the chips and munchies packed in six cartons, twenty bags to the box, Pablo and Sara begin to load the van that they will drive to the shopping mall along back streets. They point out that it would be faster to take the freeway, but neither Sara nor Pablo is driving with a valid driver's license, and they believe that their chances of staying out of trouble are better if they avoid the freeway. Sara says:

> This thing with the license is really tough. Pablo taught me to drive very soon after I got to Los Angeles, and there's no way we could make our living if I didn't share some of the driving. But as much as we can, we try to have Pablo drive because he has a fake license that he bought for $120 a year ago.

When I express my surprise that Elena, who is not only Sara's childhood friend but also Pablo's cousin, had indicated that her husband, Diego, had spent $3,000 to buy a driver's license, Sara says:

> Yes, but Diego has a "real" license with his own picture and name, the kind you get through contacts who have contacts in the motor vehicles bureau. Pablo also has a friend who told him that he could get a "real" license issued to him for only $2,000, but Pablo didn't go for it because he had just spent $120 on the fake one and he's counting on not getting stopped.

Once we reach the shopping center, Sara and Pablo pull two supermarket shopping carts from the van. They place the barrel of *elotes* in one and tie the bags of chips and chicharones up and down the sides of the cart. At this point Sara takes up her customary position in the parking lot while Pablo goes around the corner to sell ice-pops out of a cooler placed in the second cart.

I ask Sara where these ice-pops came from. She explains:

> Well, most nights Pablo makes *respados*, popsicles, in two flavors: vanilla and tamarind. The vanilla is easy because it's just made from milk, sugar, and vanilla extract. But with the tamarind, he has to buy the fruit at the market, clean and peel it, boil it down, separate the seeds, and then mix it with sugar and freeze it. But tamarind really sells well, and Pablo is known for his tamarind. He sells the pops here in the

parking lot, and he sells them at a nearby school when the kids come out of class at the end of the day.

Sara and Pablo count on selling out their whole stock, and most days they are successful. Even when it rains, Sara explains, they prepare the same amount of food, because fewer vendors appear when the weather is cold or rainy and that means more customers for the two of them.

When I ask Sara about the relations among competitors in the parking lot, she explains:

> Basically, we all get along. The truth is that there are so many people going back and forth between the parking lot and the stores on Whittier Boulevard and the corn smells so good, that you don't have to worry; there are plenty of customers for everyone, and the other vendors are decent people. They'll help you make change if you need it. You feel like you're among friends there in the parking lot.

Sara doesn't worry about competing vendors, but she does worry about the police.

> Every once in a while the police come along and they say, "I can't let you sell here because you don't have a license. In L.A. everyone who sells food has to have a license and has to be inspected. Next time I see you doing this I'm going to have to give you a fine." Then a month later, they're back and they say, "Next time I see you I'm going to have to give you a fine. I don't want to see you out here next time I come around." And then, every three months or so, they come around and I get a fine, and it comes to $80.

Sara finds the uncertainty of her relationship to the police unsettling.

> It would be better the way it is in Mexico, where you pay the police a set number of pesos to leave you alone and every-

thing is organized in that respect and you can figure out what the cost is to you to pay off the policeman and you can calculate that when you add up your expenses and your profits at the end of the day. In Mexico paying fines is more regular, more organized.

With the money Sara earns from her *elotes* and chips she manages to send her mother $100 a month, as do her three siblings and, as she notes, "In San Rafael you can live very well on $400 a month." But Sara misses her mother and is putting aside money to travel back to San Rafael to visit, even though she is concerned about what crossing back into the United States will cost and the difficulties and dangers she may face in her return trip to Los Angeles.

The last time I crossed from Mexico I was guided by a coyote from San Rafael, and he took us across at Agua Prieta, which is just south of the city of Douglas, Arizona. It used to be that people just walked from one city to the other and lost themselves in the crowd on the other side. But this time we left Agua Prieta and walked in a huge circle to avoid running into the migra who are everywhere, trying to track you down. It took us two days walking through the desert to go from downtown Agua Prieta to downtown Douglas, a distance we used to cover in twenty minutes. So I can't even imagine what I will have to do on the next crossing if I go down to visit my mom.

At this point I have to ask Sara the question I also put to her childhood friend and cousin by marriage, Elena, and to all the migrants I met along the way. I know that Pablo has been sending money back to his parents to pay for the construction of a house big enough for a multigenerational family. Does this mean that Sara will return to San Rafael?

Sara shakes her head.

The men are always talking about "when we return," but I can't see that there's anything left to return to, and I bet

Elena told you the same thing. All the people our age are here. You can't live from cultivating the land anymore and there are no jobs in San Rafael. What's more, who will send the money down for the others to live if we abandon Los Angeles and return home? I keep telling Pablo that we should save our money to buy a little house here since the eight of us are paying almost $18,000 a year in rent for this four-room bungalow.

But there is another set of reasons why Sara sees a return to San Rafael in a different light than Pablo.

San Rafael is a great place to live when you're a young girl. But once you're married you're expected to live with your husband's parents, and you're not free to walk about on the street or people will gossip about you and criticize you. It's just crazy. I'm a woman of thirty and I wouldn't have the freedom of a thirteen-year-old! I'm not kidding. When I was a girl, I played basketball every day after school with my friends. I ran through the streets alone and with my girlfriends. I even traveled by myself on the two-hour bus ride to my work as a housemaid in Puebla, and no one said anything about it.

But once you marry, you completely lose your freedom. I can remember how I felt totally asphyxiated in my in-laws' home during my first year of marriage when I lived with them, and it's still like that today back in the village, even after all the changes that migration has brought. Can you imagine someone like me, who has her own *elotes* cart, her own earnings, a woman who drives a minivan, who goes here and there in Los Angeles visiting her friends—can you imagine me shut away like a prisoner in Pablo's parents' house in San Rafael?

16

Francisco: The Hardest Place

Francisco was deeply dismayed by the drunk who staggered into El
Centro, the center for immigrant services on Castleton Avenue on the
north shore of Staten Island. The man lurched about, sang a few bars of
ranchera music, opened a bag of donated clothing, and put on a pink
wool coat that was clearly meant for a woman, and was—in the end—
gently but very firmly pushed out the door. Francisco was so embarrassed by this display that nothing I could say seemed enough to
convince him that I was not shocked and that I would not draw the
conclusion that all Mexican migrants are drunken buffoons.

Francisco explained: "We always say, '*Por uno pagamos todos.*' That
means that here, living without papers in the United States, each of us
represents all the others. Do you understand what I mean? People here
judge all of us by the behavior of the worst."

I met Francisco on a bitterly cold day in February 2006 along with
nine other day laborers at a rally for immigrant rights organized by the
Interfaith Coalition and held at Battery Park at the tip of Manhattan, a
public meeting that featured impassioned and very touching speeches
by Buddhist, Christian, Islamic, and Jewish clergy, all framed against
New York Harbor, with the Statue of Liberty in the background. The
crowd of a few hundred included immigrant aid workers of every eth-

nicity. It included trade union representatives. But two categories of people were missing.

The first category was state and national politicians. Indeed, the absence of Senators Hillary Clinton and Charles Schumer from this and similar gatherings, and their total silence on the question of immigrant rights, was a central point raised by a number of the speakers. A month later, as the immigration debate in the Senate and House of Representatives began to heat up, the two senators from New York seemed to realize that it was untenable for them to remain silent when almost every other political figure in the country was staking out a position on the issue. On March 8, 2006, Hillary Clinton—evidently preferring to be photographed surrounded by the undocumented Irish rather than other ethnic groups in the same condition—finally broke her silence by attending a small meeting that focused on the plight of undocumented Irish immigrants.

The second category of missing persons was undocumented immigrants themselves. Some migrants no doubt would never attend such a rally for fear that the migra would lie in wait to seize them if they showed up to assert their claim for rights. But most migrants would miss the rally because they work every day of the week and have no way to participate in this or any other collective action.

Under the circumstances, I was surprised to see one group of short, stocky men in baseball hats and work clothes standing clustered on one side of the crowd as the speakers exhorted the crowd to remember our origins as a nation of immigrants. This group consisted of Francisco and the other *esquineros* who had failed to find work that day, although, as usual, they had lined up at 7:00 A.M. on Castleton Avenue in Staten Island, hoping to be picked out of the crowd by a contractor for a day's labor on a construction site.

Project Hospitality, the organization that had brought the day workers to the rally, is one of an estimated 140 centers across the United States that provide a broad range of services to undocumented immigrants who would otherwise be without protection of any kind. It is ironic that some of the same feelings that were expressed to me in the Arivaca Café in the middle of the Arizona desert—a sense that government is not facing up to the reality of undocumented migration into the United States, feelings that have given rise to the Minutemen, the

Border Guardians, and the others who would take the governmental responsibility of border control into their own hands—also prompt private individuals and organizations to step forward to provide undocumented people with the services that those who work and contribute to the society might hope to receive from government.

Immigrant aid organizations across the United States not only act as social service agencies for both documented and undocumented people who lack the full entitlements of citizenship; they also fill a gap created by the decline of labor unions in the United States, where only 6 percent of all low-wage workers are unionized. These nonprofit organizations offer assistance to immigrants in claiming back pay, reporting abuses on the job, and dealing with unscrupulous landlords and others who exploit them. Often they also mount language courses, provide medical examinations and some basic medical care, counsel immigrant families on how to enroll their children in school, and give legal advice on citizenship as well as the most basic rights that immigrants can assert. Funded by private foundations, religious institutions, and even by local governments, the centers provide a crucial physical space where immigrants can find donated food and clothing, but most important, refuge from hostility that they may encounter on the street.

In the case of Project Hospitality, which describes itself as an interfaith organization, the funds for these activities come from religious groups, private foundations, and the city of New York, as Mayor Michael Bloomberg has targeted Staten Island as an "underresourced" part of the city where low-income families lack services of every kind.

One of the five boroughs that make up New York City, Staten Island is strikingly different from the densely populated neighborhoods of Brooklyn, Queens, and the Bronx and a world away from the pulse of urban life in Manhattan—although it is just a half-hour ferry ride from Battery Park at the tip of Manhattan, possibly the most beautiful free ride on the planet. Before the construction of the Verrazano-Narrows Bridge, which connected it to Brooklyn, Staten Island was part rural, part suburban backwater and largely content to remain so. Even after the completion of the bridge in 1964 set off an explosion of housing development and population growth, Staten Island remained a bastion of white, Catholic, middle-class, conservative values, with

Irish and Italian Americans in political leadership and economic power. It is the one borough in New York City that votes Republican and it proudly provides police officers and firefighters to precincts and firehouses throughout the city.

Although the dominant image of the half million people who live on Staten Island is one of a homogenous, middle-class, predominantly white ethnic population, in reality, the number of documented and undocumented immigrants from Africa, Latin America, and eastern Europe has grown at a rapid rate and the number of people classified as poor is rising more rapidly here than in any other borough of New York. As one of the coordinators at Project Hospitality explains:

> On Staten Island we have no public hospital, no publicly financed shelters for the homeless, next to no low-income housing, and only one office that processes welfare and food-stamp applications. Our food pantries are the poorest in the whole city, with budgets that are a fraction of their counterparts in Queens, Brooklyn, or the Bronx. Given how people think about Staten Island, it's like it comes as a surprise to people in government that there's anyone needy here, that there are actually people who are not comfortably middle-class.

> This is the gap that Project Hospitality is trying to fill for all poor people on Staten Island. And our work with the immigrants is just an outgrowth of this broader effort. In particular, we have a commitment to open our doors to the day laborers who are, literally, at our doorstep, standing around every day on a corner in Port Richmond at the end of the block on which we are located.

The labor shape-up in Port Richmond is only one of roughly forty such sites in the New York metropolitan area, but it has a different feel than the highly charged, threatened experience of day laborers who gather in places like Mamaroneck in Westchester County, New York, or Farmingville out on Long Island. In these far-flung suburbs, some local home and business owners have strenuously, and sometimes violently, registered their opposition to the "free market" of labor that has spontaneously formed on their sidewalks as immigrants seeking work encounter those offering minimum- (and subminimum-) wage jobs in landscaping, factory work, and construction. Indeed, the hostility of local residents to Mexican and Central American day workers in Farmingville became headline news across the United States in the fall of 2000 when two men posing as construction contractors "hired" Israel Pérez and Magdeleño Escamilla, took them to an abandoned building, and attacked them with a knife, a crowbar, and a shovel, beating them until Israel was close to death.

The Port Richmond neighborhood of Staten Island, however, provides a different context for those who seek casual work on its main street. In physical terms, Port Richmond resembles places like Freeport and Hempstead and other towns on Long Island where, over recent decades, once-thriving historic town centers had become a row of abandoned storefronts as small businesses gradually lost their customers first to large shopping malls and later to mega-malls and big-box stores. On Long Island, a number of these old town centers have been rejuvenated by the investment of immigrants who have opened small businesses that now animate the main streets of the towns. Similarly, Port Richmond Avenue, which had become increasingly shabby and deserted, has experienced a rebirth as a six-block row of Mexican and Dominican restaurants and shops began to fill empty commercial spaces.

The advantage to the *esquineros* who stand about on Castleton or Port Richmond Avenue hoping for a day's work is that rather than confronting shopkeepers who consider their presence on the sidewalk, in a parking lot, or in a public park to be a blight on their community, the Staten Island day laborers are standing in front of the restaurants where they buy their tacos and chiles rellenos, the laundromats where they wash their clothes, and the shops they frequent as customers.

Still, the life of *esquineros* is full of hardships and they are the immigrant category most likely to attract hostility because they present the most visible face of Mexican migration to the United States. Few *americanos* will ever catch a glimpse of Carlos on the pantry line in a hotel kitchen in New Jersey or Fernando pressing pants at the back of the Korean dry cleaner in Manhattan. But all the world sees the *esquineros* standing and waiting on the street corner. And in a previously insular community like Port Richmond, which now finds that just under a quarter of its population of 62,800 is composed of mostly Mexican, mostly undocumented, mostly male immigrants, the shock of suddenly coming into contact with a multicultural reality has been stunning.

For Francisco, as for the other day workers, the winter is the worst time of the year, not only because of the physical suffering involved in standing for hours in one spot hoping that someone will drive up looking for minimum-wage workers to clear a construction site or fill a rush order at his plant. Winter is the worst time because the landscaping jobs and outdoor construction jobs that make up the bulk of work opportunities for *esquineros* are not offered in the coldest season, or they are offered only infrequently. Francisco explains:

> Last week it was really cold and we had no work at all, and I went over to El Centro to see if, maybe, someone had donated a heavy jacket with a hood attached because I was wearing earmuffs over a wool hat, and still I couldn't stay warm standing around on the corner. But then this week there was this huge snowfall, like nothing that anyone had ever seen in New York or in Staten Island, and my cousin, Donaldo, who has been here a year and a half longer than me, had the idea that we should buy two shovels and make some money going house to house digging out people's driveways.
>
> We got lucky because we got the last two shovels at the hardware store. As you can imagine, coming from Puebla, I had never shoveled snow before, but I got the hang of it, and we cleared three front walks and three very long driveways, and we made out very well for a day's work because people were getting desperate to get themselves dug out. The next day the snowplow passed and blocked these people's driveways again, so we went back, dug them out, and got a little bonus on top of what we earned the day before.

While he couldn't count on another record blizzard, like other day workers, in any season, Francisco clings to the hope that a single day's work will turn into something more permanent.

My cousin and I get to the corner on Port Richmond Avenue by 7:00 A.M. and we wait there at least until noon. If we haven't found work by noon, we give up for the day because there's next to no chance that anyone will come along after that. In winter we're very lucky if we find work three days a week. In warmer weather it's completely different—it's possible to get some kind of job almost every day. The best I've ever done since I came here six months ago was a stretch when, for a full two weeks, I was working on a construction site and taking home $100 a day. Nothing even close to that has happened since. Normally the best I can hope for would be $70 for a twelve-hour day.

Thus, the prospects for an *esquinero* differ from the situation that Luis and Carlos found in food service. Fast-food franchises like Wendy's offer no hope of moving beyond minimum wage, but many restaurant jobs like the one Luis held in the deli and Carlos held at the hotel do, in fact, provide some degree of upward mobility as a worker acquires greater skill in food preparation. In contrast, the work of day laborers in construction and landscaping generally offers little hope of moving up a ladder of higher skill and higher wages. In this respect it is striking that, among all the Mexicans I came to know who had worked in construction, only one, Victor, a 50-year-old migrant day laborer who shaped up every morning in Port Richmond, had managed, by his own estimate of his situation, to make some real strides.

Victor was not merely a skilled *albañil* back in his town in Oaxaca. He explained to me that he had been a maestro—a master builder. And, he had, by his own description, been "lucky" enough to be noticed by a Staten Island contractor named Jimmy, who had randomly chosen him from the crowd of men who stood on the corner each day hoping for work. Victor explained:

This man, Jimmy, took me to a house where he was building an apartment in the basement: a single room plus a kitchen alcove and a complete bathroom. He showed me with gestures what he wanted me to do with the drywall, the wiring, the plumbing, and all the rest. And then he stood there and watched me work for a while. At a certain point, he could see that I knew how to do it all and could work on my own, even if I have only a few words of English.

After twelve hours of work on this project, Jimmy drove Victor back to Port Richmond and dropped him at a gas station near the corner where he had found him. Jimmy counted out $70 in cash, which is the sum that Victor had hoped to receive, and then he counted out another $20 and handed that to Victor as well. Then he mimed a phone call, pointing his index finger into Victor's chest, a sign that Victor took to mean that Jimmy wanted his phone number.

At that point I understood that Jimmy was going to phone me at the house I share with other Mexicans. Speaking very slowly and waving his arms, he made me understand that any time that he had work for me, he would call and say the word "tomorrow," and that meant that I should come to the gas station the next morning at six and wait for him there.

Some weeks I work only two or three days for Jimmy and some weeks I work the full week. But it's great because he always pays me $20 more than anyone else earns because he understands that I can do everything there is to do and he doesn't have to stand over me to tell me what to do. So I'm really lucky compared to the other guys. When Jimmy doesn't phone, I go to the street corner and hope for the best.

While Victor managed to attract the attention of an employer who was sufficiently alert to recognize a worker with expertise, the vast majority of day laborers, whatever their level of skill, are rarely so fortunate. When, in 2005, Abel Valenzuela and Nik Theodore carried out a national survey of 264 hiring sites in twenty states, their findings would certainly confirm Victor's sense that he was unusually fortunate. Based on interviews with 2,660 workers, the two researchers found that of those who shaped up on street corners, three-quarters of whom were undocumented migrants, more than half said that they had been cheated on wages in the previous two months, and 44 percent said that they were given no breaks during the workday. Nearly three-quarters were forced to work in hazardous conditions like digging ditches, working with chemicals, or on roofs or scaffolding. One-fifth said that in the past year they had suffered injuries requiring medical attention, and 60 percent of the injured had to miss more than a week of work. The report, published in 2006 under the title *On the Corner: Day Labor in the United States*, underscored that day laborers continue to put up with unsafe conditions and low wages because they believe that if they resist or complain, or even call attention to themselves, they will be fired or will not be paid for the work they have done.

My own contact with the world of criminally sleazy contractors came when I volunteered at Asociación Tepeyac in 2002. Like Project Hospitality, Tepeyac is a nonprofit, community-based organization that offers assistance to immigrants, including health-care information, ESL courses, and a variety of other practical services. The focus, however, at Tepeyac is on human rights advocacy and particularly on labor rights. It is in this effort that I helped out as a translator for Joe McNulty, who specialized in minimum-wage enforcement and the recovery of back pay. As Joe explained:

> You have a situation where both the Mexicans and most of the people who employ them have no idea that undocumented migrants have any rights under United States law when, in fact, they have a lot of rights, especially under New York State labor law. Whether you are here with papers or not, if you work, you have rights. Regulations on minimum wage, overtime, health and safety standards—they apply to everybody with or without green cards or citizenship. The boss cannot take a share of your tips as kickback. The employment agency cannot take more than 10 percent of the first month's wages if all they have found for you is unskilled manual labor. That's it. Papers or no papers, if you become disabled on the job, you're entitled to Workers' Compensation. And if you're ripped off or abused in any of these ways, the New York State Department of Labor will take your case.

Typical of the workers who came to see Joe at Tepeyac was Gilberto, an *esquinero*, who had worked for a week for a contractor who had picked him up on a street corner in Brooklyn. When the end of the week rolled around, the contractor told Gilberto that he would pay him at the end of the following week. Gilberto says:

> I didn't know whether to believe him, but, in fact, a lot of jobs in Mexico are paid, as we say, *cada quince días*, which for you would be "every two weeks." And I was glad to have steady work, so I decided to carry on for the second week because the guy said he would give me $600 the following Friday. Then Friday comes and he says, "You know, I'm just the subcontractor, and the contractor hasn't given me the money to pay you guys until next week." At this point, I didn't think he was going to give us anything, but I figured I better stick with it because no one is offering me anything else, so I worked for a third week.

> Luckily, there was this other guy, Dionisio, who is from Guerrero, and he was working with me picking through glass and bricks, cleaning up the construction sites. And he was smart because even though the truck that this subcontractor used to take us to the different job sites had nothing written on the side, Dionisio knew to write down the license plate number, and he was the one who knew we could come here and that you would get us our money.

In fact, Joe himself wasn't going to get Gilberto or Dionisio their back pay, but what he could do was to set into motion the process by which the two workers could recover their wages. First comes the phone call to the subcontractor, who was "counseled" in the most polite terms that he was at risk of liability under New York State labor law for violations of workers' rights. If the subcontractor claimed, as most did, that he was simply following the instructions of the contractor, then Joe would get the name of the contractor and give him a call, offering to help him avoid a citation from the Department of Labor as an "accessory to the fact" in the denial of wages, and advising him that failure to pay up means a fine and possible imprisonment if he is unable to pay the fine.

If the phone call produced no payment of back wages, Joe would follow up with a registered letter containing the same basic argument, plus an "overdue wages statement" and written excerpts from the relevant sections of the New York State law. If the registered letter failed to produce a response from the contractor, the next step would be to file a claim with the Department of Labor, and much of Joe's time was spent helping migrants do just that.

In the case of Gilberto and Dionisio, I accompanied them to the Department of Labor on Hudson Street, where they sat and waited for their case to be called, even as they fought off the impulse to flee before the migra could appear to grab them. It was incomprehensible to them that they could be seated in a government office with the New York State seal on the wall and the national and state flags on display, and that this place was filled with government workers who somehow could not and would not report them to the INS.

When their case was called, the Department of Labor officer I will refer to as Richard opened by addressing their fears:

Who do you think gets ripped off in this country? If we didn't work with undocumented people here in this office, we might as well close up shop. The bulk of our work is in securing rights for people like the two of you because you are the kind of person that unscrupulous employers will exploit. A lot of people who have no documents are afraid to come forward. Our policy, our procedure, is that we accept all claimants. If people work in New York State, it's required that they be paid. Period. We do not contact the INS, and if by some chance the INS should contact us, we tell them to go away. It's true that the INS can subpoena our records, but we will go to court to fight it.

Having established this astonishing fact, Richard addresses me:

This is what you need to do: These men have to be able to tell us exactly where they worked—which sometimes isn't so easy because the contractors haul them all over the five boroughs, often in a panel truck with no windows, and they probably don't know if they were in Brooklyn or in the Bronx. Then we need a name, at least a first name of the employer. Ideally, we have the full name, address, and the phone number of the enterprise as it appears on the side of the van, which is obligatory if it is a commercial vehicle. But some of these guys have nothing on their vans or trucks, and they even use a rent-a-car to conceal their name and ID. Anything to be able to get away with paying way below minimum. That's why we need the license plate number.

I ask Richard if going three weeks with no pay makes Dionisio and Gilberto's case extreme. He replies:

How badly can people be cheated? How about people being paid as little as $2 to $3 an hour! Do the math. A huge number of workers in this city are putting in sixty hours a week and getting $70 a day for a twelve-hour day. This works out to $5.83 an hour. Meanwhile, the minimum wage is now $6.75. And workers are supposed to be paid for resting, too. And they're supposed to be paid a half hour while they eat. Workers are not animals! They're supposed to get at least a half hour—paid—while they eat their lunch. You can't believe the stuff that goes on. Mostly these abuses happen on farms, in restaurants, dry cleaners, nurseries, landscaping, construction, nursing homes, hospitals. But absolutely the worst violations that we see are what happens to the day workers. They are really at risk.

In fact, given the great insecurity, the hardships, and, indeed, the danger that marks the life of *esquineros*, it is difficult to figure out why anyone would undertake the perilous journey across the border only to expose himself to the extreme insecurity of the day laborer's life.

When I share my perplexity with Francisco—when I ask him directly, "Why would anyone do this?"—he is, in fact, eager to explain his thinking. He is 40 years old and comes from Tehuacán, a city in Puebla that, in the course of the 1970s and 1980s, became prominent as a center of maquila production. Originally clustered in Mexican towns along the border with the United States, the maquiladoras were set up, largely by foreign-owned firms, under the Border Industrialization Program instituted in the 1960s to take advantage of low-wage labor in Mexico. The program offered special tax breaks to manufacturers who could bring parts or pieces of a product duty-free into Mexico where they would be assembled and then exported to the United States— once again duty-free—as long as they were held "in bond" during the time they were processed in Mexico.

With the signing of the North American Free Trade Agreement, it became profitable to carry out the same kind of assembly operation with low-wage Mexican workers not only along the border but also in cities throughout the interior of Mexico, wherever there was a large pool of unemployed labor and adequate infrastructure and transportation to seaports or to the border. Not only United States, but Japanese, Korean, Taiwanese, and other foreign investors took advantage of this opportunity to move plants farther south into the interior of Mexico, where even more unemployed workers were ready to offer their labor at even lower wage rates.

As early as the 1970s, Tehuacán had already attracted Mexican manufacturers to the area to produce blue jeans. By the 1990s, Tehuacán had more than three hundred foreign and domestically owned assembly plants, although if we count the clandestine sweatshops, the figure was probably closer to five hundred. Francisco, the first in his peasant family to complete high school, worked for many years as a sign painter, but in the early 1990s, he managed to secure a job in one of the maquiladoras that turned out blue jeans for Levi, Lee, The Gap, and American Eagle. He began work in the plant as a cleaner at $20 a week, but rose, over the course of two years, to the position of supervisor of the cutting tables at a salary of $130 a week, and worked at that level for another eight years. "And then," Francisco says, "it all ended."

After ten years, the plant, which had employed 2,500 people, went bankrupt and the other foreign-owned maquilas also disappeared one by one, leaving only the Mexican-owned plants in Tehuacán. Then the Mexican plants began to close as well. I received a severance payment of 5,000 pesos for ten years of work. And that was it. I was out of work and there was a ton of other people all out of work and all at the same time.

Francisco had two brothers who had worked for three years in construction in North Carolina until they put together the $30,000 they needed to buy a backhoe to launch their construction company in Tehuacán. But now those brothers were back home and could not provide the network that Francisco would need to make his way to North Carolina. Luckily for Francisco, his cousin Donaldo, who had crossed the border and joined in-laws in New York, was able to advance him the $2,000 he would need for the coyote fees and could offer him housing once he reached Staten Island.

But how would Francisco pay off his debt, cover his expenses, and still put together the $15,000 that is the figure that represents the stake he needs to transform his life in Tehuacán? Francisco outlines his calculations for me.

I need $80 a week to send home to my family. Then the monthly expenses are $120 for my share of the rent, $10 for electricity, and $40 for cooking gas. Then I need $120 for the bus, $15 for the phone in my house, and $40 for my cell, and I calculate $120 for food because we share the food shopping and cooking. Apart from these expenses, I have my debt to Donaldo. I've managed to pay the first half in the first six months that I've been here.

So if, in any month, I can get work for eleven or twelve days at $70 a day, I can cover my own expenses and provide for my family in Tehuacán. Any work I get beyond those eleven or twelve days of labor, I can put to paying off the second thousand dollars to Donaldo, and then, once I am free of that debt, everything else that I earn will be savings. It all depends on getting work more than half the days I'm on the street corner. My goal is to add two rooms to my house and to set up my wife in a fruit stall in a market, which is what she wants the two of us to do. As soon as I've put the $15,000 together, I'm out of here.

While he pursues this strategy, Francisco is adequately housed, at least in comparison with other migrants on Staten Island. He and Donaldo share a room in an apartment where the lease is held by a Mexican couple and their two children, who share the second bedroom. As modest—and crowded—as Francisco and Donaldo's dwelling may be, a few weeks into my research in Staten Island, I have the chance to tag along on a tour of immigrant housing conditions in Port Richmond that is conducted by Terry Troia, the head of Project Hospitality, for three high-ranking officials from the New York City Department of Housing Preservation and Development (HPD). In the course of this tour, it quickly becomes clear just how fortunate Francisco is in his housing arrangements.

The stops on this tour include a basement shared by eighteen single men, an unheated garage that is home to two Mexican families, an abandoned tractor trailer that houses four *esquineros*—a situation that has aroused resentment among the non-Mexican homeless people who previously called the container "home"—and an abandoned tugboat and barge, both vessels half in and half out of the water, and each providing housing to another two or three men.

When the HPD officials ask Terry why she has not reported these gross violations of city housing codes to their office, Terry explains, very simply, that there is no place to put any of these people if the spaces they currently occupy are taken out of the housing pool.

"Right now I have a family of immigrants living in my living room," Terry says. "Where would I find refuge for other people if I phone 311 and report all the violations I come to see in the course of my work? Is the city going to house these people?"

In fact, this is not the only knotty problem or paradox that confronts the HPD officials in Staten Island. Among many other responsibilities, this city agency is charged with the obligation to prosecute cases of discrimination on the part of landlords toward would-be tenants. However, in their talks with Project Hospitality social workers, an altogether unexpected form of discrimination comes to light. It turns out that in Port Richmond and surrounding communities in Staten Island, the owners of substandard rental properties greatly prefer to rent to undocumented Mexicans over all other potential tenants. Indeed, with the help of firsthand testimony from Mexican migrants they had assembled for this encounter, the Project Hospitality people were able to document numerous cases in which landlords showed a preference for undocumented Mexicans or Central Americans over Puerto Ricans, Dominicans, or African Americans—in short, over the other potential customers in this low-end housing market. As Alfredo, one of the Mexicans who spoke at this meeting, explained:

> The landlords don't want to receive a welfare check in payment for the rent. They want to be paid in cash. And the Mexican and Central American day laborers are the people who are earning all their wages in cash. These are the people who will pull a roll of bills out of their pocket when the time comes to pay up.

> More than that, the landlords think of the Mexicans and the Central Americans as people who will put up with any abuse. The landlords are like the contractors who hire you to work for a day. They figure that we're not here legally, so there's no chance we're going to be running to the authorities to report unsafe conditions, violations, or abuses of any kind.

Alfredo also reports that the landlords make their own distinctions among potential tenants, and they discriminate among migrants on the basis of these stereotypes, which, in the case of Mexicans, are positive.

> We Mexicans have this reputation for being "quiet living," because we can't afford to draw attention to ourselves in any way. Have you ever walked around in a Dominican neighborhood? A place like Washington Heights? Everybody's sitting on their front stoop with a CD player or a radio

blasting. Music is coming out of every window of every apartment, but I mean really loud music. People having fun, people dancing and partying on the sidewalk. Undocumented Mexicans aren't going to do that.

Thus, in the lowest-end housing market in Staten Island, landlords prefer to rent to Mexicans over all other potential tenants, in the same way that employers prefer undocumented Mexican workers over other low-wage workers who might be more assertive in claiming their rights. And the Mexicans' reputation as submissive in these respects inspires great resentment on the part of other poor people in New York—particularly African Americans, but also Puerto Ricans, Dominicans, and other longer-term immigrants, who see Mexicans as undercutting their wages and working conditions and beating them out in the competition for bottom end housing.

These perverse forms of discrimination in favor of Mexicans were dramatically illustrated to me when I sat one day at a large communal table at the back of a Korean salad bar in the garment district in Manhattan. There I met Enrique, a Salvadoran refugee who, twenty-five years earlier, had escaped the civil war in his country and been fortunate enough to get his citizenship papers after only a few years in the United States. Enrique explained to me:

I've been working twenty years in the garment district and I have a good job running the shipping department in this factory. But the guy who is directly over me, a Puerto Rican, is a real SOB, like a totally authoritarian person, and if I take off for lunch, like I did today, he's on me as soon as I get back, yelling at me that I have no business taking even a half hour for lunch—never mind that the stock I'm supposed to be shipping hasn't even arrived yet from the supplier.

So you know what I tell him when he starts in with me? Like, every time he gets on my case. I say, "Go get yourself a Mexican! You want someone who won't take even a half-hour lunch break? Hire a Mexican."

When, some days later, I share this exchange with Francisco, he says:

> Well, it's not a nice thing to say, the way he said it, but it's true. We do work harder than anyone else. But it's not like we're all the same among ourselves, either. Among Mexicans, when there's a job that's so tough or so badly paid that we think is not really worth taking, we always say, "I'm not going to work for crap wages. Let them find a *oaxaqueño* to do the job!"

As we have seen, the preference shown for Mexican workers on the part of employers and for Mexican tenants on the part of landlords plays out as tense relations between Mexicans and other people of Latin American origin, and between Mexicans and African Americans. As Francisco says:

> I'm not scared of white people. The worst is, they're going to cheat you out of your wages. The people I'm scared of are the *morenos* [African Americans] because the only place that I'm going to be able to afford to rent is going to be in a bad, black neighborhood, filled with drugs and criminal activities. That's what frightens me.

> Here in Staten Island, we've had three cases of Mexicans being beaten savagely for no reason at all. Three different Mexican guys who ended up wasted by people who just picked them out to beat up. In one case it was two Dominicans and a Puerto Rican who beat up a guy from Puebla. But in another case it was African Americans who started beating on a guy from Guerrero, who was just walking down the street.

> Then there was the case of Edgardo, a guy who was mopping floors and cleaning the grill in a diner. A black guy comes in around midnight and insists on being served eggs and bacon. When Edgardo says, "I can't cook you breakfast. The

place is closed. And besides, I'm the cleaner, not the cook," the black guy actually leaps over the counter and punches Edgardo in the face and breaks his nose. Luckily for Edgardo, the owner of the diner comes in at this point, calls 911 on his cell, grabs the black guy, and the two of them, Edgardo and his boss, sit on the black guy until the police arrive. But Edgardo is bleeding all over the place and now his nose is smashed up so bad he can only breathe through his mouth.

An abiding fear of African Americans was one of the most striking elements in all the interviews I carried out in both New York and Los Angeles, and these feelings were most intense among migrants who had found housing in predominantly black neighborhoods in Brooklyn and Queens. In fact, only one person I interviewed, Raimundo, an undocumented migrant from Honduras, felt that he had somehow surmounted the difficulties of this situation.

I live with my sister in Jamaica, Queens, in a really bad neighborhood with lots of guns, lots of drugs, everything. It's really ironic because the reason that I left Honduras was that my family lived in a part of Tegucigalpa that has always been poor, but is now totally overrun by gangs. It got to the point that I couldn't leave the house, for fear of getting caught in the crossfire. I was like a prisoner in my parents' house. So that's why I came here.

Of course my sister and I would like to live someplace safe. But we're right on the subway line, on the F train, and we pay only $1,250 a month for a two-bedroom place and there's nowhere else in the city that we can get a rent like that. Basically, our apartment house, which is a six-story walk-up, is about half crack house and half just poor African Americans—plus my sister and me. What can we do? We just get along as best we can. We greet everyone we meet in the hall, "Hi, how'ya doin'?" But we don't really have anything to do with these people because so many of them are involved with drugs.

The funny thing is, though, that they've accepted us. Somehow they've taken a liking to us. They always call out to me, "Hey, Papi!" or "Hey, Nigga'!" and "How's it goin', Nigga'?" and greetings like that—just the way they talk to their friends, to the people they really like.

And so Raimundo has found an accommodation with his black neighbors. And, strikingly, Vicente, from Nopal Verde, who labored as a housepainter in Oklahoma, spoke to me very fondly of an African American with whom he had worked for two years in Tulsa. Moreover, in describing his work as a deliveryman, Angel underscored the kindness and empathy of Puerto Rican and Dominican doormen, who were always helpful to him. Unfortunately, these experiences represent significant exceptions to a dominant tale of tension between blacks and Caribbean Hispanics and the Mexicans they often perceive—and not incorrectly—as their rivals in the housing and job markets.

But these are not the only areas of resentment toward Mexicans among those who share with them a place at the bottom of society. One of the most stunning outcomes of the new population mix in New York plays out in the Catholic Church as a competition for space and prominence for different expressions of the Virgin Mary.

As a priest in the Bronx whom I will call Father Robert explained to me:

Of course this parish used to be Irish when I was a kid growing up here, and then it was black and Puerto Rican, and later people came from the Dominican Republic. What we do is we try to serve everyone who comes into the church and to give them a home in the church.

But when the Mexicans came here, it was different. Because of the way they worship in Mexico, and the customs they practice there, the Mexicans' way of encountering the church is completely different from any of the people this parish has served in the past. They are very silent and very strong in their worship. And they constantly surprise me: the men just ask me for a ladder, and next thing they are up on the roof, repairing the roof. I never asked them to do this; they just do it. Next they tell me they want to whitewash and paint the interior. The women want to embroider vestments for the saints and for me to wear when I say Mass. They want to prepare food.

It's never about what I can do for them. It's about the way they give expression to their love of Christ, which is that they want to work, they want to contribute. They're used to cooperating to look after the church in their village in Mexico, and they want to do the same thing here in the Bronx.

Father Robert underscores that the Mexicans come with no expectations of handouts. He says they wouldn't expect the priest back home to help them economically because everyone is poor in the village. In Mexico—where Father Robert customarily travels on vacation—poor people have to find the resources to donate to the church to assure that the key festivals are celebrated properly. And because they are not accustomed to a priest who provides tuition for Catholic school or rent money for a parishioner on the verge of eviction, he says, "they are very shy in making any request of me."

So when they ask me to bring the Virgin of Guadalupe into the church, how could I deny them? And when they ask to see her closer to the Christ on the cross at the front of the church, I couldn't say no. The prominence of our devotion to the Virgin of Guadalupe has created some uneasy feelings among the Dominicans, who venerate the Virgin of Alta Gracia and Divina Providencia, and the Puerto Ricans, who venerate Nuestra Señora de Lujan. But everyone is welcome here and the Mexicans are now the lifeblood of this parish and I want them to feel that this is their house.

So it is that in every aspect of their lives, in the workplace, in housing, and at worship, Mexicans have to work out relationships not so much with the "dominant society" but with others at the bottom of the ladder. Francisco once confided to me that for fear of his *moreno* neighbors, he always carried a pocketknife. Yet, when I asked him what was the most distressing encounter he had had since coming to the United States, he surprised me by saying,

> Basically, to put together the $15,000 I need in order to get out of here and back home to my family, I can put up with anyone and anything. It doesn't matter. But for sure, in terms of other people, the worst thing I have suffered since coming here is the arrogance and disrespect of some of the Mexicans who have been here longer than me, and who make clear that they look down on me because I don't know English and I don't know my way around.

Part IV

To Stay or to Return Home

17

Julio: A Quick Exit

Julio's first day on the job was a bust. He set out early on a Monday morning pushing a supermarket cart filled with soft drinks and ice-cream sandwiches. The jobber who supplied the cart, the coolers, the ice, the soda, and the ice cream had assured him that this area was a prime zone for Mexican and Central America migrants, who would stop for a snack on their way to work in sweatshops, and surround his cart three deep on their lunch hour.

But Julio never got to see the crowd three deep. He had barely installed himself on a corner in Los Angeles when another Mexican with a similar cart rolled up to the same spot and said, "Sorry, 'mano, this is my corner."

I asked Julio if the other street peddler had threatened him.

No, he didn't have to. I can figure out that you can't take another guy's territory, and I also understood that I had been screwed around by the jobber. So I wheeled the cart back to his house near I-10, and I stood there until he returned the $60 I had paid him to take the cart for the day. But he wasn't real happy about giving me anything back because he said he was now stuck with the melted ice-cream sandwiches.

Julio had crossed the border at Tijuana only two days earlier and was feeling lucky about the ease with which he and his cousin—on their second try—had climbed over the fence, crossed the dry riverbed, and made it to the McDonald's in San Ysidro on the California side. That's where their contact, another migrant from Atlixco, Puebla, was waiting to drive them to Los Angeles. Julio was feeling lucky that his older brother, who sponsored his trip, had a room he could share with Julio in a house with nine other undocumented Mexican men in South Central, a neighborhood in downtown L.A.

Julio did not want to go into detail about his reasons for leaving Mexico. But he did make clear that his decision to join his brother in Los Angeles had less to do with economic aspirations than with his need to extricate himself from a romantic relationship that had, as he put it, "gone bad."

Under the circumstances Julio was just glad to be on the other side and his setback with the ice cream didn't upset him. He spent the next week "freelancing" with his cousin in pizza sales. The pizza venture was much less complex than the ice-cream cart rental. With the pizza, he explains, you buy a whole pie and you walk around selling it by the slice, and the difference between the cost of the pie and the eight slices is your profit to take home. You can also carry a bag over your shoulder with some cold sodas, straws, and napkins.

> That's the whole operation: very neat and very simple. But I couldn't make any money at it because at least once a day a gang of African American kids would see me walking along with my pizza, and they would surround me, grab the box, and take off. There really wasn't anything you could do to defend yourself against that kind of thing in the places where I was peddling the pizzas. The whole pizza thing lasted less than a week.

Still, in spite of these nonstarters, Julio felt certain that his luck was running, that something else would come along. And indeed, a few days later, one of his housemates said, "Don't worry. I've got something good for you."

The "something" turned out to be a small-time crack distribution

ring in an area of L.A. that—unlike the ice-cream sandwich operation—
was, for the time being, uncontested by rival distributors. All Julio had to
do, his new friend said, was to walk around dressed in a Lakers sweatshirt and an L.A. Dodgers cap, and customers—he was assured—would
find him.

So Julio walked around and waited to be approached by the customers who would recognize his sweatshirt and hat. And it wasn't more
than ten minutes before two short men who, from their accents, Julio
took to be Nicaraguan, approached, bought a little glassine envelope
for $20, thanked him, and then slapped handcuffs on him, and—
wreathed in smiles and laughing hard—said, "Listen, you Mexican
piece-of-shit son of a whore, you have the right to remain silent."

Well, silent was just how Julio remained, as they drove him down
to the station house, stripped him naked, and stood him, spread-
eagled, against the wall of an interrogation cell. This is when one of the
Nicaraguans noticed the Mexican Air Force tattoo on Julio's bicep. See-
ing the Battalion 5 insignia, they returned his clothing, took him out of
the cell, sat him down in a metal chair next to a metal desk, and went
off in search of someone they referred to as Jaime and a cup of burnt
coffee that Julio didn't want, but accepted politely.

As Julio and I sit talking in a public park in Puebla years after the
event, he tells me that even when this Jaime returned, accompanied by
two other narcotics officers, he never lost his composure. "That's one of
the things that, all my life, I've always been good at."

Julio explains that when he was 15 he enlisted in the military with
the hope of becoming a paratrooper and possibly even a pilot. His
mother had to sign a permission slip because he was underage, "but she
understood that I really needed to get away from home and I pointed
out to her that if anything happened to me in the army, she was going
to receive a pension for life."

> The training they gave us in those days was beyond brutal,
> even for a man, not to speak of a boy like me. The boys in my
> platoon were mostly older than me, but some didn't last a
> week. They actually deserted after three or four days. But I
> stuck it out because I didn't want to go home and I would
> have been too ashamed to go home. My father didn't live

with us, but he had been a *militar*, he had served in the cav-
alry. I had uncles on both sides who had been soldiers, and a
great-uncle who rode with Pancho Villa in the revolution.
So I didn't see that I had any choice but to stick it out, even
if I died in the course of the training.

But, imagine. In the second year of my military service, we
had the earthquakes in Mexico City, and it was the soldiers
like us who had to dig the dead bodies out of the rubble because the city police were too busy looting and pulling jew-
elry off the dead to get on with the job. But even that wasn't
the worst I had seen. The year before, in 1984, there was the
huge explosion and fire at the oil refinery in San Juanico in
the state of Mexico. It destroyed the tanks and the area all
around the refinery where squatters had built their shantytown because they were too poor to find open land anywhere else. So you can just picture it: I was sixteen years old
and I was digging out dead people, but that time, they were
people who had been incinerated in a fire rather than
crushed to death.

Julio explains that these experiences were ghastly, but he doesn't
think of them as dangerous.

Dangerous? Well the most dangerous thing I had to do was
to jump out of a plane that the U.S. Air Force had given to
the Mexican Air Force for training purposes. It wasn't that I
was scared to jump. I was glad to jump. It was flying in this
plane that was terrifying because these were C-46s, C-47s,
and C-54s that had been used in World War II. We saw that
the gringos themselves absolutely refused to fly in these
planes because they knew they were so obsolete and badly
maintained that they were like flying coffins. In the end the
Mexican Air Force had to borrow a Hercules from Pemex,
the national oil company, so the gringos could show us how
to jump, so they could give us the training they'd come
down to Mexico to give.

Julio says that all these difficult experiences contribute to explaining why he was not—perhaps—as shaken as I would have imagined him to be to find himself in police custody. Even the fact that he had been picked up, not by the migra as an undocumented immigrant, but by the narcotics squad as a drug dealer, did not upset him as much as I would have thought.

> Look, I spent almost five years in the Mexican military, and you see so many terrible things when you are a soldier that—well, it's sad—but nothing that happens later in your life is really going to frighten you. I was in Guerrero during the war on drugs, and there were whole villages of poor peasants destroyed and unarmed people killed: old men, women, and children. It was no different from the massacre in Acteal, Chiapas, in 1996 that everyone in the world knows about, where unarmed people took refuge in a church and the paramilitary types machine-gunned them. The thing is that when the army was carrying out the war on drugs back when I was a soldier in the 1980s, there were no television crews running around with cameras. Things went on all the time in places like Guerrero. The Mexican army carried out raids on people in isolated places, and no one in Mexico, outside of that zone, even knew what was happening, let alone people in other countries. In those days you wouldn't have foreigners marching around protesting in front of Mexican embassies.

> The fact is, I had seen some really terrible things even before I turned twenty, and I had participated under orders in things I can't talk to you about. So I am a person who isn't easily rattled.

I asked Julio whether he realized what he was getting into when he accepted the job of selling crack in Los Angeles.

> Well, I certainly didn't expect to be arrested my first day out. But in the army we were often involved in transshipment of drugs all over the country under orders of our superior offi-

cers. Not all the officers were tied in with the drug lords. But there's no question that many did business with the *narco-traficantes*. For sure, it wasn't what I wanted to do when I came to the United States. There would be no point in crossing the border if you didn't think you could have a better life. But I guess I was more used to the idea of moving drugs than another guy might have been if he'd never been in the army.

So Julio, now dressed again in his Lakers sweatshirt and his Dodgers cap, sat in an office drinking his coffee and trying to work out what the five narcotics officers—two Central Americans, one Venezuelan, one Cuban, and, strangely enough, a Spanish-speaking Korean woman—had in mind to do to him. It was clear that once they saw his air force insignia, their attitude toward him radically altered. It wasn't just that they stopped referring to him as a prick and a son of a whore. He says they started treating him with a certain familiarity, as if he were a colleague. Julio says they were respectful toward him and they became very interested in having him describe all the weapons he knew how to fire. Then they popped the question.

They told Julio that more Mexicans were dealing crack, but they had no one in their squad who could infiltrate a Mexican drug gang because they had Chicanos, but no Mexicans, in their unit. They told him that he could be that agent, and he would have an excellent salary and all kinds of benefits. They would also help him bring his family to live in Los Angeles, and they would help him get his United States citizenship.

"Were you tempted to take up the offer?" I asked.

No way. In fact this was the hardest moment for me to stay cool, because it was so clear that they intended to use me as cannon fodder and that I was going to end up dead. But I had to sit there looking enthused and eager for the chance they were offering. So I just said that, yeah, it would be great to work with them and what time did they want me back the next morning to begin my training.

And then?

And then I just walked out of the police station. They even offered me a ride home, but I said, no thanks, I could walk. Then I jumped on a bus back to South Central, packed my bag, borrowed some money, took a bus to San Diego, and went by trolley to San Ysidro on the border with Tijuana, walked back into Mexico from the U.S. side, and caught the first flight back to Puebla.

Julio never returned to the United States. He concluded that it is not the kind of society where he thinks he would like to live. He is now married, has three children, and a job selling food in a covered market, and he hopes his children, who are getting toward the age of longing, will not decide to try their luck on the other side. Still, as we conclude our talk in the park, he says:

My whole life now is centered on my children. Right now I'm working to pay for them to go to a private school rather than the state school, to give them a better start in life. I'm not sitting around like when I was young, trying to figure out how to get to be a pilot. I'm focused on the kids.

But, yes, sometimes I wonder if I threw away a really good chance to be a policeman in Los Angeles. Maybe I would have been killed, but maybe not. Maybe I would have survived to be a good cop, to be able to serve people. Maybe it would have been like when I was a young soldier digging out the bodies after the earthquakes and people were thanking us and bringing us tortillas and beans and water and telling us that we were the only ones who were really there to help them.

18

Manuel: Life After Amnesty

In the dream, Manuel was sharing a bed with his three older brothers, Gerardo, Alejandro, and Felipe, just as they had as boys in the village. And even though in real life Gerardo was back in Tepec, in the Mixteca region of Puebla, rather than with his brothers on East 118th Street in the heart of what outsiders called "Spanish Harlem" but the brothers always called "El Barrio," in the dream, Gerardo was there, sleeping sideways across the bed with his feet in Manuel's face, just like when they were kids. At this point in the dream, Manuel hears a knock at the door. He looks at the clock, which says 6:00 A.M. He jumps out of bed and dives into the cupboard under the kitchen sink because, at 14, he is still very small, and of the nine Mexicans sharing the apartment at the time, he is the only one who could possibly wedge himself into the space between the drainpipe and the garbage pail and still manage to close the cupboard door. Manuel says:

> So I woke up, all cramped up in a ball and pouring sweat, as if I really had been in that tiny space, and I shook Alejandro and I said, "Ale, the migra was coming for us and I was under the sink, and you and Felipe were trying to run down the fire escape, but they had the place surrounded." So, of

course, my brother says to me, "*¡Hijole!* It's four in the morning. It's just a bad dream. Go back to sleep!"

Well, it's going to be hard for you to believe, but at six that same morning, we're getting ready to go to work and we hear this pounding on the door, and we just freeze in place and my brother signals to me not to make a sound, but when I look over my shoulder out the window, I see that one of the migra is coming up the fire escape and he gives me a little wave, and the others are shouting from the hallway: "Open up, *amigos!*" In those days the migra didn't know much Spanish, but they all knew the word *amigo* and that's how they always addressed people as they were arresting them.

Manuel explains that with one officer on the fire escape and the others blocking the door, the only one of the nine who "escaped" was Celestino, one of the roommates who was lucky enough to have left for work at five that morning and must have been very surprised when he returned home that night to find himself all alone in the apartment Manuel says.

The funny thing about this raid is that I dove under the bed, hoping that in the confusion, the migra wouldn't figure out that there were actually nine people living in this one-room apartment. But my feet were sticking out, so it took the migra about ten seconds to spot me, and I remember the guy saying to his *compas*: "Look! A rat with shoes!"

"This would have to have been in 1977," Manuel explains, "because, I recall that I had only been in New York six weeks and I hadn't quite paid off the $1,500 I owed for the coyote fees."

You see, this is why it was such a problem if you were caught by the migra not long after your arrival—because once they sent you back to Mexico, how were you going to pay off your debt for the trip you just made, except to go into more debt to get yourself smuggled back into the United States? Between the deportations and some trips home for Christmas, I ended up crossing ten times—five at the Tijuana border and the rest in Laredo or Piedras Negras—and for each of the crossings I went into debt and had to spend the first months in New York, in effect, working for the coyote—or at least to pay back whoever had put up the money to hire the coyote.

Manuel explains that from 1972, when his seven older brothers arrived with other young men from Tepec and neighboring towns, until the early 1980s, "it was a really tough time. The migra actually ran around in New York actively searching for undocumented people to arrest."

In restaurants, in the street, in factories, on the subway, in the movies, the migra was everywhere. They would wait outside The Prospect or The Boulevard, which were these two movie houses in the Bronx that showed Mexican films on weekends—like Cantinflas and cowboy films with Vicente Fernández—and the migra would just grab people as they walked out of the theater. The migra even staked out the Catholic church on the corner of Union and Tinton in the Bronx because guys like us would go to the Spanish language Mass there on Sunday mornings. You could end up going straight from communion to the clink.

"The rumor was that the migra would arrest people and then offer them the chance to go free if they would give up a bunch of other illegals they knew of." And that, Manuel thinks, is how he came to be arrested on East 118th Street and later at his job in a Greek restaurant at Madison and 85th Street, a location, he tells me, now occupied by a Banana Republic store. "In the restaurant," Manuel recalls, "the migra walked in and asked for me *by name*! And all I could do was to wonder who had ratted on me." In all, Manuel was apprehended three times in as many years and, indeed, the raid on the apartment was not his first arrest and deportation.

The first time, I guess you could say, I gave myself up, because I was standing on 42nd Street near Times Square with Alejandro and we were trying to decide which movie to see. This would have been in 1976 and there were so many big movie houses there, with big marquees and flashing lights, and you could end up just standing and staring for a long time. In fact, I was looking at the poster for a kung fu movie with Bruce Lee, and when I turned around I saw that right there in the street, the migra had got hold of my brother, who was trying to signal to me to walk away, just to lose myself in the crowd.

But, they had my brother, so I didn't see how I could walk away. And I was only fourteen, so I really didn't understand what we were going to face once they put us in the *corralón*, the "big corral," as people called it. So I hung around and they arrested and handcuffed me as well, and the next thing we were being "processed" at the offices of the INS near the Brooklyn Bridge.

Manuel and his brother were transported from the INS headquarters to the *corralón*, the immigrant detention center in Flushing, Queens, where they joined more than five hundred undocumented people who were awaiting deportation.

It was unbelievable. There was every kind of person you can imagine: people from all over Latin America, plus Russians, Jamaicans, Greeks, Africans, people from every part of the earth, and really, it was very nice because my brother and I made a lot of friends in the *corralón*. People treated each other decently and everyone was especially good to me because I was just a kid.

The women were in another section, but all the men slept in a huge room in triple-decker beds. They gave you a towel and we had showers every morning and they gave you three meals a day, and a dollar a day if you wanted to do some of the work, like serve up the food at mealtime.

"The only bad part," Manuel says, "was that you made all these good friends and then you realized that you would all be sent home to different places and you'd probably never see each other again for the rest of your lives. I cried when they took me away to the airport."

> I was there for twenty days and I really learned a lot. People would tell you their life stories, and all the places they'd been in the United States, and how they had made out in New York, and how they were apprehended, and by the time the migra finally got around to deporting me to Mexico, there wasn't much I didn't know about how to get along in the United States. The only problem was that once I was back home in Mexico, I had to work for another six months to raise the money to make my way back to New York.

I confess to Manuel that I am astonished to hear his story because one of the most surprising things I have encountered in my conversations with migrants in all parts of the United States is how little the migra figures in their thoughts once they are safely over the border and beyond the main transportation nodes like Union Station in Los Angeles or the major airports and bus stations in California, Arizona, and Texas—the points from which an undocumented immigrant who has successfully crossed into the United States might hope to travel on to Chicago, New York, Atlanta, or other cities or agricultural regions farther afield. Indeed, during my years of fieldwork *before* the mass demonstrations for immigrant rights that mobilized millions of documented and undocumented people in the spring of 2006, the standard response I received to my question: "How much do you worry about being picked up by the migra?" was the one given by Angel, who said, "I don't worry. I don't even think about it. I've got plenty of other things to think about in my life."

However, after the 2006 mobilizations, the Bush administration responded with raids on high-profile targets like Wal-Mart and Swift meatpackers and an intensification of enforcement in rural areas. Following these widely publicized raids, immigrant communities were rife with rumors that ICE was descending on factories and construction sites. There was even a widespread, but seemingly unfounded story—that the number 7 subway that runs from Flushing, Queens, under the East River into Manhattan and westward to Times Square was traveling "empty," because—depending on who told the story—the migra had hauled off *all* the immigrants they found on the train, or—in another version of events—because all the undocumented people in the borough of Queens, possibly hundreds of thousands of people, had decided it was too dangerous to put a toe outside the door, let alone go to work.

But for all the fear that the federal government's response to the 2006 marches had provoked, within a few weeks, the life of undocumented New Yorkers seemed to return to what it had been before the spring demonstrations, and the answer I received to my query: "How often do you think about the migra?" was once again likely to be "Never," or "Hardly ever."

Manuel confirms that, indeed, the situation today is strikingly different from the early 1970s when his brothers first arrived, and the late 1970s when he followed them to New York, that is, from the period in which the migra seemed to be "everywhere."

> We never understood why, but once Ronald Reagan had been in office about two years, you never saw the migra again and you never heard about anyone being picked up, except for people who had been denounced by a jealous lover or by an employer who wanted to get rid of them—you know, by someone who, for whatever reason, had it in for them.

> And then, in 1986, after all that my brothers and I had been through with the multiple detentions and deportations, just like that, you had the amnesty, so we could all get papers and live without fear. It was amazing, really.

Manuel, and all the members of his extended family who were lucky enough to find themselves in the United States in that period, immediately began registering to regularize their status and to set in motion the process by which they could become citizens. Strikingly, however, there were many undocumented migrants who did not seize this opportunity. Manuel explains:

> I knew people who were convinced that it was all a trick to get you to reveal your name and address and that as soon as we had all registered, the migra or the FBI or someone else would come and grab us and carry out mass deportations. I also knew people who thought that they would no longer be Mexican if they registered to become American, and that worried them.
>
> Then there were other people who never really saw themselves living in the United States. They had just come to earn money and go home and they never understood that, even if they always meant to go back to Mexico, it would still be a good thing to have papers, to be able to come and go between the two countries safely, to visit people here, to visit people there—the way that people with legal status can do.

Indeed, Manuel says, as a young man he never thought that he would live out his days in Upper Manhattan and the Bronx. "I figured I would earn money. I would go back to Tepec and find myself a *novia*. I would build a house, invest what I had saved in some kind of business, marry and bring up my kids in my hometown. That was the plan."

Instead, Manuel found that his prospects in Tepec were few. His father, who had a small piece of land where he used to grow corn, beans, and, occasionally, peanuts, had given up cultivating his *milpa* once the youngest of his sons, Manuel, took off for the other side. Rather than work alone in the fields, his father started to produce *huaraches*, the traditional leather sandals still worn by rural people in this impoverished agricultural zone of Mexico. This artisanal production is also what Manuel worked at during the various stretches of time that he spent in Tepec between periods of residence in New York.

> I was the youngest of the eight brothers—we were twelve kids altogether—and, truthfully, I had never worked in the fields as a boy the way my older brothers had. When I was

little, my mother would entrust me with the basket of tortillas and the pail of refried beans to deliver to my father and my older brothers in the *milpa*. By the time I had left school and could have helped him on his land, I was living on East 118th Street and my father had pretty well given up on *mais* and *frijol*. So whenever I returned to Tepec, I cut leather and stitched *huaraches* with my dad. But you can imagine, we didn't earn much from this production, and basically we lived from the money my brothers sent home.

You know, it's amazing. The fields around the village, which were all cultivated intensively when I was a boy, have now gone back to a wild state. It's *puro monte* out there, which is something that hit me last time I was in Tepec and I was driving around and saw good-sized trees and bushes growing in places that used to be plowed furrows. It's just that as the men of my father's generation got old or passed on, there was no one left to take over the cultivation of their land, or if any of the sons were still around, they weren't willing to dedicate themselves to working the land.

In Tepec, as we have seen in Nopal Verde in Zacatecas, the depopulation of the town that resulted from successive waves of out-migration was, in itself, the biggest obstacle to the fulfillment of migrants' dreams of saving money in the United States to return to their hometown and open a business. There might have been a modest market for *huaraches* among the poorest of the poor peasants who were left behind, but on his trips home, Manuel could see how limited were possibilities for other kinds of commerce in a town that had emptied out. Moreover, he did not find the *novia* of his dreams in Tepec. Rather, at age 22, he found Angela in Manhattan, among the friends with whom he attended *tardeadas*, weekend parties organized by Tepequeños.

So it was that Manuel carried on working in restaurants, raising a family in Manhattan, and saving his money, until his brother Felipe, who had returned to Tepec, came up with the perfect business in which to invest. Both of them remembered that when they were first in New York, people who were planning a trip home would often sneak away in the night without telling any of their friends they were off to Mexico. They said nothing of their plans for fear their friends would "entrust" them with multiple suitcases stuffed with gifts for loved ones back home, gifts for which overweight charges would be levied by the airlines and bribes might have to be paid at customs, gifts that would need to be transported all the way to Tepec and then to surrounding communities, to be delivered firsthand to their recipients.

This gave Felipe and Manuel their idea. Together they would become *paqueteros*, transporting *paquetes*, or packages, between Tepec and New York and, before long, the "Tepec Express," as they called it, employed more than two dozen people receiving, distributing, and traveling with parcels. They were hardly alone in this field. Other Tepequeños were running similar operations. But with well over half the population of Tepec living in the United States, mostly concentrated in the greater New York and tristate area, the brothers were confident that they could make a success of a *paquetero* business.

Manuel says that developing an immigrant-related service makes perfect sense in a town like Tepec where, at any given time, the majority are in the United States but remain closely connected to family back home. Moreover, in comparison with towns that only recently became sending communities, the proportion of Tepequeños who were in the United States in 1986 and thus qualified to become citizens under IRCA and to sponsor family members for permanent residency, is relatively high. For these Tepequeño–New Yorkers, the annual family vacation in Tepec, in a new home constructed with their remittances, is not a abstract wish but a concrete reality.

Indeed, the very look of the town reminds visitors to Tepec of the peculiar history of migration in the 1970s from the state of Puebla. Elsewhere in Mexico migrants traveled to California and—in a great architectural irony—those who returned have built structures that resemble houses in California that, for their part, seem to be trying to look like Mexican haciendas. In Tepec, in contrast, the new houses often have gables and steeply sloping roofs, like the houses Tepequeños came to admire in the Northeast of the United States, even if the runoff of ice and snow would not be a concern in Puebla or Veracruz or other migrant-sending zones where the influence of New York suburban architecture is very obvious.

The impact of migration is obvious as well on the main street of Tepec, which features gift and clothing shops offering consumer goods generally within the reach only of those who receive remittances. But perhaps the most striking physical aspect of Calle Independencia, which runs through the heart of Tepec, is the number of businesses that offer services directly related to migrants and migrant-sending families: money-transfer operations, travel agents, Internet hookups, cell phone stores, and *paqueteros* like Tepec Express.

Relying on a core of eight cross-border couriers, all of whom have dual citizenship and can travel freely between Mexico and the United States, Manuel and his brother recruited associates who deliver parcels to Tepec's neighboring towns and villages in a wide district that covers Puebla and the closest parts of the states of Guerrero, Oaxaca, Morelos, and Veracruz. As their business expanded, Tepec Express's northern reach also came to include outlets in all five boroughs of New York City plus Long Island, Camden, New Jersey, Newburgh in the Hudson Valley, and Monroe in the Catskills.

The goods that move in each direction are quite different. Migrants living in New York will phone or e-mail their relatives in Mexico and request homemade tortillas, dried hot chili peppers, *mole*—the spicy chocolate-based sauce in which chicken is cooked—peanut brittle, cactus jam, and an assortment of other "nostalgia products," as such delicacies are increasingly called by the economists who assess the impact of these goods on the local economy in places like Zacatecas where they are beginning to be produced on a mass scale and exported commercially to Mexican consumers in the United States.

In addition to the foods, the religious objects, and other handicrafts, *paqueteros* arrive from Mexico bearing the original copies of birth, baptismal, marriage, and death certificates as well as other documents that migrants may find they need in the United States. For example, Edgardo, one of the migrants lined up at the Tepec Express branch that is, in fact, the living room of an apartment in Staten Island, was waiting for the arrival of a series of personal photographs that should enable him to prove that before his nose was broken in an unprovoked attack—an incident for which he hoped to win Workers' Compensation—it pointed forward, not sideways, on his face. Another customer was hoping that his parcel would contain a video of the *quinceañera* celebration of his teenage daughter and the baptism of his first grandchild. Manuel explains:

> The food parcels, as people would say in the United States, are more or less our bread and butter. Even though Mexican delicacies like *chapulines*, dried grasshoppers from Oaxaca, are available in stores in New York, it's amazing how much migrants here will spend to eat their mother's tortilla or their mother's *mole*, even if these foods—freshly made—are all on sale up and down East 116th Street in Manhattan, or on Port Richmond Avenue in Staten Island, or in hundreds of tiny Mexican eateries in the Bronx, Brooklyn, and Queens. Relatives in Mexico can send any home-cooked products they like, as long as they don't send meat or fresh vegetables. But tortillas and tamales made with real white corn, preferably from the *milpa* of a relative, is probably the most prized food that anyone can receive.

Emotion also plays a big role in the content of packages that travel from the United States to Mexico. Manuel explains that, apart from money, his customers in New York also send videos and photographs that provide details of their lives in the city: the apartment where they live, the people with whom they share their dwelling, the soccer team they play with on Sundays, the Cinco de Mayo celebrations in Corona Park, excursions to the Empire State Building or the Brooklyn Bridge or up the Hudson River to Bear Mountain.

However, the bulk of the packages, Manuel explains, are clothing, appliances, bicycles, toys, and electronics of every kind. And as he explains the process, it becomes clear that migrants in New York are paying three times: first for the goods themselves, and then by the pound to send these goods to Mexico, and finally, an extra charge to cover the import duties that Manuel's broker in Mexico has to pay on these products to clear them through customs.

> Obviously, it's going to cost a lot more to send a microwave from New York to Tepec than to send the money for your wife or mother to buy the same Asian-made product in the

appliance store on Calle Independencia. But that's not the point. The point is that people back home in Mexico want their running shoes and their baseball hat and their VCR and their blender to come from the United States. And the immigrants here want to express their emotions and their continued connection by sending things that—let's face it— these same loved ones, with the remittances they receive, could buy for themselves right in Tepec.

In general, a *paquetero* like Tepec Express charges strictly by weight, with the exception of extra charges levied for electronic devices and appliances that require special handling and on which import duties are due. In addition, for products like dried chile peppers, which weigh next to nothing in relationship to their bulk, the price is set according to the size of the package.

On average, once a week, Manuel and Felipe's eight regular couriers move hundreds of pounds of bags, boxes, and containers packed in huge suitcases, ten to fifteen cases per trip. They travel on regular commercial flights, are met by brokers at the airport in Mexico City and Newark International, and are well-known to the customs officials at both ends. Manuel says they rarely have any problems in either airport because of the care with which every parcel is opened and inspected at the sending point before it is placed in a suitcase.

People come in with their parcels all taped up, but we explain that they have to open them so that we can make sure they are not shipping anything that will be confiscated or that will get us into trouble. Once we found drugs stashed in a hole cut for that purpose in a stack of tortillas! And, of course, there are the customs officers at the Mexican end who might ask for their *mordida*, their payoff, to speed things along. Even into the early 1990s it was kind of standard for these guys to hit you up for $10 or $20 "for a can of soda pop." "*Ponme algo para los refrescos,*" they would say. But now there's much less of that kind of corruption than we used to see. Much less.

For all that Manuel, Felipe, and their associates—mostly extended family—seem to have the whole operation running smoothly, only three months before our conversation they were rocked by a major reversal. For reasons they never clearly understood, the Mexican customs agents seized fifteen suitcases, which they took apart piece by piece. Seven of the suitcases were never returned to the courier, while the contents of the eight that reappeared had been dumped out, scrambled, and randomly stuffed back into suitcases, with all their packaging and labels stripped off.

> Under the circumstances there was no way we could match up the goods with the delivery addresses. We couldn't make out who belonged to what. It was a total mess and we had to pay customers as much as $500 in some cases as reimbursement for the packages we had never been able to deliver. We also had more than $800 in phone calls to Mexico, just trying to sort it all out.

> The truth is this kind of near total loss of a shipment in Mexican customs happens from time to time to all the *paqueteros*. It was a huge monetary loss for us, but we were not ruined because we made good on our customer's losses and people have even more confidence in our service today than before this incident.

I ask Manuel how long he figures on running the New York end of the operation and when he thinks he can find someone to take over for him in Manhattan so that he can work in the Tepec headquarters and move into the house that he has built for his family in his hometown. Manuel gives me the kind of smile that I have come to recognize is the prelude to a viewing of baby pictures of a grandchild, and he confesses that, now that his daughter is settled in New York with a child of her own, the long-anticipated return to Tepec may not play out exactly as originally planned.

19

Patricia: Weighing the Good and the Bad

When Patricia and I first talked, we sat in a tiny living room in the Bronx that was dominated by the double bed she shared with her husband, Daniel, in a one-bedroom apartment that looked as if sunlight might penetrate for only a few hours right around the summer solstice. When we spoke in New York, I guessed that she was one of the immigrants who would, in fact, carry through her plan to return to Mexico, and that "one day soon" as she put it, I would indeed have the chance to sit with her on the veranda of the house that she and Daniel would build in "Santa Rosa," a village in Puebla with anywhere from two to four thousand inhabitants depending—as it always does—on whether we count only the resident population or the full diaspora of migrants from Santa Rosa who live in the United States. As she spoke, it was evident that Patricia's warm description of life in Mexico was more than nostalgia for an idealized past. She was quick to compare her circumstances in the Bronx with her prospects in Santa Rosa in very precise terms that made clear that she had carefully weighed the various advantages and shortcomings of the two settings.

It was striking that among the shortcomings Patricia noted were features of life in New York that had been cited to me by other immigrants as major benefits. Others would say, "Here we have a lot more to eat than the corn and beans we had back home." But Patricia remarked, "The way people eat here in the United States makes you fat and gives the children diabetes." Likewise, access to consumer goods that would have been unknown in Mexico, a phenomenon that, for other immigrants, represented a big plus of life in the United States, was something that Patricia saw in strictly negative terms:

> Here people begin to live on credit cards just the way the *americanos* do, and they end up accumulating debts that are totally different from the kind of indebtedness they knew in the village. In the pueblo it would be a debt held by the *acapador*, the moneylender. With the *acapador*, you borrowed money to buy seed and plant your crops. And, sure, he would charge usurious rates on his loan, and you could get unlucky and have your crop fail and you could fall further into debt. But it was all about growing food to live, I mean to eat or to sell. It wasn't this crazy life that people have here in the United States, where people borrow to have things they don't need and had always gotten along without.

And some of her assessments were negative with respect to the broader society even as she recognized some advantage for herself.

> When we came to New York, we lived in Brooklyn and we furnished our apartment right off the streets. You can't believe what people throw away in the United States. We just waited for garbage day and went out the night before, and we found a bed with a new mattress, a TV, a vacuum cleaner, dishes, pots, new clothing, and a beautiful rug. That's how we got everything we needed to live. Who knows why people would throw away such nice things?

After joining Daniel in Brooklyn in 1995, Patricia worked almost entirely in factory jobs of the most unstable nature. The first was one that she found through an employment agency at 188th Street in Washington Heights, which, every morning at seven, filled a van with Dominican, Peruvian, Ecuadorian, Colombian, Central American, and Mexican women who were then hauled across the George Washington

Bridge into New Jersey, where they worked a ten-hour day at $5.15 an hour. After the agency deducted its $15.50 fee and another $25 for a week of transportation to New Jersey, and Patricia calculated her subway fares from Brooklyn to West 188th Street, she cleared $202 a week for fifty hours of stuffing CDs into paper envelopes on an assembly line. Between the paper cuts and the damage to her hands from scooping the CDs off the rough surface of the belt, Patricia soon came to understand why there were no *americanas* at this workplace, and she was relieved when, through a friend from Santa Rosa, she was able to get a job making Christmas decorations in a factory in Brooklyn.

The daily commute to this job required a subway ride and a bus, but Patricia had only one fare to pay, no "finder's fee," and none of the anxiety of the previous job, where she would have to reach the employment agency at 188th Street early lest she be one of the unlucky women to be left on the pavement when the van filled up and pulled away. So she was grateful for the factory job in Brooklyn.

Alas, inasmuch as the production of Christmas ornaments is about as seasonal as a job can get, she was laid off in the fall and once again had to rely on the employment agency until a *comadre* of her cousin found her work in a garment factory owned by Russians. Here she moved around from the positions where workers are paid for piecework, which included the cutting tables, the sewing machines, and the pressers, to the jobs paid by the hour at minimum wage, which were those that involved cutting the bolts of cloth, organizing them by size, and spreading the cloth on the tables to prepare for the cutters. In the longer run, this more varied factory experience with the Russians would enable Patricia to find work as needed in other small apparel firms operating in Sunset Park, and once the Russians closed up shop, she was never out of work for more than a week or two.

Thus, by the time I met and talked with Patricia in 2003, she had experienced all that was numbing and exploitative in the labor market that is open to undocumented migrant women. She had also lived the best part of the equation, which was to see her take-home pay pile up week by week until it amounted to a considerable sum that would begin to alter the prospects for her family in New York and back in Santa Rosa. But Patricia says that although you may be very clear in taking the measure of all the good and bad features of life in the United States, it is still very difficult to figure out when to go back to Mexico, even if it was always your plan to stay only long enough to buy a piece of land or to build a house or to set up a business. "The hardest part," she says, "is to think through whether the kids are going to be better off here or there. Does it makes sense to send the kids back to live with their grandparents while the wife stays on with the husband and keeps working in order to shorten the time that it will take to raise the money?" Alternatively, as Daniel has proposed, it could be better for Patricia to go back with the children and stay in the village to oversee the construction of the house. She explains:

> Some really bad things can happen when people just send their money down or send their kids back to the pueblo. The grandparents are a lot older now than when you left, say, ten years ago, and in any case they will be raising grandchildren who aren't obedient in the ways we were when we were little. And the kids aren't used to the physical freedom they have in a village.

> In New York, the children are very grown up in some ways, but they've never had the experience that we had as kids in Santa Rosa, where you just run around with the other boys and girls your age and you look after yourselves. And meanwhile, everyone else in the village looks out for you because that's the good part of having everyone minding each other's business in the village: grown-ups keep an eye out for kids and anyone can and will scold children if they see them jumping around on a roof or doing something stupid. What's more, big kids feel responsible for the little ones. We all grew up raising brothers and sisters only a couple of years younger than us, and that's still what goes on back home in the pueblo.

In the Bronx, Patricia says, her children aren't used to having that kind of space. Either they are in school with the teacher or they are in lockdown in the apartment, watching TV, with strict instructions not to open the door to anyone. This is why Patricia doesn't know how they

will adjust to the freedom that she remembers from her own childhood. As it is, Patricia still hasn't recovered from her oldest son's first
days in elementary school.

> At school they have to join a gang to protect themselves, but,
> like, in first grade! My son went to school and on the third
> day, a boy came up to him and said, "What are you?" My son
> didn't even know what the question meant, so the other lit-
> tle boy said, "What are you? Mexican? Guatemalan? Salvado-
> ran?" So Pancho says, "I'm Mexican" and the other boy says,
> "Okay, you have to be in our gang and that way you won't
> get beat up." At age six!

Patricia thinks that it is difficult for parents to figure out how to
do the right thing for their children because, in some ways, the opportunities seem so much better for kids in the United States:

> Computers in the classrooms. Equipment you would never
> find in Mexico. Trips to the museums, to the zoo, and above
> all, learning English, which will give them all kinds of ad-
> vantages in life.

> But there's a lot they can't learn here, like how to be on their
> own with their friends and work things out among them-
> selves. The other things they can't learn in school here is that
> not everything can be fun every minute and that some
> things are hard to do or boring to do and you have to do
> them anyway.

Patricia says that she went to parents' night at the school and the
teacher told them that children can't learn things they don't want to
learn.

> But that doesn't make sense to me. As a girl, I learned a lot of
> things I wouldn't have chosen to study. While Pancho's
> teacher, who is a very nice Colombian lady, spoke, I keep
> thinking of my old primary school teacher, Maestro

Osvaldo. You didn't fool around in his class, that's for sure. And you weren't busy having a good time. You were busy staying out of trouble with the maestro. But everything I learned from him is still in my head. I use it every day of my life. This is why I can calculate numbers in my head faster than anyone can punch them into a cash register. That's why I can write in a nice clear handwriting that anyone can read.

Here my kids come home with prizes and stickers and award certificates just for showing up. All three of my children have been Student of the Month more than once. When this happened with Pancho, my oldest, we thought he was really outstanding, and it kind of scared us because we didn't know if his father and I could give him everything that a boy that special might need. But when the middle one, Eddy, came home with his Student of the Month certificate, we knew something was strange because he's not great about doing his homework and he's lazy about everything at school, not to mention his chores at home.

Patricia thinks that the problem is that in the children's school the kids don't get used to sitting still and digging in to learn the things that are not easy to learn. This, she says, is why the children who have been in school in the United States are behind their classmates in math when they go back to Mexico and enroll in the school there. "Of course" she says, "they're going to be at a disadvantage in Spanish—they'll be able to speak and understand, but not to read and write. But there's no good reason for them to be behind in math in comparison with kids in the village school who've been sitting on wooden benches in a crowded classroom."

Because they always had in mind that they would return, Patricia and Daniel have been reading with the children in Spanish from the time they were tiny and could barely turn the page of the picture books. Although both parents consider themselves lucky just to have completed six years of primary school, they have given a lot of time at home to working on reading and writing in Spanish. Patricia says, "the kids who never learned to read or write in Spanish, the ones who have never had this kind of extra help from their parents, are totally lost in school their first year back in Santa Rosa, and some of them never catch up."

However, Patricia notes that, once they have returned to their country, Mexican parents face many more expenses for their children's schooling than they would in the United States. In New York, she never had to buy the children special materials or school uniforms, and the most the teachers might ask of a parent would be to send the children to school with a colored pencil or some crayons. Moreover, her two sons and her daughter were all in a free-lunch program.

In Mexico, she tells me, it is the opposite. "Apart from the textbooks, the government doesn't provide much of anything. Parents have to get together and "cooperate" with a contribution in order to have electricity running in the schoolroom or a functioning toilet." Moreover, parents have to chip in for the cleaning of the school, they have to come up with lunch money and they have to purchase three different uniforms: one for every day, one for sports, and one for assemblies and the formal ceremonies which the schools hold for all the national holidays and graduation. "What's more," Patricia says, "if the teacher is sick, there's no substitute."

> All this makes it very hard to figure out what's the right time to go back to Mexico. Should we wait until the kids are reading and writing English? They were all born in New York and are U.S. citizens and you would like them to have the choice to work in the United States, if that's what they want when they grow up. On the other hand, if we wait too long, the oldest will be a teenager and then we have to worry about violent gangs and drugs and teenage sex, and all the things that happen to kids in New York that don't happen back home.

"But do you mean that no teenagers ever get pregnant in the village?" I ask.

> Well, the women in my generation, we all became *novias* in our early teens and were married by the time we were six-

teen or seventeen. So we had teenage sex, but it was with our husband!

At times, Patricia explains, the *novio* would be only a few years older than the girl, but most often the men were in the twenties before they decided to settle down and find a wife, and when they went courting, they would be looking for a young, "innocent" girl, which is to say, a girl so young that she could never have been with anyone else. In Santa Rosa, a young man might see that kind of adolescent girl walking with her girlfriends from church. But, as I had learned from Marta, in Pantla, the most common way in which would-be suitors would meet their future wife was in the combi, the van that plied a route from the village to the city of Puebla.

Then, there's another kind of sexual initiation of teenage girls that Patricia recalls from her life in the village.

> There were always young girls who went as domestic servants to work in the houses of middle-class people in Puebla or in Mexico City. You know they had their little "maid's room" with no lock on the door, and, of course, they had no rights inside the houses of their employers. So lots of times they were used sexually by the sons of the family or by the father himself. When they got pregnant, the señora would want to send them packing—unless she really knew that the baby was her grandchild, in which case she might relent and let the girl stay on with her baby.

> I never heard of a girl in that situation who ever came back to live in the pueblo. There was really no place for women in the village outside of marriage, and even today, in effect, there's no divorce, although people do separate. Generally, when a couple is unhappy, the parents on both sides intervene to press the young people to reconcile, because if you remarry you could lose control over land. When people actually divorce in Santa Rosa, it almost always comes as a result of conflict between mother-in-law and daughter-in-law, not a direct problem between the husband and wife.

All of these factors—the quality of life, the opportunities, the education, a parent's assessment of the perils that await young people in one place or the other—make the decision to stay or return difficult. Moreover, the nature of a small village in which behavior is firmly controlled by what anthropologists call a "shame culture," in which people—for better *and* worse—mind each other's business, cuts both ways in the decision to stay or return. Patricia mentions this dynamic again and again, but, interestingly, so, too, did Ignacio, a 45-year-old migrant from Zacatecas I interviewed in his bodega in East Los Angeles. "I'll tell you one thing I don't miss, back home," he said to me,

> If you come from a small town like mine, there's no end to the jealousies and gossip. In Los Angeles, the pace is fast and people don't have time for that kind of pettiness. It's one of the things I like here. But, strangely enough, when I go back to my village, I have to admit that there are actually fewer conflicts underway there, maybe because people are too wrapped up in their effort to make it to Los Angeles. Like, who's going to fight over some little piece of parched land that two different people claim as their own when the real issue is to get to L.A.? You hardly hear anymore about those kinds of fights between neighbors. Or who knows? Maybe it's just that the kind of people who used to get into that kind of argument have all left for the other side.

As Patricia emphasizes, the hardest part of weighing all these drawbacks and advantages of village life is that she is planning a project that involves her husband, herself, and her three children as a family unit, but each member of the family experiences life in the United States differently. For example, Patricia says that she is very attached to her mother, and being so far from her is very painful. In contrast, Daniel was the last of twelve children and he was effectively raised by an older sister, not by his mother, and this sister now lives in Texas with grown children of her own. So he doesn't feel the same pull that Patricia feels to return to his mother in Santa Rosa.

"You can imagine," Patricia adds, "if the balance of the good and the bad is so different for people within the same family, you can't be surprised that it is very different for each of us migrants who has made the journey to the United States and more or less made a life here."

This was a thought that Patricia repeated to me the next time we spoke as we sat in a space suffused with sunlight in the ample front room of her new home in Santa Rosa, which was now all but complete. The house itself was a mixture of Mexican and North American architectural elements, including elaborate wrought-iron grillwork on each window, blue-and-white floor tiles, a veranda with arches, and large terra-cotta urns filled with succulent plants, both indoors and out. But it also featured the peaked roof that Patricia and Daniel had come to admire when they visited their *compadres* in Dover, New Jersey, and sliding glass doors that opened onto a deck at the back of the house. Most important, there were three bedrooms, including a large bedroom for Patricia and Daniel. And although, at this stage, none of the plumbing had been connected, two bathrooms, one with a bathtub that had the appearance of pink marble and the other with a shower stall, had been roughed in.

As we sat in her new house and reflected on the adjustments that Patricia and her children had made over the previous two years, Patricia confided:

> My friend Teresa is always saying: "My children miss New York. Pepito was crying the other day and he said he was homesick for PS 150, and that he really missed Ms. Valdéz, that he doesn't love any of the teachers here in Santa Rosa the way he loved Ms. Valdéz."

> But I can tell you, what's really going on is that it's Teresa who is homesick for New York, for her life in Long Island City. She doesn't want to say it straight out like that, but she's the one who is unhappy to be back. She always talked about what a sacrifice it was to live in New York so far away from Santa Rosa, and how she could only bear it because it was the best thing for the children. But, for sure, she really liked it there.

Just as I had learned in my conversations with Marta, Dolores, Sara, and so many other women, Patricia says that in Santa Rosa women are completely under the thumb of their in-laws. If they managed to build their own house with the money they saved from their work in the United States, they may escape the tyranny of their *suegros*, but they are under the control of their husbands in a way that they would never be in New York.

I am struck by Patricia's observations because in all my interviews with Mexican women in New York, I have rarely heard a woman say: "I really like it here. This works for me." Mostly, I heard long tales centered on sacrifice for the children and for the children's future, but little—except when speaking with younger, unmarried women—on any possible pleasures of life in New York for undocumented Mexican woman.

When I say as much to Patricia, she says, "Sure. A lot of people only talk about the hardships that we face, especially the hardships of women."

> But think about it. In New York, Teresa used to leave the house at six-thirty in the morning and jump on the number 7 train and then change for the R and then the bus to the garment factories where she worked in Sunset Park in Brooklyn. So who gets the kids up and makes them breakfast and gets them out to school? Her husband, Pepe! Has anyone ever *heard* of a man doing something like that every morning in Santa Rosa so that his wife can get to work?

> So, yes, it's hard to take two trains and a bus to a factory where you're going to sew all day for minimum wage. But, it's very nice to receive your own paycheck, and to have your own friends from the factory who you eat your lunch with. And it's not so bad to ride back and forth on a train by yourself and to look around at the other passengers and to sit there and think your own thoughts. For a woman from Santa Rosa, who was not allowed by her *suegra* to cross the street to visit her sister or her parents, it's an amazing kind of freedom just to be among strangers without people gossiping about you all the time, and reporting you to your *suegros* or your husband.

In general, Patricia believes that at some level the men understand that in the United States they lose control over their wives. They know that the need for two incomes in order to realize the migratory project—whatever it might be—gives women authority in the family that they would never have enjoyed in Mexico even if their contribution in maintaining the family was always as crucial in Santa Rosa as it might be in the more ambitious family projects in which they are involved in the United States. Moreover, whether the wife joined her husband who was already established in New York, or if the couple met in New York, as was the case for the *paquetero*, Manuel, and his wife, Angela, wives know that their husbands have been food shopping, cooking for themselves, and washing clothes in laundromats for months or years, and that they have no justifiable reason to abandon these tasks if the wife is working outside the home.

And then, there is the matter of the famous 911 call. No woman I interviewed in Los Angeles, New York, Massachusetts, or upstate New York could cite for me anyone of her acquaintance who had actually picked up the phone and dialed 911 to report an abusive spouse. However, every woman with whom I spoke had *heard* of the woman who had finally had enough and had called the police on her undocumented husband. Men, as well, knew these same stories and gave them credence, and as such, whether reliable or not, the rumors had a powerful restraining effect on men's absolute authority in the home and their propensity to abuse either their wives or their children in the manner they would have felt free to do back home.

In Mexico, where the police are seen by ordinary people almost entirely as the extorters of bribes, the runners of drugs, and the collaborators of criminals, the idea of government intervening in the private lives of citizens—and specifically, the prospect of the police coming into the home to intervene on the side of women and children—is so far outside the experience of Mexicans as to be incomprehensible and unthinkable. Under the circumstances, when I asked male migrants, "What did you like most and what did you like least in your experience in the United States?" I was not surprised to find men who were prepared to ignore racism, exploitation, and a host of other wrongs that a migrant might suffer in the United States, arguing instead that the worst thing by far is that the father's authority in the family is undermined not only by law but also by the teachers in school.

This is an understandable response because there is no shortage of examples of clumsy misunderstandings and cultural incomprehension on the part of social workers, teachers, and other representatives of the dominant society who have some legitimate means to intervene in the lives of the migrants. And this is the case even when these members of the "helping professions" are themselves Spanish-speaking people from longer established immigrant groups.

I observed this for myself while sitting in on a talk given in Spanish by a second-generation Caribbean American social worker for a group of recent immigrants from Puebla who had gathered for this session in a parish hall in the Bronx.

In the first part of her presentation, the social worker outlined the laws that apply to child abuse in the state of New York. In a manner that was sympathetic to the women in attendance, she put forward the idea that abuse could be psychological as well as physical, and that battered wives often suffer a lack of self-esteem so complete that they come to believe that they *deserve* to be beaten. This idea met with a reasonably receptive response from the women, if not the men in the room. But then the speaker went on to say that, whether for lack of self-esteem or for any other reason, the failure of an adult to intervene to protect children who are being abused in her presence is a crime, and that the law sees this person as complicit in the abuse.

This idea seemed to be a somewhat larger pill for the women to swallow insofar as it required women to confront an abusive father and husband in a manner that could carry great personal risk to the woman, and possibly to the children as well.

Having pushed the theme that far, the social worker closed the session by hammering away on the idea that to allow a child to see sexual acts performed on TV or on a computer screen constitutes a serious form of child abuse, and that adults who engage in sexual relations while children are in the room are similarly guilty not only of a crime punishable by law, but of a misdeed that may well destroy the life of a child.

At this point in the presentation, a heavy silence hung over the gathering. These people had all grown up in Mexico in one-room dwellings, shared with multiple generations of relations, and most of them currently live in only slightly less crowded conditions, often with their children sleeping in their room in an apartment that the family might share with other families. And it was at this moment that I really understood why Patricia had insisted that people were afraid to send their children to school: not only because they might be uncovered as undocumented migrants, not only because the children might be spirited into gangs, but because, as she put it, "at any moment the teachers can say that you are not fit to be a mother and can take your children away from you and never give them back"—a source of terror to Mexican mothers, and not merely an irritant to those Mexican fathers who might prefer to have a freer hand in disciplining their children.

Another telling example of cultural incomprehension struck me at a workshop I attended on the school problems of Mexican agricultural worker families in North Carolina. I already knew from the very approximate statistics that are available for immigrant groups in New York City that well over half of Mexicans ages 16 to 19 are not in high school and, of those who have attended high school, almost 40 percent drop out before graduation, the boys to go to work in unskilled jobs, and the girls to look after their newborn babies or even to marry the father of their child. Likewise, in California schools, Hispanics in general have the highest dropout rates when compared with Asian, African American, and white students, and among those classified as Hispanic, the largest number are Mexicans or Mexican Americans.

But the world of the Mexican student in rural North Carolina is marked by challenges of an altogether different order. Settled as farmworker families in the poorest, most isolated rural areas of the state, the Mexicans, if they attend school, will find themselves in the lowest-income school districts with the fewest resources and the worst-paid teachers in the state—teachers who already have to cope with the cultural deficits of exceedingly poor people whose roots in those rural communities go back for generations. When their parents enroll them in school, Mexican children enter a world that has always been divided along black-white lines. Now, they enter the mix as people labeled "Brown" and encounter teachers who previously have never had any reason to know Spanish or understand Mexican customs. And among the countless problems generated by the mutual misunderstanding between teachers and Mexican immigrant parents are the teachers' widespread concerns that Mexican girls of 14 or 15 have boyfriends in their mid-twenties who blithely risk charges of statutory rape while the girls' parents remain—in the teachers' view—incomprehensibly undismayed by a grown man's romantic designs on their daughter.

Of course, if the teachers had a common language in which to speak to the parents, they would find that often the girl's father is ten years older than her mother and that in these Mexican parents' experience, a twenty-something man courting a teenage girl is normal, not aberrant behavior—and certainly not cause to call the police or even to register distress.

Thus, fear of being denounced to authorities *not* for the usual reason of having entered the country illegally, or for inventing a Social Security number in order to get a job, or for driving without a license, but for being a *neglectful parent* haunts the lives of Mexican immigrants, and especially Mexican immigrant mothers. And as Patricia explains, her own preoccupation with being misunderstood in these ways, and being unable to explain or defend herself, was central in pushing her to return to Santa Rosa.

And so, while Daniel has stayed on to work in New York to generate remittances, Patricia has returned with her children to her hometown. But living the consequences of that decision has been difficult because with this move, she has joined the countless immigrant wives in the village—women like Marta, Dolores, and Celia, whose circumstances are described in Part 1—who live their marriage at huge distance with only phone conversations to hold the family together.

On the other hand, as Patricia notes, had she had not gone back to Santa Rosa, their house project would never have taken off. Indeed, the interviews I collected were full of stories about people who had sent all their remittances back to family members who, rather than faithfully proceeding with the purchase of land and the construction of a house, effectively appropriated those funds for their own use. In Morelos, I heard the story of a father who meticulously carried out his son and daughter-in-law's directions to buy land and build a house, according to actual drawings they sent down to him. But only when the couple returned to take up residence in their dream home did they discover that both the land and the house were registered in the father's name, and he had no intention of turning any of it over to them.

Then in Pantla, in the state of Puebla, Marta's friend Margarita told me this story.

> My in-laws kept saying, "We're building your house," but in fact, when we came home we found it was a skeleton with no windows, no water pipes, no bathroom, only a latrine, and we couldn't live in it. We had to go back to living in one room of my in-laws' house, and all this after we had sent anywhere from $500 to $700 every two weeks for six years. In fact, it was in order to raise the funds to build this house that I left my children behind with my *suegros* and joined my husband in Atlantic City, just to speed the day when we could actually move out of my in-laws' house and into our own home. For years we were spending my salary to live in Atlantic City and sending his home to Pantla. But then we came back to the village and we discovered that his parents were spending it on themselves and lying to us. All we could do was to cover the openings of our frame with heavy plastic to keep the weather and animals out.
>
> At this point, my husband wants to go back to Atlantic City to work so that we can finish the house, but by now our three oldest are teenagers, and they've lived a crazy life in Pantla with us away in New Jersey and their grandparents neglecting them the whole time that they were telling us that the children were fine. So that now my husband is scared that if he leaves for the United States the kids will turn out to be wild. Not so much the oldest, who is a very quiet boy, but the second, who is very rebellious. "What's the point," he says, "of having a house if you lose your children?"

At the other extreme are Angel's sisters and brothers, who decided one day that they could no longer allow him to work for another twelve years in the United States, always sending remittances to them and their parents and never putting aside anything to build a future for himself in their hometown. So they agreed that he was to have a piece of land and a house and some kind of business, and they took the project in hand to develop something for their brother who refused to spend on himself. When I visited them in Morelos in 2006, construction on a handsome four-room house was complete, and on the edge of the property, they had also built a chicken coop and a pen for beef cattle that they were fattening for slaughter.

Finally, Patricia points out that there are some people who seem unable ever to make up their minds. Such is the case, she says, of her cousins, who are still in New York, have built their house, and say they want to come home, but never feel they have put aside quite enough money to reestablish themselves properly in Santa Rosa.

> Ricardo keeps saying, "Look at the four of us squashed into two tiny rooms in a basement apartment in Brooklyn when we have a beautiful house waiting for us in Santa Rosa." At one point, in fact, his wife, Marisol, did go back with the girls to supervise the house-building project. But every time that Ricardo phoned home, his oldest, Evelyn, always said, "Papi, I don't want you to send me things. I want to be with you!" And this just broke his heart and made him so lonely that he came up with almost $4,000 to pay for a coyote so that Marisol could cross back into the United States while his two daughters, who were born in the United States and had passports, could fly into JFK.

In more lively places, like Tepec, enterprising people like Manuel and his brother, Felipe, can start up a business that corresponds to the impermanent, migratory nature of the town. But even in Tepec, the majority of migrants who left, gained U.S. citizenship, and built lives in the greater New York area tend to think of the town as the place where they will retire when they reach old age. If their children and grandchildren are in the United States, as was the case for Don Juanito, the returned immigrant whom I met sitting under the eucalyptus tree in the *zócalo* in Tepec, a retired man might content himself simply to come south for the winter months like any other sensible New Jersey–based gentleman of 75 might choose to fly off to Florida.

On the other hand, as we have seen in the lives of Sara who sells her corn on the cob in East Los Angeles, and her friend and cousin by marriage, Elena, who described her border crossing in Chapter 7, some people never dream of building a *casa de retorno*, a home to return to, because they can't really picture themselves ever going back except to visit loved ones, or marry, or be buried in their village. When I asked about their plans to return, both Sara and Elena were definitive in saying: "No, my life is here in L.A." But to understand their feelings on this issue, it is important to recall that their village, San Rafael, is like Nopal Verde, one of the hundreds, perhaps thousands, of small towns in Mexico that have reached that critical point described by Silvia, the nurse-practitioner in Nopal Verde: they are no longer viable, they no longer offer more than a handful of people any economic and social possibilities beyond sitting passively and receiving remittances from "up north."

But Sara reminds me, when I visited her at Easter week in 2006 during a break she took from her work as a street vendor, that there is often a difference between men and women in their thinking about the prospects for return to Mexico. "Remember," she said, "I'm the one who wants to stay in L.A. and Pablo is the one who always talks about going back to San Rafael, even if he doesn't talk about it very often or very seriously."

> Here in California women can earn wages in a factory job, cleaning houses, or lots of other activities, just the way I earn selling my *elotes*. And it's women, not men, who receive money from the state because all of these forms of help for needy families are given to the mother, not the father of the family. So there are a lot of ways that women can end up better off than their husbands.

> Look at my friend, Estela. In San Rafael, Estela used to take a combi to go to work for a Korean in a sweatshop near the city of Puebla. Now she lives in Los Angeles, and she's working for another Korean in another sweatshop. But she's much better off, not only because here in L.A. the boss is not allowed to lock the workers into the factory the way these guys do in Mexico, but also because she receives assistance from the government, which provides food stamps and milk and cheese and health coverage for the children.

Last year, Estela's husband, Arnoldo, lost his job. So while Estela was sewing in the sweatshop, Arnoldo was home looking after the baby. I said to Estela, "Arnoldo was okay with that?" And she told me that she just said to him something that our parents always used to say in San Rafael, which was: "Either you work or you work. Those are the two choices." And he was okay about it.

"Then, there's also our friend, Elisabeta," Sara says. It seems that when Elisabeta arrived in Los Angeles, she came to live with her uncle and three male cousins. These men had previously paid a neighbor, another migrant from San Rafael, to cook for them. When Elisabeta joined their household, they told this woman that their cousin would now take over the food preparation and they began to pay Elisabeta the $60 a week that they had previously paid to the Señora. Elisabeta told Sara that she insisted on receiving only $50 a week because, after all, these men were her cousins and her uncle. But the principle was clear, even to a newcomer like Elisabeta. Everyone in the household had to chip in for rent and a share of the utilities, and therefore she needed to be paid by her relatives for the domestic work that she performed or else she wouldn't have the money to cover her share.

Initially Elisabeta was astonished to have monetary compensation for cooking for male family members, but she soon began to see that she was not alone in finding herself with cash in hand for performing traditional women's tasks. Among migrants from San Rafael in Los Angeles, grandmothers of children with working mothers would walk the children to school and pick them up after school and look after them until their mother returned from her job. But the *abuelas* are paid a few dollars a day by their daughters for performing this service, something that would be inconceivable in San Rafael. Sara says:

> There are lots of ways in which women can end up with more money than their husbands, and that's why women don't have to stick with a husband who gets drunk and abusive. This is a huge difference between our life in Mexico and our life here in the United States, and one that makes a lot of men want to return to the village and a lot of women want to stay in L.A.

Conclusion

I'm a retired cop. I was in the Marine Corps. I have a lot of respect
for the laws of the United States. If I lived in Mexico and I knew I
had some advantage here to help my family back in Mexico, I'd be
wading across the Rio Grande myself. I'd be on a raft floating from
Haiti. I'd be crossing the border from Yugoslavia into Germany.
I'd be going into England. I'd do anything I can to help my family.
Again, I'm a humble citizen, and I'm here to remind everybody
these are children of God. . . .

—Testimony filmed in *Farmingville*

In following this journey from Mexico to the United States and back, a
trip that has taken millions of Mexicans from one set of difficult circumstances to another, we have looked at the experiences of Mexican
migrants from the inside out. The idea has been to set aside the usual
question: What are *those* people doing *here*? to ask, instead, Why would
any of us make the decisions and choose the courses of action that millions of Mexican migrants have taken?

Viewed from this perspective, the answers are full of surprises.
People leave their home for reasons we could easily have imagined, but
also for complex reasons that, short of living in a Mexican village, we
might never have suspected. To be sure, poverty figures as a dominant

push factor. But more intimate knowledge of the satisfactions and the limitations of village life reveals some compelling reasons that prompt migration—reasons that are better understood as cultural, rather than economic, even if these cultural problems could be said to be exacerbated by poverty.

Likewise, the understanding that comes from a closer acquaintance with the world of Mexican migrants in the United States confirms some of the generalizations we might have formulated about who they are, how they survive, how hard they work, and what it is that they hope to achieve in the United States. At the same time, this more intimate picture also provides many surprising insights that bear on the question of what is to be done about undocumented migration—a question that we will take up at the end of this chapter.

The Economic and Social Roots of Migration

When attempting to identify the causes of Mexican migration to the United States, most analysts focus on poverty, or, better said, they focus on the imposition of neoliberal policies like NAFTA and the intensification of poverty that these policies have produced.[1] Certainly there is no need to be a rigid economic determinist to find, in all the cases presented in this book, ample evidence of the power of economic explanations. The most fleeting visit to a sending community like Nopal Verde or San Rafael would be sufficient to demonstrate the near complete lack of viable economic prospects for poor and middle-class Mexicans in their own country.

The free-market commitment of neoliberalism promises "a tide that will lift all boats," but no one who has looked at the migrant-sending areas of Mexico could be under any illusion that there are boats are bobbing up and down in places like Tepec, Tenango, or Pantla—and even less in depopulated towns and villages like Nopal Verde or San Rafael. It is no secret that the framers of NAFTA calculated that small-scale agricultural activity in Mexico was a thing of the past, and that the peasants as a social class would die out or be absorbed—if they were lucky—into the workforce of the large-scale commercial enterprises of the agribusiness giants. But it is fair to say that the boosters of NAFTA in Mexico, President Carlos Salinas, and his successors, Ernesto Zedillo and Vicente Fox, never doubted that the agreement would bring industrial jobs to Mexico. It is hard to imagine that they actually believed that these industrial jobs would ever be sufficient to absorb the surplus rural population plus urban youths entering the labor market—but they did believe that NAFTA would promote industrial expansion.

Whatever their beliefs may have been, the sad outcome is now clear. As we have seen, a person like Francisco, who was born forty years ago in a peasant village, for lack of arable land moved to a large town, Tehuacán, precisely to grasp the opportunities afforded by NAFTA which had brought foreign and Mexican-owned assembly plants into the interior of Mexico. But after a mini-industrial boom in the Tehuacán valley, competition from other low-wage zones around the globe made these operations unprofitable. At this point, the maquiladoras picked up and moved elsewhere, and so, too, did Francisco—to a street corner in Staten Island.

Thus, anyone who is trying to account for increases in the flow of undocumented migrants into the United States would have to begin by looking squarely at the economic policies that the United States has pushed so hard around the globe through its commanding role in the World Trade Organization, the International Monetary Fund, and the World Bank. In all of this, the United States has found a compliant junior partner in the Mexican government. Over the last three decades, Mexico has been dominated by a political elite that is dedicated to a neoliberal model that requires an end to spending by the state either to underpin industrial development or to guarantee the survival of the majority of Mexicans who are poor. The Mexican government still makes a show of providing some social assistance to impoverished Mexicans. But even a cursory look at the actual operation of these programs confirms what Don Claudio told us on the road to San Rafael: Procampo and Progresa don't even begin to meet the basic needs of the poor, and recipients of these "benefits" often come away economically worse off than if they had never become involved in the program in the first place.[2]

Still, it is important to underscore that the impulse to migrate to the United States does not spring from economic causes alone. The experiences of women like Marta and Dolores show that there are also some significant social changes in Mexican society that have intensified the desire to leave Mexico for the United States.

One stimulus to rural exodus is that migration offers women an escape from the most oppressive village-based forms of patriarchy. The ideological commitment of many progressive people to denounce neoliberalism and its pernicious effects has led some analysts to ignore the simple fact that many women like Sara or Patricia who migrate, or others, like Marta, Dolores, and Celia, who support the migratory projects of their husbands, do so in order to raise the funds to build an independent housing unit, that is, a "neolocal household," in order to escape the absolute tyranny exercised by the mother-in-law over the daughters-in-law in the patrilocal household.[3]

Another motivation for migration that reflects the kind of social change that is stimulated by the process of globalization is the shift in poor people's conception of the basic necessities of life. Any consideration of the migratory process that does not sentimentalize the migrants points to the astonishing lengths to which migrants go— leaving loved ones behind, running great personal risk crossing the desert, living without formal rights as an underclass in an often hostile society—all in the interest of acquiring material goods. To be sure, migrants direct their first remittances to improving their dwellings, acquiring land and better agricultural equipment, purchasing a car or truck, or underwriting a modest business venture. Moreover, an estimated 20 percent of Mexican families are absolutely dependent on remittances to meet their need for food, clothing, and shelter. Yet, a careful survey of sending communities is likely to highlight what Don Beto found so troubling with respect to his own sons and daughters. Televisions, computers, cordless phones, cell phones, DVD players, and a variety of consumer goods that, in very recent memory, would have been seen as luxuries, if they were known at all, have come to be redefined as basic needs. And to some degree, the desire for these goods plays a part in stimulating migration.

Networks

We know that those who leave are by no means the poorest in the village or neighborhood because financial and human capital are needed to finance the trip. Indeed, if we can find any factor that would account for the decision to undertake the journey northward, it is the availability of family, neighborhood, or village networks that facilitate the journey.

Experts on migration use the term "pioneer migrant" to refer to the individual who sets out alone, establishes himself, and is later followed by family and neighbors. In this study, the only person who might qualify for that title would be Alberto, who ended up working in a Chinese restaurant in Mapleville in upstate New York as a consequence of his chance encounter with a labor recruiter on a street corner in Brooklyn. It took more than a decade before Alberto was finally joined in Mapleville by family and the impulse for his wife, Graciela, and his children to come north was the post-9/11 crackdown at the border, which made it too dangerous and expensive for Alberto to return regularly to Mexico as he had done in the past.

However, although Alberto became the pioneer Mexican in a small town in upstate New York, he himself was originally brought to Brooklyn by a cousin. Likewise, everyone who appears in these pages reached the United States though the classic process of sponsorship by those who had gone before. Depending on whether they wished to go only as far as southern California or hoped to reach destinations on the East Coast or the northern United States, the cost of transportation and coyote fees would have been $3,000 or more. For people like Luis, Elena, Carlos, Sara, Francisco, Julio, and Manuel, the expense was underwritten by a relative who was already established in the United States and could provide not only an advance on future wages to pay for the trip, but also housing upon arrival and help in finding a job.

Alternatively, migrants may be sponsored by relatives back home in the sending community. Indeed, the acceleration of international migration has led to the revival of the traditional system of *acapadores*. These moneylenders historically provided credit to peasants who mortgaged their future crop for cash to meet basic family needs or to buy seed and other agricultural inputs to cultivate their land. Nowadays, as Silvia, the nurse at the clinic in Nopal Verde explained, parents mortgage their land to finance their children's crossing. If the remittances don't begin to flow back to the village very soon after the migrant's arrival in the United States, the parents stand to lose everything they have.

In the southernmost states in Mexico, in small towns where local strongmen still hold sway, migratory journeys may be underwritten by the local *cacique*, or political boss, who expects to be repaid with votes as well as cash. Yet another source of funds may be the village priest. While some, like the priest in Tepec, take a passionately strong stand against migration, especially of women and young people, others play an active role in facilitating the trip northward, in part because they recognize that the entire life of the village is unsustainable without remittances, but also because remittances have become a key resource for an underfinanced church, supporting both religious festivals and the repair and upkeep of the church buildings.

Ironically, the strength of migrants' networks provides key advantages to employers in the United States as well as to the migrants themselves, as Carlos observed in his hotel kitchen in New Jersey and as Wayne Cornelius noted in his study of labor markets in San Diego county. "No costly advertising is required; no employment agency fees need be paid. Job vacancies can be filled almost immediately; in most cases, immigrants already working in the firm know that a vacancy is about to occur even before the employer does."[4] In some sectors— notably restaurants, landscaping, building maintenance, and low-tech manufacturing—Cornelius discovered that 80 percent of those employed had found their job through their migratory networks.[5]

However, as we have seen in the lives of the people profiled in this book, not all networks can provide a migrant with the same level of support. Carlos recognizes his great fortune in having his cousin David as his principal contact. David, as Carlos puts it, "is a really smart guy and a well-liked guy and a person who knows a lot of people." Francisco, on the other hand, is connected only to his cousin Donaldo, who, in turn, was sponsored by recently arrived relatives on his wife's side. None of these people is well-established in Staten Island, a lack of grounding that is evidenced by their continued status as *esquineros*, rather than as workers with some fixed employment. Indeed, it is telling that, in the case of Francisco and Donaldo, it fell to me to teach them a range of useful skills, including reading the map of the New York subway system, how to obtain one of the five places on the line at the Mexican consular office in Manhattan that are reserved for Mexicans from Staten Island, and even how to use an automatic elevator without getting stuck between floors, something I discovered was a preoccupation of theirs. In the case of immigrants who have better established networks, the roles were reversed and migrants were teaching *me* how to get around, how to get value for money, and other useful lessons they had learned from friends, relatives, and their own direct experience.

A good example of migrants who are more successfully established is provided by the group from San Rafael: Sara, Pablo, Elena, Diego, and Dario. These Rafaeleños have a thick network of *comadres*, *compadres*, and extended family in East Los Angeles, and they are people who *really* know how to get around. They know where to buy their ingredients at the lowest prices. They know how to acquire real fake driver's licenses and fake fake driver's licenses. And no one who has ever driven in Los Angeles with Sara in the passenger seat would think it made any sense to upgrade the rental car to a model that features a global positioning device. Sara can guide you on or off any freeway or provide you with an alternative nonfreeway route. Most impressive is Sara's anticipation, as when she would say: "Olympic Boulevard is coming up and you're going to have to make a left, but they're not going to let you make a left, so get over to the right now and you're going to see a gas station and you can pull in there and go out the other end and you're going to have a light that will let you into the stream of traffic."

For all the advantages that their friends and relations can provide, what the Rafaeleños lack in their network are people with papers. Because their large-scale migration dates only to the mid-1990s, they do not enjoy the great advantage that Tomás has, which is to have in his acquaintance a lot of people with legal status. Tomás may have missed his own chance for amnesty in 1986, but he has a network of people with papers who can help him in many ways, such as lending him their licensed-plumber number when needed. Similarly, Samuel, the dentist from Nopal Verde, may be undocumented, but when he wanted to bring his dental office equipment back to Nopal from Oklahoma, he had a range of people with papers whom he could call on for help, people who could buzz down to Zacatecas in their truck, enjoy the weekend "at home," and return to Tulsa with no problem at all. Meanwhile, Manuel, the *paquetero* in New York, comes from Tepec, a town that started sending migrants to the United States in the 1970s and that now has a relatively high percentage of people, like himself, who were around when the amnesty was offered. For this reason, Manuel and other "Tepequeño Americans" are available to help more recently arrived undocumented migrants from their hometown.

Then there are those who have no network of family and neighbors already settled in the United States and these migrants must pick up on the migratory networks of others. Jan Rus found that often migrants from the southern state of Chiapas made their way to California by latching onto the migratory networks of Guatemalans they met while working in the lowest rungs of the tourist industry in Cancún, on the Yucatán coast. In fact, sometimes the Guatemalans actively recruited Mexicans from their workplace who shared their ethnic origin as Mayan Indians. In this way, as the group made its way north through Mexico to the U.S. border, the Guatemalans could pass themselves off as Chiapanecans, rather than undocumented Central Americans. Moreover, if apprehended at the border, Guatemalans who successfully passed for Mexicans would only be deported to Mexico, not all the way to Guatemala. Once safely across the border into the United States, however, the Guatemalans could return the favor as their own networks, which dated from the solidarity movement with Central Americans of the early 1980s, provided help to the Chiapanecan newcomers.[6]

As all these cases make clear, people need their networks, and if they don't have any, they must construct them. In 2006 I visited a household in Brooklyn made up of seven men from four different Latin American countries (Mexico, Guatemala, El Salvador, and Peru), who had met on a street corner waiting for work, and who lived in what appeared to be a very well-organized and harmonious, if crowded, apartment. Haroldo, the member of the group whom I first met on the subway and who had invited me to share the hearty *comida* they customarily prepared for themselves on Sundays, explained.

> It works out okay because we've got two guys here who are Pentecostals and the rest of us might have a beer now and then, but there's no one who drinks a lot and that's really the key thing. Basically, we get along because we have to. None of us has family here and there's just no way you can live alone.

The universal agreement among the people I met of the necessity to have family or, failing that, to create a household out of the people who come to hand, will be interesting to anyone who has read Barbara Ehrenreich's excellent book, *Nickel and Dimed: On (Not) Getting By in America.* In what she describes as a journalistic experiment, Ehrenreich lived as a low-wage worker in Florida, Maine, and Minnesota, taking only minimum-wage jobs and only the kind of housing that would be available to a person with no car and insufficient money for a security deposit and one month's rent, both normally required for long-term leases. After living like this for a year, Ehrenreich concluded that it is mathematically impossible for a single person to rent the housing that is available to the working poor on the take-home pay offered in minimum-wage jobs. Indeed, she found that the only workers in this situation who could survive were those who shared a household with at least one other wage earner, be it a spouse, a relative, or a friend.[7]

When I mentioned Ehrenreich's striking finding to Patricia in one of our talks on her sun-soaked veranda in Santa Rosa, all she could say was, "Well, of course. Everyone knows that!"

The Hard Place

Unquestionably there are some very sad passages in this book; the loneliness of Dolores, left behind in San Pedro, and the close-to-hopeless situation of the peasant Claudio are two that stand out for me. But the reader may have noticed that there is no one chapter in this book that describes a classic downtrodden immigrant who lives poor at the fringe of a rich society, exploited as cheap labor, cheated out of wages, overcharged for housing by slum landlords, without medical insurance, Social Security, or unemployment insurance, and hunted at every turn by the migra.

Certainly, all of these conditions and concerns *do* frame the lives of the migrants I interviewed in the "hard place," which is to say, the world that they have come to inhabit when they reach the United States. Yet, as these interviews make clear, the lives of Mexicans in the United States are made up of a complex assortment of experiences, including some very positive ones, albeit many that fall under the heading of "the good that can come from something bad." If this were not the case, if it were not a mix of good and bad, it would not be so difficult, as Patricia points out, to figure out when to go home to Mexico.

In one of the many ironies that this work uncovers, I found the people I interviewed in Los Angeles and New York to be optimistic, even as they related to me incidents of mistreatment and exposure to dangers that could only inspire dismay. To a degree, this finding reflects the need that the migrants feel to justify *to themselves* why they stay in a place so far from home. It also reflects what we could call a sampling bias: the people I met in the United States were those who had stayed on. The migrants who become discouraged go home.

This point was highlighted for me by Alfonso, a former neighbor of Don Beto in San Jerónimo, who now lives in New York.

> I was nineteen when I first traveled to the United States, and after three weeks, I was ready to leave. I said to my cousin, "Lalo, I gotta get out of here. Give me some money so I can go home and I'll pay you back." But Lalo, who was already holding my debt to the coyote, said he wouldn't have enough to live on if he paid my way back. So I stayed and after six months he said, "Okay, I have the money for you to go home." But by then I wasn't so ready to leave. Somehow I had got to like it in New York.

Another case, that of Julio, the would-be crack dealer, represents a particularly dramatic example of this general problem of sampling. Given the quick exit he made, in the pool of people available for me to interview in Los Angeles, it would be unlikely that I would find someone like Julio, that is, a person involved in criminal activity. If he were still in Los Angeles, he would be much better concealed than, say, a street vendor of popsicles like Pablo. Or as Julio was quick to point out, he might have "ended up dead." In short, it is no accident that Julio is someone I interviewed as a returned migrant in Mexico. He had a story of failure that I would be unlikely to hear from a migrant still resident in the United States, unless I had access to Mexicans who are incarcerated in the United States. This, indeed, was a form of access I did have with Javier, whom I visited in the Berkshire County jail in Massachusetts. But lacking the personal connection I had to Javier through my friendship with his family and their desire for my intervention, neither prison authorities nor the Mexican consulate—which has information on all Mexicans incarcerated in the United States—will entertain requests for interviews with prisoners.

Thus, those migrants I met and interviewed in the United States were likely to be optimistic either about their prospects of making a life for themselves here or—in the great majority of cases—accumulating enough capital to create the basis to build a life for themselves in Mexico. And if they weren't wildly optimistic, at least they had developed some solid justifications to meet their own needs, evaluating in positive terms the choices they had made and the situation in which they found themselves.

In assessing the positive features of their life in the United States, one that is particularly striking to observe is the closeness that migrants come to feel for others who are sharing their experience. Some of these people may be *compadres* and *comadres* or relatives from their hometown with whom they form a community in, say, an apartment house in the Bronx or a few square blocks in East Los Angeles. Others could be Mexicans from other regions, or immigrants from other countries with whom, in their isolation, they manage to form a kind of fictive community, bound together by the sort of mutual help, caring, and responsibility that would have been central to their culture back in small-town Mexico.

Another source of satisfaction, mentioned by interviewees many times in these pages, is the accumulation of capital that is possible even in the lowest-wage jobs that immigrants can hold in the United States. Migrants who never build a nest egg, people who really have nothing to show for all their hours of hard labor, may exist, but by definition they are virtually impossible to find. Carlos did speak to me of other immigrants who grew lonely and began to drink away all they had earned or who got carried away and ran up credit card debt. But these tales usually ended with the return of that person to Mexico, so he would be unlikely to be anyone I could find to interview in New York or Los Angeles or, if he were still around, he would be unlikely to make himself available for an interview. As Carlos reports in Chapter 14, it often takes longer than planned to accumulate enough money to return home because many things cost more than the migrant may have anticipated before coming to the United States. But, in general, one of the pleasures of this work was to meet people who, albeit with setbacks and difficulties and only with a great deal of effort, were actually succeeding in meeting goals they had set for themselves. And to know something about the structure of opportunity back in Mexico, that is, to have met Don Claudio on the road to San Rafael, a peasant who was thrown into complete financial crisis by the necessity to come up with 350 pesos— $35—for his share of digging a well, is to understand better why an *esqinero* like Francisco in Staten Island would consider $70 take-home pay for a ten-hour day to be a day well spent, even if it does and *should* upset us to know there are people working in our society whose labor is exploited by contractors in this way.

Yet, ironically, for all that I encountered a good measure of cheerfulness and satisfaction with the choice they had made in coming to the United States, one of the words that most frequently cropped up in the narratives I collected was "sacrifice." Indeed, it occurred so often that it seemed that people felt somehow *required* to tell me that the entire exercise was about sacrifice, lest I carry away the impression that they were actually having a good time. Yet one of my findings was that many people *were* having a good time, insofar as a good time might be defined not only as taking a rare day off from hard work to go to the pier at Santa Monica or the Bronx Zoo, but also learning to make your way around a new city and a new society, connecting with other people in a workplace who come from outside your world, and generally learning a remarkable number of new things in a remarkably short span of time, all the while that you feel gratified by your capacity— though your labor—to care for the people you love back home.

These are some of the findings that make the study of the receiving society a relatively upbeat experience for the researcher, above all in comparison with time spent in the sending communities. For sure, the United States is a "hard place," but the people who make the journey have self-selected for all kinds of good reasons, and they bring to the task they set for themselves a strikingly positive spirit.

The Rock

If the hard place provides a mixed picture of exploitation and injustice on the one hand, but also growth, mobility and accumulation on the other, the "rock" is a more unambiguously difficult place to be. Indeed, the benefit of an approach in which we begin with a look at the conditions that migrants have left behind in Mexico before we consider the life that immigrants lead in the United States, is that this comparative perspective explains things that might otherwise be incomprehensible.

The need for this perspective struck me in the course of my chance encounter with the officials from the New York City Department of Housing Preservation and Development on their tour of Staten Island. It was clear as Terry drove us through the suburban streets of Port Richmond and along the shore of New York Harbor, that the HPD officials—all of whom were both sympathetic and empathetic in their responses—were groping to imagine what kind of life, what kind of housing, people would have in Mexico that could make a basement shared with seventeen other men, an unheated garage, an abandoned tugboat, or a freight container seem like an acceptable condition in which to live. The answer to this question, in a sense, is that it is the wrong question. Sharing a basement with seventeen others is not a housing choice as such; it is an element in a larger strategy for accumulating capital to meet long-term goals. But to grasp this requires knowledge of the life the migrants have left behind.

However, in looking at that life, we inevitably face the same kind of sampling problem that I referred to earlier. People who are interviewed in Los Angeles and New York explain how and why their choice adds up to a decision to stay in the United States. Back in their village, the very same people (not to mention those who have never left the village and never wished to leave) often evaluate life in Mexico more positively because they also need to justify the decisions they have made. A reflective person like Patricia is unusual in her ability to weigh the return to Santa Rosa and consider the characteristics of life in both settings in a neutral and rational manner. In the end, she chose to return to Mexico aware of all there is to appreciate in village life, but conscious, as well, of the positive characteristics of the life she had known in New York.

The case studies drawn from the sending communities give us a sense of what it is that Mexicans value in their society when living there or far away. Don Beto is clear about his attachment to the soil, as well as the satisfaction of creative artisanal work as an expression of religious belief. Many people I interviewed in the United States were similar to Don Beto in their expressions of appreciation of the natural setting they had left behind. They also placed great value on the cycle of religious festivals, although some had managed to recreate these moments through their involvement in churches in Los Angeles and New York that had taken up the celebration of the saints venerated by the immigrants in their parish. The closeness of family and the food— especially the white corn—are inevitably mentioned by Mexicans in the United States as some of the things they miss most, while the irritants of small village life, where people mind each other's business, is sometimes transformed though nostalgia into something closer to pure "caring and sharing."

Not everyone I interviewed spoke spontaneously of the dignity of living in one's own society rather than as a person without status on the fringes of another, but many did, and all agreed, when asked, that this was one of the key elements that would make life in Mexico preferable to living anywhere else. Perhaps the advantage of living in Mexico rather than the United States that was mentioned most often was the quality of life offered to children. There is no question that small towns and villages give children a great degree of freedom to run and play and to organize their own games and their own time. Parents emphasize that in Mexico their children enjoy physical security from drug-related crime that their mothers and fathers could never offer them in the kind of neighborhoods where Mexican migrants are constrained to live in the United States.

These are features of life in Mexico that people value. And if it were really possible for them all to build their dream homes, set up viable small businesses, prepare their children for the educational and social transition of a return to Mexico, and move back at the same time with their full network intact so that they could reconstruct their lives in the company of the *compadres* and *comadres* in their age cohort, then life would be just about perfect. But no one I interviewed ever suggested that this could be more than a consoling fantasy.

Overwhelmingly the people I interviewed shared a "best possible scenario," which would consist of living in Mexico with the kind of income that people like themselves can only enjoy while working in the United States. This is the logic that lies at the core of business ventures that are transnational in nature, like the *paquetero* business and money transfers. It is also at the heart of the nostalgic food industry that some returned migrants are trying to develop in Zacatecas growing prickly pear cactus and similar crops to make jam and candy for the ever-increasing market of immigrants in the United States who long for this taste of home. But it is important to note that the only migrants who can feasibly plan a transnational existence where they can combine the best of both worlds are the migrants, like Manuel, who have legal status in both countries. For those who cannot easily move back and forth, the sending community remains a rocky place where even energetic, determined people find no way to make a living.

And yet, as we have seen, only Sara and her *comadre*, Elena, bluntly state that they are now firmly planted in Los Angeles with no realistic prospects of returning to San Rafael. Manuel has his papers and can freely move between the two countries. But now that he has a grandchild in New York, he has begun to reconsider the timing of a return to Tepec. Strikingly, these are the *only* people among the scores of Mexican migrants whom I interviewed in depth in the United States who even entertained the idea that they might be "here to stay." However rooted they might have seemed in their U. S. setting, all the others continued to nurture plans for their return to Mexico. And Father Robert, commenting on the outlook of his rapidly expanding congregation of Mexicans in the South Bronx, told me: "We have yet to have a burial here in New York. In my parish, a collection is always taken up so the body of the deceased can be sent home to Mexico to join the ancestors in the village cemetery. No one has wanted to be buried here."

What Is to Be Done?

The responses I received when I asked migrants about their future plans are striking because they are totally at odds with the way the entire immigration debate in the United States has been framed, both in

Congress and in the media. Discussion of the immigration issue generally presupposes an immigrant who comes to the United States, drawn by "all that is wonderful" in U.S. society, who then embraces its values, makes a place for herself or himself in the fabric of national life, and wishes for nothing more than to be *allowed* to "become an American." The idea that millions of people might wish to work very hard to accumulate capital and return to their homeland with the resources to live out a Mexican, rather than an American Dream, is virtually absent from any public discussion on the question.

It is important that we confront the disjuncture between this reality and the image that Americans themselves often cherish: that they are the envy of people around the world, all of whom would make their lives in the United States if given half a chance to enter and gain legal status. It makes no sense to discuss what could be an effective policy to resolve the problem of undocumented migration to the United States in the absence of understanding what we have covered in these chapters: why people come to the United States without documents and whether they hope to stay or return home.

As I argued in the introduction to this book, the presence of Mexicans in the United States is so ubiquitous and widespread that anyone in the United States who looks around intuitively understands that closing off the border to Mexicans (as well as the Central and South Americans who may cross with them) has not significantly slowed the continued flow of undocumented migrants into the country. Would-be migrants find their way across in any case, and the intensification of the effort to exclude migrants has only made the crossing more dangerous and a lot more expensive for those who would attempt it. The response of undocumented Mexicans to these measures has been, logically enough, to give up their annual trip to their homeland, stay longer in the United States, and often to make the sacrifices necessary to pay for their families to join them. Thus, the policies intended to tighten the border and keep migrants out have, instead, had the effect of containing more of them within the United States.

Recognition of this reality is now reflected in public opinion in the United States. For example, a *Washington Post* survey carried out in January 2005 found that 61 percent of United States citizens thought that undocumented migrants should be allowed to keep their jobs and apply for legal status.[8] Clearly, if it is the political will of U.S. citizens *not* to have undocumented immigrants living and working among them, their political representatives will need to find a formula through which these immigrants can receive proper documents and the full range of rights and guarantees available to legal residents. The construction of higher fences and the deployment of more troops and machinery at the border will not accomplish this goal.

U.S. federal policy on immigration is clearly contradictory and bespeaks a profound ambivalence of a political elite that advocates and promotes a free market in goods, while prohibiting a free market in labor. The official position that excludes the free movement of labor across borders produces policies that are at odds with the manifest need for these workers in the economy.

This contradictory nature of federal policy gives rise to some of the strangest coalitions in U.S. politics. The Essential Worker Immigrant Coalition lobbies Congress and the White House on behalf of fast-food restaurant chains, the hotel industry, slaughterhouses and meatpacking companies, nursing homes, and agribusiness. This kind of "pro-immigrant" coalition faces off against populist anti-immigrant groups that fear that a decline in wages will be the inevitable consequence of the entry of more immigrant workers, both documented or undocumented. Social-justice advocates who are concerned with immigrants' welfare find themselves linked to small-business people who are eager to employ immigrant workers if only to exploit them as cheap labor. Business interests hope to meet the challenge of lower production costs abroad by employing undocumented workers in the United States find themselves in the same Republican Party with those who want to stem the flow of foreigners at all cost, including racist vigilantes who have appointed themselves as "minutemen" to guard the border.

Immigration Reform Before and After September 11

Given the complex and the contradictory nature of the interests at stake, it is not surprising that every official unilateral or bilateral attempt to address the problems of labor market mobility, border security, and the rights of immigrant workers has ended in an impasse.

Whether we look only at the debates and the results under the most recent two administrations or begin with the long, sad history of bilateral
negotiations from the bracero program of 1942 to 1964, through the
1986 amnesty, to the 2006–2007 congressional debates and stalemate,
we can only conclude that these are intractable problems that are unlikely to be resolved easily. Certainly from the time that the United
States' superior bargaining position enabled its representatives to take
labor mobility off the table in the negotiations leading up to NAFTA,
the goal of guaranteeing rights and security and the chance for a digni-
fied life in the United States for all who live and work there has come
no closer to fulfilment.

Perhaps the greatest hopes were raised during George W. Bush's
first presidential campaign in 2000. In an effort to attract Hispanic vot-
ers to the Republican Party, Bush met frequently in a series of folksy,
cordial encounters with his "friend," "neighbor," and "fellow rancher,"
the governor of the state of Guanajuato, Vicente Fox, himself the leading candidate for the Mexican presidency and, by July 2000, president-
elect of Mexico. Once in office, Bush appointed a cabinet-level panel
charged with formulating recommendations on how undocumented
Mexican workers might apply for legal status if they could meet eligi-
bility requirements based on their employment history and length of
residence in the United States. Of course this proposal, coupled with a
program of recruitment of "temporary workers" who would hold
short-term work visas, immediately set off protests from non-Mexican
immigrant groups that demanded similar opportunities, as well as
counterprotests from xenophobic groups that simply want the exclusion of foreigners in general and nonwhite foreigners in particular.

Nonetheless, the proposal won the backing of the AFL-CIO leadership, which had come to see that legalization of the undocumented
workforce would enable organized labor to unionize low-wage workers
and to fight the kind of exploitation that occurs when a huge pool of
cheap labor is readily available to employers.

On September 6, 2001, Bush and Fox announced their intention
to pursue these changes, but the terrorist attacks five days later brought
the entire discussion to an end. In fact, following September 11th, the
INS simply stopped processing immigration and visa applications. It

would not be until 2004 that Bush's second presidential campaign prompted a brief reprise of the immigration policy discussion. Once again, he hoped to attract Hispanic votes by offering a program that would allow undocumented workers to apply for temporary guest-worker status for an initial period of three years, a permit that could then be renewed an indefinite number of times. To guarantee that the workers would leave the United States at the conclusion of their contract, the plan called for part of their pay to be withheld and turned over to them only on their return to their home country.

It is disheartening to see that in the 2006 round of congressional debates, the most *progressive* position on what would be a viable program, the original McCain-Kennedy bill, proposed a return to the old bracero-type guest-worker program, the prospect of some provision for acquisition of full citizenship after a period of guest-worker status, and the payment of a fine to be slapped on those who have entered illegally to punish them for having walked across the desert for three days.

When we consider what the people who share their stories in these pages risked to cross into the United States, it is easy to imagine that a $2,000 fine might have seemed like a reasonable deal, if only to put the experience of illegal entry and coyote fees behind them forever. It may seem reasonable even when we calculate that the fine would be the equivalent of six to seven full weeks of labor for those lucky enough to earn the standard $300 or $350 per week income that comes with the best and steadiest jobs available to undocumented migrants in the current labor market.

No doubt, many Mexican migrants would have willingly paid the fine. But the ugly part of the punitive provision was that it reinforced the image of undocumented migrants as people who have done something very wrong and who have compounded their wrongdoing by inventing Social Security numbers or purchasing false documents so that they might work and drive a vehicle where necessary. That there should be debates in which U. S. senators and representatives rise to ask with straight faces whether this punishment is sufficient to the crime speaks very badly for a society that is not shy about proclaiming its greatness and generosity. Likewise, the issue of whether a guest-worker program could ever meet the standards that we would want to provide for people who live and work in our society is another fundamental question that tells us more about ourselves than about the workers who may be brought into the country under such an arrangement.

Reviewing the congressional debates on the McCain-Kennedy bill, it is not surprising that this proposal found little favor either with immigrant advocates or with right-wing anti-immigrant groups.

At this writing, with the revival of the initiative on an immigration bill in May 2007, we find that even with the Democrats now in control of both houses of Congress, the terms under consideration are even more mean-spirited than the bills debated the previous year in a Republican-controlled House and Senate.

Tellingly, the fines to be levied on those who have entered without documents have jumped from $2,000 to $5,000. Any hope of applying for legal status from within the United States has disappeared. Perhaps most damaging to the hopes and expectations of poor migrants is the shift from family unification to a "merit-based" point system based on education and skills, a policy that emphasizes "workplace competitiveness" and gives far less weight to family ties.

What makes the most recent proposal even worse than the 2006 bills is the concept of "triggers," that is, the idea that there can be no effort to regularize anyone's status until border security is reinforced and a "virtual wall" of unmanned vehicles, cameras, and sensors is in place. Accordingly, the 370 miles of triple-layered fencing, the 500 miles of vehicle barriers, the 14,000 additional Border Patrol agents, the construction of holding facilities for another 10,000 detainees, along with systems for tougher enforcement in the workplace, would all have to be installed before any action could be taken on the requests of those who would wish to gain legal status in the country.

So it is that we begin to read estimates suggesting that it would be roughly fifteen years before any of the current 12 million undocumented immigrants in the United States might hope to gain permanent legal status or green cards: two years to put the triggers in place, eight years to clear the existing backlog of immigration applications, and another five years to process candidates for green cards. Of course, over that period, millions more undocumented migrants will likely have arrived, a possibility that has received remarkably little discussion in the debate.[9]

In reality, there is little chance that any socially just legislation could be put forward because of the contradictory nature of the demands on policymakers. Immigrant labor is crucial to the United States service economy. Moreover, the future competitiveness of the United States in a global economy depends absolutely on a continued supply of unprotected, low-wage labor, that is, of people who will work *inside* the United States at wage rates and in conditions that approximate those of the export zones in the poorest countries of the world.

Of course, U.S. manufacturers cannot match the rock-bottom wages and deplorable conditions of, say, Chinese factories. Yet, the logic of global capitalism demands that manufacturers reduce their production costs to the lowest possible level. From the employer's perspective this is best achieved by exploiting those whose legal status is insecure and labor rights are unprotected.

Under the circumstances, only the countermeasure of reinforcing labor's capacity to organize workers is likely to bring any improvement in this situation.[10] This is because in spite of the many changes in migration patterns, the plight of recent migrants to the United States is, in so many respects, the same as that faced by the "huddled masses" at the turn of the last century. Migrant workers' desperation to find and hold jobs makes them vulnerable to exploitation. Thus, the answer to the question of how best to counter this vulnerability is the one that Joe Hill, the legendary labor organizer of the International Workers of the World, would recognize and surely endorse on the basis of his own experiences almost a hundred years ago.[11]

If there is a solution to be found it is not a particularly novel one. It is a response that is called forth by the conditions that are widespread today, but were also characteristic of a period of immigration a full century before anyone ever thought to impose a model called neoliberalism. The answer consists of a call for recognition of the crucial role that immigrants play in the economy and society of the United States and other industrialized countries. It requires those lucky enough to hold citizenship in the receiving country to think hard about the kind of society in which they wish to live, and in which they wish their children to live. And it depends, as it always has, on the success of the struggle to strengthen labor rights and human rights in general.

A Note on Methodology

Working to understand the lives of people who are vulnerable raises an assortment of ethical and methodological questions to which a researcher must respond. The rules are generally spelled out by the ethics committee of a researcher's own university, a body on which I myself have served. The guidelines are usually very explicit, but often correspond more closely to the challenges that arise in clinical experimentation in—yes—a *clinic* than to a situation in which the field of study is the real world. The rules, in either case, require the researcher to produce an "informed consent" document *before* opening a conversation with a "research subject" whose words could possibly become part of the findings of the study. The form is supposed to spell out the purpose of the project, the goals and objectives of the study, the procedures to be employed, the possible risks to participants, the research subject's right to remain anonymous, to decline to participate, or to withdraw from the experiment or study at any point, and the direct future benefits, if any, for the participant in the study. Other sections of the ethics code anticipate the ethical questions that could arise for anthropologists in the field, but generally the picture of fieldwork to which these rules correspond is that of a small-scale society, and the guidelines presuppose that permission to study the "community" will be obtained from the "elders" or even from the chief!

Overall these guidelines may be of relevance for physiologists wiring up experimental subjects with electrodes or for social psychologists running a simulation that explores the relationship between prisoners and guards in a psychology lab. In short, the rules apply best to research in settings in which the "experimenter" has a great deal of control over the experimental situation. Even the fact that at many universities the ethics code is labeled "Guidelines for Research on Human Subjects" suggests a model drawn from biology rather than the world of social science. However, as I will show, the awkward fit between ethics committees' requirements and the real-life situation in which a study like this unfolds can be illustrated by any of a large number of examples I could give from this project.

To cite but one, a very interesting moment I had in my fieldwork came in a laundromat as I waited for my own clothing to dry. A young man from Bangalore explained that he was very sorry to occupy all three of the tables provided for folding garments with foot-high stacks of white tablecloths, but that it fell to him to launder the linen from a nearby Indian restaurant during the slack time between lunch and dinner service. If I had thought to bring a consent form along to the laundromat, could I have whipped out this piece of paper at that moment? Could I have made clear that I am studying the immigrant experience in the United States, and that thoughts and observations he might share with me as we chatted about his journey to New York, the family he left behind, his work, and his experiences as an undocumented migrant might end up in my head, eventually in my thinking, and ultimately on the printed page? Gopal was too forthcoming, too pleased to pass the time with me, too eager to share his life story to give me so much as a moment in which I might have provided even an oral version of the formal written "permission slip" that the ethics committee requires before the researcher might speak a word to such a potentially vulnerable—and potentially interesting—research subject. The best I could do was to interrupt Gopal's narrative long enough to squeeze in a few words to the effect that this was all very enlightening to me because I was writing a book on the subject of migration.

In short, the ethics committee model presupposes a process of "recruitment" of "subjects." It does not foresee situations in which subjects recruit themselves, in which marginalized people speak very readily, sometimes very eagerly, to someone like me, a person they perceive to be part of the dominant society and whose interest in their lives they sense is genuine and sympathetic. It also does not foresee the occasions in which the tedium of low-wage work can be broken by a chance conversation with a stranger, especially in New York, a setting where, as I can attest as a native, people engage with strangers far more often than non–New Yorkers might imagine.

This question of passing the time in a tedious work situation or on a long subway ride became particularly significant for me in the New York–based part of this research. Notwithstanding the precariousness of their general situation and the particularly tense period of debate over immigrant rights that coincided with my fieldwork, the willingness and enthusiasm that met my efforts to interact with undocumented immigrants in New York was remarkable and is worth reflecting upon. On the one hand, my ability to chat with people in fluent Spanish was a conversation opener with countless people I met on the subway or bus whose own expectations of who is likely to break into Mexican-inflected Spanish were challenged by the lack of fit between my physical appearance and the words and expressions that I used in conversation. And, as their surprise turned to interest, it was often possible to connect with these people in a manner that made them not only willing but eager to talk to me. Often it would turn out—in the case of both men and women—that I was the first person from the dominant society (other than, perhaps, the Spanish-speaking Irish American priest in their parish)—with whom they had ever spoken *at length*. And, luckily for me, once these conversations began, I could easily ride an hour to the end of the subway line in Brooklyn or the Bronx and establish sufficient rapport to enable me to make an appointment to interview my seatmate more systematically.

On the other hand, even in encounters with immigrants like Gopal, whose first language was not English, the opportunity to converse with someone *in English*, who was happy to speak slowly and clearly, provided ample motivation for many people to talk to me.

My discovery of this disposition, this desire to connect and communicate, became a key element in the method I used to find people willing to tell their story, and it impacted on the results that this method yielded. Often researchers rely heavily on networks of "people like us," which would normally include other scholars, social workers in immigrant service organizations, activists in nongovernment organizations, and similarly engaged people. However, the problem with relying exclusively on research subjects found through these kinds of contacts is that by definition, migrants I might meet sitting in the reception area of Asociación Tepeyac on West 14th Street in Manhattan, or Project Hospitality in Staten Island, or any number of similar organizations would, by definition, be people who had the knowledge and links to find those with resources to assist them in making their way in the new environment. But while there may be thousands of people who are served by each of these organizations, there are, literally, millions who have never found their way to such a place, and it is important to capture their story as well: hence, the subways in New York and the buses in Los Angeles.

Thus the codes of ethics surrounding interactions with people who are defined as research subjects are explicitly spelled out. They are meant to protect such people from embarrassment or harm and, indeed, research funds are not released until the "principal investigator" signs on to these protocols. However, as these experiences illustrate, the matter is not a simple one. Readers have often asked me, "How many people did you interview for this study?" The answer is, it all depends on what we mean by "interview." When is a chat a chat? When is a chat an interview? The answer is that sometimes we don't know until hours, days, or months later that someone has provided us with important insights. Often only after reflection do we realize that a chance conversation was, in fact, rich in material that is of use. In short, in studies that are carried out not in the lab but in the real world where every sight that passes before the researcher's eyes and every chance conversation may become part of the findings, the best we can do is to respect the spirit of the regulations on informed consent.

A good "feel" for the spirit of these protective rules is crucial because the real problem is not whether people speak to you and you copy down what they say, either in written or recorded form. The key issue is what you do with the material that people have willingly given, conscious of the fact that their story may be published in a book. The central ethical challenge is not whether you induce people to talk to you or how you explain what will become of their story, but the judgment you exercise in determining which details you can safely incorporate into a book like this without compromising the safety, well-being, and future status of the people who have spoken to you, including people whose eagerness to "speak to the world" and whose confidence in their own future safety may exceed your own expectations and projections for them.

In my previous work in Mexico, I interviewed people who were living in an authoritarian political system dominated by a single party in which the press was far from free. But there were millions of other people who lived in the same circumstances. Although the official party, the Institutional Revolutionary Party, the PRI, sustained itself in power in part by coercing dissidents and violently suppressing political opposition, to grumble about the corruption of the PRI and the social inequality its programs promoted was like breathing in and out to a huge proportion of Mexicans. Thus, complaining, as "Josefina" did (and as I reported in my book *Mexican Lives*), that "the PRI always comes around and makes promises. . . . But then, after the elections, things are always worse than before," was not likely to bring down a heavy fist of repression on the person who might share this thought. Even if someone were to say, "The police are all gangsters and thugs," provided these words were not uttered directly into the face of a thuggish policeman, the remark was not likely to bring misfortune to the person who expressed this view. Indeed these were perceptions that were pretty much universally held, and how would anyone find the "Josefina" or the "Miguel" who had spoken these words if this person is described in my book as living in a settlement of half a million people on the outskirts of Mexico City?

Nonetheless, although the people who shared their ideas with me and whose stories appeared in my book effectively enjoyed safety in numbers, in *Mexican Lives* I followed the practice of giving a pseudonym to each of the fifteen Mexicans I profiled, along with all their friends and relations. And even as I did so, I met the objections of a few people who, like Josefina, *wanted* to be called by their real names and clearly identified so that readers would be able to come to Mexico and find them. As Josefina told me a few years after *Mexican Lives* was published:

Everything I said in your book was the truth and I am not
ashamed of it, so you can put my first name, last name, address, and the telephone number of my neighbor who will
call me to her phone if anyone wants to talk to me from
North America.

To be sure, it would have been gratifying to have respected Josefina's wish and it was difficult to deny her the notoriety that she clearly
hoped to enjoy. However, I was constrained from doing so by consider-
ations other than the ethics codes to which I had signed my name.
Rather than obedience to the ethics code in the formal sense, I was constrained by my knowledge of the notorious case of Oscar Lewis and
The Children of Sánchez. The Sánchez family were poor Mexicans interviewed by Lewis in the late 1950s. Lewis then crafted their direct testimony into a collective autobiography so compelling in nature and
moving in its impact that although he clearly believed he had adequately disguised the identity of all family members, based on Lewis's
vivid descriptions, Mexican journalists were able, with relative ease, to
locate the paterfamilias, Jesús Sánchez, at his place of work and un-
cover the identity and whereabouts of all those who had shared their
intimate secrets with Oscar Lewis, and through him with readers
around the world.

In an age in which people offer up their most private thoughts
and experiences on *Oprah* for all the world to know, the Sánchez scandal may seem a small matter. But the thought that personal material,
willingly shared with a researcher, could come back to damage the in-
formants in some way haunts anyone who works with direct testimony.
It is not only that people might suffer political repression for their
ideas or behavior at some future point because they have been exposed
in your writings. Equally worrying is the possibility that, because of a
frank thought they shared with you as a researcher, they may come to
be embarrassed or compromised with people important to them: with
their family members or friends and neighbors.

And while Margaret Mead might have hoped that her book *Coming of Age in Samoa* would one day be translated into dozens of lan-
guages and read around the world, she was clearly taken aback when

her research subjects themselves, the Samoans, eventually read her account of their lives and in many cases, found it to be objectionable, hurtful, and, by their reckoning, stunningly inaccurate. Today we have no illusion that people interviewed would not want to know what has been said about them and would not want to read about themselves at some future point. But it is also the case that almost anything we write about people may disappoint them. I discovered this when Josefina, a person whose integrity and courage and spunkiness in the face of misfortune I greatly admired and hoped to convey to readers, confided to me that although she recognized that all I had written about her life was accurate, she was very let down that I had, in her eyes, left out the most important part. This was the hours of taped conversation in which she described to me in detail each of the romantic disappointments she had suffered with men.

In the case of this book, all the concerns that preoccupied me with respect to the future safety and privacy of research subjects in *Mexican Lives* were also present. But even more pressing and immediate issues were at play.

First of all, people I interviewed in small towns in Mexico need their anonymity from their neighbors of whom—as we have seen—they are often quite critical.

Second, with few exceptions, everyone I interviewed in Los Angeles, New York, New Jersey, and Massachusetts was in a precarious condition precisely because of having no legal status in the United States. The consequences were potentially very grave if I were to write about them and locate them in a way that could lead the authorities to them. This was a danger that, when I began the study, was only a very remote possibility, and certainly one that was regarded by the people I interviewed as highly unlikely. One person after another told me, "I don't spend my time worrying about being picked up by the migra."

However, after the congressional debate on immigration reform that unfolded in the winter of 2006 and the mass protest demonstrations that followed in the spring of 2006, enforcement increased and the likelihood of being apprehended by the authorities as an undocumented migrant is greater than when I began this work. *How* much greater is difficult to say. What we can say for certain is that, for its own citizens, the United States may not be as authoritarian a society as Mexico under the PRI. But for immigrants without papers, the United States is a randomly authoritarian setting in which one minute you may be walking your child to school, taking up your position on the cutting floor at a meat-packing plant, or sorting bricks on a construction site—and the next you are handcuffed, imprisoned, and deported.

Under the circumstances, for this book it was obvious that I would have to employ all the usual protective practices that a researcher would think to use: the assignment of pseudonyms and the alteration of place names and some nonessential details. In short, I needed all the standard methods that conceal individual identities.

But, in practice, how can this work? If I interview an undocumented 30-year-old man named José who is in charge of flowers and vegetables at a Korean-owned deli "somewhere" on the Upper West Side of Manhattan, and if, out of fear of exposing José to apprehension and deportation I identify him in my account as "Carlos," I may successfully disguise José only to expose a man named Carlos—who also sells flowers and vegetables at another Korean-owned grocery a few blocks away—to the very dangers from which I hoped to protect José.

Interestingly, in decades of research in Mexico, I have interviewed people with names so extraordinary—in the literal sense of that word—that it was a real temptation to use some of these names, such as Teofilia, Everista, Dagoberto, or Ubaldo, as the pseudonyms of the people who are presented in this book, thus to protect both Carlos and José. However, in the end I stuck to my usual practice of assigning the most common names I know to the people I wanted to profile and quote. I also tried, insofar as possible, to use names like Luis or Patricia that have cognates in English, so they would be easier for readers to remember. Moreover, I was careful not to use the names that I had given to the people profiled in *Mexican Lives*, which is also a book based on interviews and oral histories. My concern here was to avoid any confusion that could arise for the readers of that book who might wonder if the Miguel I interviewed when he was a street vendor near the Basilica of Guadalupe back in 1992 is the same Miguel who is now standing on a street corner in Staten Island hoping for a day of work on a construction site. To be sure, it *could* be the same person. But since, with the exception of Pedro, the coyote, none of the people in this book are the people from that book, I thought it best to come up with new pseudonyms, and this is what I have done.

In summary, as noted in the Prologue, all the names of people are invented, with the exception of two that belong to people so passionately attached to their names that I acceded to their request to be called by their own names, which, in any event are very common ones. Similarly, I have used the real place names of towns and cities of more than ten thousand inhabitants and I have invented names for small towns and villages both in Mexico and the United States.

As it turned out, my desire to conceal the exact whereabouts of these small towns and villages was at odds with my desire to acknowledge the friends who brought me to these places. That is, anyone who peruses the suggested reading section at the back of the book will be able to connect the friends I mention in the text to their writings, and the writings to the research site. In these cases, my decision on which of the two conflicting obligations to privilege is based on the fact that the stories in the book that come from these settings are, in one way or another, public, as, for example, in the case of Don Beto, whose work has been featured at the Museum of Anthropology and who was the subject of a newspaper article in the Netherlands.

Notes

Introduction

1. See Jeffrey S. Passel, "Estimates of the Size and Characteristics of the Undocumented Population," *Pew Hispanic Center Report*, March 21, 2005, available at http:pewhispanic.org/files/reports/44.pdf. By far the most commonly accepted data come from the Pew Center report, which uses monthly population estimates based on U.S. Census Bureau statistics, and an estimate of 850,000 undocumented arrivals each year since 2000, to project the 12 million total.

2. Some of the ideas I present in this introduction have been developed at greater length in Judith Adler Hellman, "Give or Take Ten Million: International Migration of Mexicans," in Eric Hershberg and Fred Rosen, eds., *Latin America After Neoliberalism: Turning the Tide in the 21st Century?* (New York: The New Press, 2006).

3. See Maxwell Cameron and Ricardo Grinspun, eds., *Critical Perspectives on North American Integration* (New York: St. Martin's Press, 1993).

4. Sandra Polaski, *The Employment Consequences of NAFTA: Testimony Submitted to the Senate Subcommittee on International Trade of the Committee on Finance* (Washington, DC: Carnegie Endowment for International Peace, 2006), 1–24.

5. José E. Iturriaga, *La Estructura Social y Cultural de México* (Mexico, DF: Fondo de Cultura Económica, 1951), 33.

6. A good number of the men in this category whom I have interviewed in Mexico—beginning as far back as my first fieldwork in 1967—have commented that they worked for employers who asked them to stay on and who offered to help them get papers, an opportunity that today, as we will see, would be viewed by most undocumented migrants as an extravagant daydream. Yet, appealing as this scenario might be to current-day migrants, in the mid-1960s, gaining status in the United States would have made these Mexicans subject to the military draft, and the former braceros who spoke to me in Mexico were the ones, by definition, who rejected this offer because they were afraid of being sent to war. Others did accept and ended up fighting, and some dying, in Vietnam.

7. These figures, together with a wealth of other data, are available on the Mexican Migration Project website, a collaborative research project based at the University of Guadalajara and Princeton University. See http:mmp .opr.princeton.edu.

Conclusion

1. An example would be the arguments put forward by Louis Uchitelle, "Nafta Should Have Stopped Illegal Immigration, Right?" *New York Times*, February 18, 2007, Week in Review, 4.

2. As we know, in the United States there are conservative elements who are outraged by what they view as the hordes of Mexicans pouring over the border. These are the U.S. citizens who are the most eager to criminalize undocumented migrants and to build what they think will be impenetrable walls to keep Mexicans out. Ironically, they are also the same people who, in 2006, celebrated the contested victory—by less than 1 percent of the final, dubious, tally—of the conservative presidential candidate, Felipe Calderón, over the center-leftist candidate, Andrés Manuel López Obrador. Yet López Obrador was the candidate most committed to making the lives of the people in places like San Rafael or Nopal Verde sustainable. That is, he was the leader most likely to develop programs for the transfer of resources to communities in the sending regions of Mexico. This speaks to the remarkable level of ignorance of what goes on in Mexico on the part of those who are the most vocal in their fear of the "Mexican menace": these conservatives could not grasp that the continuation of the neoliberal model under Calderón is unlikely to produce a drop in the number of desperate Mexicans trying to make their way across the border and into the U.S. economy.

3. In a personal communication, Nancy Churchill Connor explains: "In the countryside, peasant women are subject to patriarchal vigilance by men, boys, and older women, all of whom are responsible for watching over their virtue, and by extension, the honor of the family. When women marry, the responsibility for vigilance passes from their fathers and brothers to their husband and his father and mother." Also see Nancy Churchill Conner, "Trabajadoras domesticas y migracion internacional: Cambios en la vida cotidiana en Santo Tomas Chautla," in Leigh Binford, ed., *La Economia politica de la migracion internacional en Puebla y Veracruz: Siete estudios de caso* (Puebla, Mexico: Benemerita Universidad Autonoma de Puebla, 2004), 277, 290–92.

4. Wayne A. Cornelius, "The Embeddedness of Demand for Mexican Immigrant Labor: New Evidence from California," in Marcelo M. Suarez-Orozco, ed., *Crossings: Mexican Immigration in Interdisciplinary*

Perspective (Boston: David Rockefeller Center Series on Latin American Studies, Harvard University, 1998), 126.

5. Ibid.

6. Jan Rus and Salvador Guzmán López, eds., *Chamulas en California: Testimonios de Tzotziles indocumentados en los Estados Unidos* (San Cristóbal, Chiapas: INAREMAC, 1996).

7. Barbara Ehrenreich, *Nickel and Dimed: On (Not) Getting By in America* (New York: Henry Holt and Company, 2001).

8. Cited in "Special Report: American Immigration," *The Economist*, March 12, 2005, 28–29.

9. Associated Press, "Tighter Border First, Immigration Later," *New York Times*, May 8, 2007.

10. See Ruth Milkman, "Critical Mass: Latino Labor and Politics in California," *NACLA Report on the Americas* 40, no. 3 (May/June 1997): 30–36.

11. Joe Hill was executed in Utah in 1915 on trumped-up charges. Just before his execution, he reportedly wrote to Bill Haywood, an IWW leader, saying, "Don't waste any time in mourning. Organize."

Glossary

abuela	grandmother
abuelita	granny, grandma
acapador	moneylender
agrarista	agrarian, as in the agrarian struggle, that is, the fight for land
albañil	house builder; traditionally someone who worked with adobe bricks, now applied to almost anyone involved in house construction
al otro lado	the "other side," that is, the other side of the border, the United States
cacique	a political boss, in pre-Columbian times, a village chief
campesino/a	a person from the countryside, a peasant
campo	the countryside
cantina	a bar
casa de retorno	literally, "the house of return"; the house migrants save money to construct in their hometown, in the hope of returning one day
centavo	cent
cerro	hill
Chicano/a	Mexican American

chicharón	fried pork rind
ciudades perdidas	literally, "lost cities," i.e., shantytowns
comadre, compadre	godmother, godfather; co-parents; godparents to one's children
comal	the flat metal sheet on which tortillas are cooked
combi	van or minibus
comida	food; also the big midday meal
compañero/a	friend, companion, comrade
compas	short for *compañeros*; friends or companions
corralón	"the big corral," the holding facility where undocumented migrants would be held prior to deportation
coyote	people smuggler
cuate	the Nahuatl word for "twin" used to mean pal or chum
cuñado/a	brother-in-law, sister-in-law
ejidatario	a person who holds an *ejido* land grant
ejido	a family-sized parcel of land granted to a peasant applicant by the Mexican state under the agrarian reform provisions of Article 27 of the Mexican Constitution; also the community in which the *ejidatarios* live
elotes	corn on the cob
esquineros	day laborers who stand on a street corner, or *esquina,* waiting for work
frijol/es	bean, beans
gordito/a	chubby, a chubby person
gordo/a	fat
gringo/a	a person from the United States
grupera	a type of music blending traditional *ranchera* music from Sinaloa with more modern instrumentation
güero, güerito	blond or, in the diminutive form, "blondie"; these terms may be affectionately or derisively applied by Mexicans to people from the United States and to other foreigners who are fair in coloring if not necessarily blond

hijole	an exclamation
huaraches	leather sandals, sometimes with pieces of auto tires for soles
indirectas	indirect comments, usually meant to insult
jornaleros	day workers
limón	lemon or lime
linea	the demarcation line between the United States and Mexico
maestro/a	master, as in schoolmaster, master builder, or a highly skilled artist or artisan
maís	corn
'mano	short for *hermano*, brother
maquiladoras	assembly plants
medio loco	half crazy
mestizo	a person of mixed indigenous and European heritage
migra	the Immigration and Naturalization Service (INS) or its successor agency, the Bureau of Immigration and Customs Enforcement (ICE); the term is also used to refer to individual INS or ICE officers
militar	soldier
milpa	cornfield
mojado/a	wetback
mordida	a bribe—literally, a "bite"
morongo	blood sausage
narcotraficante	a drug trafficker
novio/a	a steady boyfriend or girlfriend, generally with the status of a fiancé
nuera	daughter-in-law
oaxaqueño/a	a person from the state of Oaxaca
pan dulce	sweet rolls
parcela	parcel of agricultural land
prepa	short for *preparatoria*, the equivalent of high school, the educational option that leads to university studies
primaria	primary school

pueblo	village
pulque	an alcoholic beverage derived from the maguey plant; served in a *pulqueria*
puro monte	uncultivated, uncultivable lands; badlands
quinceañera	the coming-out party of a teenage girl, celebrated at the time of her fifteenth birthday; marks the passage to womanhood
ranchera	Mexican country music
rancho	a ranch or a very small village, a dot on the map
rebozo	shawl
refresco	soft drink, soda pop
retablos	devotional images, a religious folk art form, generally little drawings or paintings invoking the intercession of a saint
secondaria	secondary school
suegro/a	father-in-law, mother-in-law
tardeada	an afternoon dance or social gathering
tejano/a	Texan
tianguis	the Nahuatl word for market
tortilleria	the store where tortillas are mass-produced and sold
zócalo	the main square of a city, town, or village

Suggested Reading

With the Internet at our disposal any suggestions to readers interested in the topics covered in this book must begin with directions to a number of websites and their links. One of the first to consult would be the website of the Pew Hispanic Center, pewhispanic.org, which provides studies of patterns of Hispanic population growth and settlement across the United States as well as statistics on educational attainment, wages, income, and other indexes of well-being of the Hispanic immigrant population over time and in comparison to other ethnic groups. Pew reports also highlight the role of Hispanics in the labor force as well as their party preferences and levels of participation in politics. Other Pew reports focus on migration, including the total dollar and peso value of remittances, how the remittances are sent, and how they are spent.

The Center for Comparative Immigration Studies at the University of California, San Diego, is another rich resource. At this writing, it has posted 150 PDF versions of working papers that have been presented at the center from 1999 onward. All can be found at www.ccis-ucsd .org/PUBLICATIONS/working_papers.htm. These articles cover the full range of topics related to immigration with an emphasis on Mexican migration to the United States. As with the Pew Center materials, readers will find policy-focused papers as well as studies that highlight the attitudes of different sectors of the U.S. population toward migrants in general and toward Mexican migrants in particular. Readers will also find links to the online newsletter *Migration Information Source* with its own links to data sources, statistics, and the rest.

The Red Internacional de Migración y Desarrollo (International Network of Migration and Development) is based in Mexico and can be found at www.migracionydesarrollo.org. Currently this network brings together roughly 160 experts in the field of migration studies who post their work to this site. Both the Spanish- and English-language articles found here cover not only national and international migration in Mexico but also migration studies from other countries. This source is particularly strong in providing Mexican scholars' research on the conditions in sending communities and the impact of migration on sending communities all over Mexico.

The Mexican Migration Project (MMP), mmp.opr.princeton.edu, is a multidisciplinary research collaboration between investigators in Mexico and the United States. It has a center in Mexico at the University of Guadalajara and another in the United States at the Office of Population Research of Princeton University. The MMP Database (MMP107) is a data set with statistics on 107 sending communities in Mexico. It offers findings based on surveys of more than 17,000 households in Mexico and more than 800 households in the United States. The website has a "Descriptions area" with background information on the MMP research strategies and database construction and a "Data Files" area containing all the files that are available to be downloaded by the public. The actual questionnaires used by the MMP to gather statistics in households on both side of the border are also available to download.

Readers who seek background material, particularly statistical information on Mexican migrants to California, should go to the website of the Public Policy Institute of California, www.ppic.org, where they can download reports including: Laura E. Hill, *The Socioeconomic Well-Being of California's Immigrant Youth* (July 2004); Belinda Reyes et al., ed., *A Portrait of Race and Ethnicity in California: An Assessment of Social and Economic Well-Being* (March 2001); and Laura E. Hill and Joseph M. Hayes, "California's Newest Immigrants," *California Counts: Population Trends and Profiles* 5, no. 2 (November 2003).

An excellent starting point for material of this sort for New York is the Population Division of the New York City Department of Planning, especially the department's report *The Newest New Yorkers, 2000: Immigrant New York in the New Millennium.* Go to www.nyc.gov/html/dcp/html/census/popdiv.shtml.

Apart from these web-based sources, some recent books offering comprehensive views of migration are: Douglas S. Massey, Jorge Durand, and Nolan J. Malone, *Beyond Smoke and Mirrors: Mexican Immigration in an Era of Economic Integration* (New York: Russell Sage Foundation, 2002); Marcelo M. Suárez-Orozco and Mariela M. Páez, eds., *Latinos: Remaking America* (Berkeley: University of California Press, 2002); and Raúl Delgado Wise and Margarita Favela, eds., *Nuevas tendencias y desafíos de la migración international México-Estados Unidos* (Zacatecas: University of Zacatecas Press, 2004).

The following works are more specifically focused on some of the issues raised in this book.

On socioeconomic conditions in the sending communities: Wayne Cornelius, "The Impact of NAFTA on Mexico-to-U.S. Migration," in Edward J. Chambers and Peter H. Smith, eds., *NAFTA in the New Millennium* (La Jolla, CA: Center for U.S.-Mexican Studies, UCSD, 2002), 287–304; Wayne Cornelius and David Myhre, *The Transformation of Rural Mexico* (La Jolla, CA: Center for U.S.-Mexican Studies, 1998); Jeffrey Cohen, *The Culture of Migration in Southern Mexico* (Austin: University of Texas Press, 2004); and Leigh Binford, ed., *La Economía política de la migración internacional en Puebla y Veracruz: Siete estudios de caso* (Puebla: Benemérita Universidad Autónoma de Puebla, 2004).

On women's role and the family in both sending and receiving communities: Jennifer Hirsch, *A Courtship After Marriage: Sexuality and Love in Mexican Transnational Families* (Berkeley: University of California Press, 2003); María Eugenia D'Aubeterre, *El pago de la novia: Matrimonio, vida conyugal y prácticas transnacionales en San Miguel Acuexcomac, Puebla* (México, DF: Colegio de Michoacán, 2002); Pierette Ondagneu-Soleto, *Gendered Transitions: Mexican Experiences of Immigration* (Berkeley: University of California Press, 1994); and Sara Poggio and Ofelia Woo, *Migración femenina hacia EUA: Cambio en las relaciones familiares y de género como resultado de la migración* (Mexico, DF: Edamex, 2001).

On transnational life lived between New York and Mexico: Héctor Cordero-Guzmán, Robert C. Smith, and Ramón Grosfoguel, eds., *Migration, Transnationalization, and Race in a Changing New York* (Philadelphia: Temple University Press, 1999), 1–34; Robert Courtney Smith, *Mexican New York: Transnational Lives of New Immigrants* (Berkeley: University of California Press, 2006); Alyshia Gálvez. "'I too was an immigrant': The Transformation of Affinities and Identity Through Time in a Mexican Migrant Devotional Organization in the South Bronx," *International Migration* 45, no. 1 (January 2007): 87–121; Blanca Laura Cordero Díaz, "Viviendo en el capitalismo global: La organización de la sobrevivencia transnacional entre Huaquechula y Nueva York," *Canadian Journal of Latin American and Caribbean Studies* 29, nos. 57–58 (2004): 117–46.

On transnational life of migrants in California: Wayne A. Cornelius and Enrico A. Marcelli, "The Changing Profile of Mexican Migrants to the United States: New Evidence from California and Mexico," *Latin American Research Review* 36, no. 3 (2001); Christian Zlolninski, *Janitors, Street Vendors, and Activists: The Lives of Mexican Immigrants in Silicon Valley* (Berkeley: University of California Press, 2006); Jonathan Fox and Gaspar Rivera-Salgado, eds., *Indigenous Mexican Migrants in the United States* (Berkeley: University of California Press, 2004); and María Eugenia D'Aubeterre, "Procreando ciudadanos: Trabajadoras mexicanas indocumentadas residentes en California," *Canadian Journal of Latin American and Caribbean Studies* 29, nos. 57–58 (2004): 147–72.

On relations between Mexicans and African Americans in Los Angeles: Rene P. Ciria-Cruz, "To Live and Let Live in South Los Angeles," *NACLA Report on the Americas* 40, no. 3 (May/June 2007): 37–40.

On hometown associations: Luin Goldring, "The Mexican State and Transmigrant Organizations: Negotiating the Boundaries of Membership and Participation in the Mexican Nation," *Latin American Research Review* 37, no. 3 (2002): 55–99; Miguel Moctezuma Longoria, "The Migrant Club of Remolino: A Binational Community Experience," in Timothy Wise, Hilda Salazar, and Laura Carlsen, eds., *Confronting Globalization: Economic Integration and Popular Resistance in Mexico* (Bloomfield, CT: Kumarian Press, 2003), 195–210; and Rodolfo

García Zamora, *Migración, remesas y desarrollo local* (Zacatecas: University of Zacatecas Press, 2003).

On day workers: Abel Valenzuela Jr. et al., *On the Corner: Day Labor in the United States* (UCLA Center for the Study of Urban Poverty, 2006), available at www.sscnet.ucla.edu/issr/csup/pubs/papers/item .php?id=30; and Abel Valenzuela Jr., "New Immigrants and Day Labor: The Potential for Violence," in Ramiro Martínez Jr. and Abel Valenzuela Jr., eds., *Immigration and Crime: Ethnicity, Race, and Violence* (New York: New York University Press, 2006), 189–211.

On immigrant-aid centers: Janice Fine, *Worker Centers: Organizing Communities at the Edge of the Dream* (Ithaca, NY: Cornell University Press, 2006).

On border enforcement and immigration policy: Wayne Cornelius and Jessa M. Lewis, eds., *Impacts of Border Enforcement on Mexican Migration: The View from Sending Communities* (La Jolla, CA: Center for Comparative Immigration Studies, UCSD, 2007); Belinda I. Reyes, *Holding the Line? The Effect of Recent Border Build-Up on Unauthorized Immigration*, Public Policy Institute of California Working Paper, December 2002; Wayne A. Cornelius, "Death at the Border: Efficacy and Unintended Consequences of US Immigration Control Policy," *Population and Development Review* 27, no. 4 (December 2001): 661–85; and NACLA, "Of Migrants and Minutemen: Inside the Immigration Battle," *NACLA Report on the Americas* 40, no. 3 (May/June 2007).

On education: Regina Cortina and Mónica Gendreau, eds., *Immigrants and Schooling: Mexicans in New York* (New York: Center for Migration Studies, 2003); Enrique T. Trueba, "The Education of Mexican Immigrant Children," in Marcelo Suárez-Orozco, ed., *Crossings: Mexican Immigration in Interdisciplinary Perspectives* (Cambridge, MA: Harvard University Press, 1998), 253–75.

On the impact of migration on education in Mexico: Saúl Macías Gamboa and Araceli Reyes Vergara, "Migración laboral y deserción educativa," *Canadian Journal of Latin American and Caribbean Studies* 29, nos. 57–58 (2004): 173–202.

On the impact of migration on education in the *United States: Carola Suárez Orozco and Marcelo M. Suárez-Orozco, Children of Immigration* (Cambridge, MA: Harvard University Press, 2001).

On educational attainment: Héctor Cordero-Guzmán and Pascual Padró Collazo, "Changes in the Demographic Characteristics, Educational Attainment Levels, and Labor Force participation of the Youth Population in Puerto Rico and New York City: An Analysis of 1990 and 2000 Census Data," paper presented at the Russell Sage Foundation, May 21, 2004; Christopher Jepsen, Hans P. Johnson, Laura E. Hill, and Deborah Reed, *Educational Progress Across Immigrant Generations in California,* Public Policy Institute of California report, January 2006; and Laura Hill and Joseph M. Hayes, *Out-of-School Immigrant Youth,* Public Policy Institute of California report, April 2007.